THE LION
OF THE RAF

THE LION
OF THE RAF

THE EXTRAORDINARY LIFE OF GEORGE BEAMISH,
SECOND WORLD WAR HERO AND RUGBY STAR

PAUL McELHINNEY

AMBERLEY

In memory of my late parents, Brian and Mary McElhinney,
and thanks for the day-to-day support of
the loyal and irrepressible Maggie.

First published 2019

Amberley Publishing
The Hill, Stroud
Gloucestershire, GL5 4EP

www.amberley-books.com

Copyright © Paul McElhinney, 2019

The right of Paul McElhinney to be identified
as the Author of this work has been asserted in
accordance with the Copyrights, Designs and
Patents Act 1988.

ISBN 978 1 4456 9061 2 (hardback)
ISBN 978 1 4456 9062 9 (ebook)

British Library Cataloguing in Publication Data.
A catalogue record for this book is available
from the British Library.

Typesetting by Aura Technology and Software
Services, India. Printed in the UK.

CONTENTS

FOREWORD BY
WILLIE JOHN MCBRIDE

My career was in banking and I was transferred to the Coleraine branch of Northern Bank in 1964. At that time, I was a cashier and I remember well one day a gentleman appeared at my desk. He reached out a hand to greet me, which was surprising because bank tellers didn't normally get that type of greeting. This gentleman had a presence and indeed an aura. He introduced himself as George Beamish and then congratulated me on playing for Ireland and the Lions. We had quite a conversation about rugby when I learned he was a former Irish International and a Lion, having toured Australia and New Zealand in 1930 on that Lions tour.

George Beamish came across to me as a very serious man who would take no nonsense and he obviously had the qualities of a leader. I did some research afterwards on his life, particularly his rugby career, and it was only then that I realised what a brilliant history this George Beamish had. It was only after more research that I realised that he had captained the Irish team and also had a most distinguished military career in the Royal Air Force, rising to Air Marshal – he was obviously a man of considerable leadership qualities. George lived in the lovely little village of Castlerock, close to Coleraine, and when I attended a sub-office there, he used to call on me to discuss rugby.

Many a time I wondered what it would have been like to travel to Australia and New Zealand on a rugby tour in 1930 – by boat, which would take many weeks. He obviously thrived on it and played in all five Test games. I remember he called me after I had been to Australia and New Zealand in 1966 and we had not done so well. Sadly, George died the following year, but I am always grateful to have known him. It has been an honour to have been asked to write a few lines for his biography.

Willie John McBride
November 2018

Willie John McBride's Biography

Willie John McBride was born in Toomebridge, Co. Antrim, in 1940 and now lives in Ballyclare, Co. Antrim. He played rugby at club level with Ballymena, with Ireland and, ultimately, the Lions. His first cap was against England in February 1962.

He shares the record for playing in the most Lions tours, with five. He was a member of the Lions tour to New Zealand in 1971, the first ever Test series win there for the Lions. Probably the pinnacle of Willie John's achievements was his captaincy of the Lions in South Africa in 1974, when the Lions registered their first-ever series win against the Springboks – something even the All Blacks had not yet managed to do – and emerged from the tour unbeaten. He retired from international rugby in 1975. After retirement, he managed the Irish team and in 1983 was called upon to manage the Lions tour to New Zealand. Remembered fondly by all those who have come across him in Irish and international rugby for his effort, commitment and character, few others have left such a positive legacy on world sport.

INTRODUCTION AND ACKNOWLEDGEMENTS

One was a hero of the British military and a rugby international; the other was a leading Irish republican and Gaelic games enthusiast. Two men from similar religious and social backgrounds in late nineteenth- and early twentieth-century west Cork could not have ended up in more different circumstances. They were cut from the same broad cloth, yet the paths they took in life were hugely different. Air Marshal Sir George Beamish, rugby international and RAF hero, and Sam Maguire, the senior anti-Treaty republican of Gaelic games fame, both started off in the unassuming town of Dunmanway, along the road from Bandon to Bantry in west Cork. Although separated in age by about thirty years, both were part of an Anglican Church of Ireland community in the area, relatively large by Irish standards. A significant population of that faith remains in and around Dunmanway even to this day. In a very Irish way, the contrasting lives of Beamish and Maguire exemplified the quirks and the twists and turns of Irish history, which have often confounded the outward labels and symbols of 'official' Irish history.

Maguire took a path that led him towards the republican struggle in the early part of the twentieth century, and along the way became a leading figure in the Gaelic Athletic Association (GAA), a path not too often trodden by his co-religionists. During his time living and working in London, Maguire became an active republican and a close associate there of fellow Cork man Michael Collins, the charismatic leader of republicanism. Such were the divisions in republican politics at the time that Maguire fell out with Collins when the latter decided to give support, albeit reluctantly, to the Anglo–Irish Treaty following the War of Independence.

Beamish, a little younger than Maguire, also lived in an Ireland politically undivided, even though it was part of the British Empire at that time. He was to go on to travel as a combatant to several theatres of war during the Second World War and to excel at rugby on the international stage.

By contrast, Maguire became a leading figure in the organisation that vigorously espoused Irish games, and in a similar vein he became an activist in Irish republicanism. The divide between those who played 'foreign games' and members of the GAA was to remain intense for most of the twentieth century. Stories abound of the animosities and misunderstandings between those camps. For many, sport was 'war by other means'.

As Ireland was then undivided politically in a formal sense, Belfast, Cork and Dublin were very much in the same country. Indeed, in 1912, Beamish's father, a school teacher and later an Inspector of Schools, moved seamlessly from west Cork to Dublin in 1912 and then to Antrim and Derry, exemplifying this very fact. Although he was born in Dunmanway, George grew up mainly in the northern part of Ireland. As a young man, he joined up with the fledgling RAF in the 1920s. In so doing, he followed the example of his elder brother, Victor, who went on to have an illustrious career as a fighter pilot in the early part of the Second World War before being killed in action in 1942. Indeed, Victor blazed a trail for all the remaining five Beamish siblings who joined the RAF and served during wartime. Victor's own story, in many respects more exciting and action-packed than George's, forms part of the overall narrative of *Wings Aflame*, the book by Douglas Stokes.

Victor might best be viewed as the sprinter with the explosive, blistering pace over a short distance. George, by contrast, is best viewed as the long-distance runner who, with a combination of patience, hard work and dedication, rose to the heights over a longer period. Although they were quite different personalities, George's exploits should really be seen in tandem with that of his elder brother who set such an example to George and his younger siblings. There was clear evidence of rivalry between the two, particularly in the boxing ring. Victor first bested George in that arena in RAF competition, but the tables were eventually turned as George matured and grew stronger.

George had a very successful RAF career. His career included being involved in the Battle of Crete, the Desert War, the Sicily Campaign, life as an aide-de-camp to the King, an appointment to the rank of Air Marshal and also to Commandant of the RAF College at Cranwell. While firmly loyal to the RAF, he also managed to maintain a great pride in being Irish, something he was not shy of displaying to his friends. In a very visible way, this was also evident in his illustrious career as a rugby international for Ireland from 1925 to 1933. During that time, he captained Ireland and toured with the 1930 Lions on their tour of Australia and New Zealand. While rugby was his premier sport, he was also an accomplished golfer, boxer, cricketer and shot. A big bear of a man, it was said that he was so strong he could bend a penny between his thumb and forefinger. He was also able to use this strong physical presence to his advantage on the rugby field and as an RAF officer. 'Don't mess with Texas' is the phrase that immediately springs to mind.

George joined the RAF at eighteen years of age in 1923. While George's career was on the ascent, it was at this stage that the life and career of his fellow townsman, Maguire, went into decline. Having been on the losing side of the Irish Civil War, as a civil servant in the new state, Maguire faced the wrath of the incumbent government when they sacked him and denied him a pension. He retired in penury and died prematurely of a heart attack in 1927 while also suffering from TB. His name has arguably become more renowned after his death. Every September, the country waits in expectation for the new winner of the Sam Maguire Cup, or 'Sam' as it is colloquially known, the final of an annual football knockout competition. That kind of perennial publicity virtually ensures the kind of longevity in the public mind most public figures would envy.

Beamish would, no doubt, have identified with Maguire's sporting achievements, if not his political aspirations. Over time, a respect would surely have developed despite their contrasting outlooks. Indeed, it has often been said that a shared Cork heritage has been a way of uniting people of otherwise different backgrounds.

Another element in the formation of George's outlook was his participation in rugby at the highest level. Rugby was one of only a few sports which maintained its 'all Ireland' structure after independence. Players from North and South, despite their political affiliations, all played in a spirit of harmony in which political differences were set aside. This tradition has held firm right up until the present day. Being chosen to captain an Irish side in the 1930s as a senior officer in the RAF exemplified the atmosphere of tolerance and harmony in which the sport was played. Indeed, many examples exist of international players of that era from the 'Twenty-Six Counties' who signed up to fight with British forces in the 1920s, 1930s and 1940s. Some of these are referred to in the text.

The overall picture of George Beamish is of a man dedicated to the service of others, whether as an RAF officer, as a High Sheriff for his county or as a dedicated member of an international rugby side. The Beamish siblings were said to be undemonstrative, humble and unquestioning in their loyalty. Their father and mother were instrumental in developing these character qualities. In the case of the sons, their schooling at Coleraine Academical Institution (known locally as Coleraine Inst.) a voluntary grammar school for boys in Coleraine, County Londonderry, and their eventual entry into the

RAF would also have been significant contributors to their character formation. George was born in 1905 and died in 1967, making him, by today's standards, a relatively young sixty-two at the time of his death. In some ways, the year of George's passing marked an end of an era. It was only one year later that violence broke out in Derry, which was to scar the political landscape in Northern Ireland for another thirty years. George did not witness any of that but would have been deeply conscious of the political fault lines that went to make up Northern Ireland society. He would have been deeply affected by the outbreak of the Troubles, but at the same time, he would not have been hugely surprised either.

The atmosphere of tolerance produced by the Good Friday Agreement has been instrumental in allowing people in southern Ireland to discuss objectively and dispassionately the lives of those who fought with British forces. In earlier times, members of George's extended family living in southern Ireland describe the 'code of silence' adopted in relation to the membership of British military forces, particularly during the Troubles period. Events such as the Queen's visit to Ireland in 2012 and the visits of the English rugby team in the early 2000s to play at Croke Park, the HQ of the GAA, played a considerable part in the developing tolerance and understanding towards a community once regarded as pariahs. The Beamishes were one of these families. They never hesitated to declare their Irishness while also being resolutely British. Altogether, George Beamish was a proud Ulsterman, Irishman and British citizen. He saw no contradiction between any of these attachments.

George's story does read a little like a classic *Boy's Own* story, full of excitement either at war or on the international rugby field. Yet, as a man, he was quite humble and anything but a self-publicist. His exploits emerged out of doing the right thing, of doing what was expected of him. A measure of George's character was his reluctance to speak about his war service, but equally his pride in his own achievements. It was out of that mindset of dedication that his career developed into the great story that it is.

The timing of this publication, I hope, is apposite. Last year was the centenary of the establishment of the Royal Air Force as well as being the centenary of the end of the Great War. Both centenaries were marked by several commemorations culminating in Armistice Day in November 2018. It was a particularly poignant event. Not only were the commemorations recognised in Britain and much of Europe, but also by many Irish people who had relatives who fell during the Great War or who simply wanted to mark its importance.

George's story is as much a story of the events and key characters of the time as of the man himself. As the text will show, the character of the man was very much shaped by his associations and interactions with the cream of rugby talent and the upper echelons of the armed forces. A significant amount of attention is focused on these key individuals and the key events in which they participated. In doing so, I have endeavoured to elucidate the flavour and the spirit of the times which George played no small part in shaping. George also had the benefit of associating with several very influential figures, particularly in the Second World War, who left lasting marks on his development.

I want to extend a special thanks to Irish rugby legend Willie John McBride who agreed to write a foreword to the book. Willie John knew George personally and benefited as a young rugby player from George's advice in advance of the Lions Tour to New Zealand and Australia in 1966. He had very much the same type of experiences and challenges as George did, whether it was captaining Ireland or playing for and captaining the Lions. His own wise comments reflect his commitment and experience in the game. Willie John's contribution is greatly appreciated.

I am also indebted to the help and generosity of Leicester Rugby Football Club and of the library at Royal Air Force Cranwell, where George was Commandant in the late 1940s and early 1950s. Assistance provided by the staff of the Archives at Churchill College, Cambridge, and the National Archives at Kew in relation to RAF matters was of particular value. Family members were hugely helpful during my research on George. These include Val Beamish, Michael Beamish and Gail Neill. Several residents of Dunmanway including members of the local parish church and of Castlerock and Coleraine, Co. Derry, also provided useful information and insights into George's life and career. Of huge assistance was Stuart Farmer of Leicester RFC for his encyclopaedic knowledge of rugby and Ian Pierce of RAF Cranwell for his wide knowledge of all matters relating to the RAF. Considerable thanks are also due to Major (Retired) R. A. H. Barber, 2nd Gurkha Rifles for his invaluable advice on matters military, in particular military protocol. The final responsibility, of course, lies with the author for the accuracy and authenticity of the text.

George lived in an era when Corinthian values were cherished and promoted as the norm, long before the arrival of a more individualist, self-orientated generation. Beamish – taciturn, naturally modest and reserved as he was – would have been greatly surprised to hear of his life and career being described as 'heroic' or 'action-packed'. Blowing your own trumpet was considered decidedly bad form by George Beamish; this, I suppose, is a measure of the man. The following pages will seek to shed more light on the 'measure of the man' and where appropriate, to blow trumpets on George's behalf.

I

EARLY YEARS IN DUNMANWAY

George Beamish was born in Dunmanway, Co. Cork, in 1905, the second son of Francis and Mary Elizabeth Beamish. His father was a trained schoolteacher and later became the school principal at the local Model School in the town. Model Schools were creations of the nineteenth century and part of a push to expand education in Ireland. As their name suggests, they were seen at the time as quite modern and innovative.[1] As was the norm then, Francis's wife, Mary, worked at home where she was to provide an anchor for the family and a strength that translated to her children over time. George's elder brother, Victor, was born in 1903. Charles was born in 1908, Cecil was born in 1915, Eileen and Kathleen were the youngest of the six siblings by a number of years. Victor, George and Charles were all born in Dunmanway.

The eldest three Beamish children attended the Model School in their very early years before their father's career took them away from Dunmanway. For young boys, it must have been a double-edged sword having a father as head of the school they attended. It could have provided you with an added advantage or could have been a wedge in your relations with your peers. In the end, it left no lasting scars. Francis was certainly committed to his children's welfare and ambitious for their progress. This inevitably would have conveyed an advantage. Their education and training were then only at a preliminary stage and would flower over the coming years in ways few could predict.

Model Schools were set up in Ireland in 1831, one of the aims of which was to provide trained teachers to work in the new non-denominational national schools. Between 1848 and 1857, these schools were built in several towns and cities around Ireland including Limerick, Galway, Clonmel, Waterford, Kilkenny, Trim, Dunmanway, Newry, Ballymena, Coleraine, Belfast and Athy.[2] In 1870, a Royal Commission recommended that the schools should be closed. Pressure from both the Catholic and Protestant communities to maintain control of education were the main factors behind the move.[3] Nevertheless, the school at Dunmanway and a few others survive to the current day. Tensions between non-denominational education and parochial education were to remain in Ireland in the subsequent period right up even to the present.[4]

To set George's early years in context, 1905 was the final year in government of a succession of Conservative administrations headed successively by Lord Salisbury and his nephew, Arthur Balfour. These years were marked by the Tory policy of 'Killing Home Rule by Kindness', which broadly had the desired effect of maintaining a general peace throughout Ireland. The year 1905 was also when Albert Einstein developed his theory of relativity. In that year, the humiliating defeat took place at Tsushima of Russia's Asian fleet by the newly emerging Japan, an emergence that over time would have momentous, destabilising effects on the geopolitical environment.[5] It was into this world of international turmoil and uncertainty that George was later to be catapulted when he served as an RAF officer before and during the Second World War.

Beamish Family Origins

The area in and surrounding Dunmanway is notable for having had a higher concentration of Protestants than almost any other part of the southern part of Ireland. Its population in 2006 was 2,300.[6] George's father and his ancestors were members of the Church of

Ireland, as were most of the west Cork Beamishes. Although they were in a minority, they were a significant and influential minority. Francis and his family worshipped regularly at the local Church of Ireland, St Mary's. Established in the Elizabethan era, the original church known as Fanlobbus is east of the town of Dunmanway. The ruins of the church still stand beside the Famine Burial Ground.[7] Records suggest that the first Beamishes were Huguenots who settled in Ireland from Normandy in the mid-seventeenth century. In those years of religious persecution, Huguenots became subject to the Revocation of the Edict of Nantes, which had previously extended civil and religious liberties to Protestants in France. As a result, many Huguenots migrated to Ireland, but also to South Africa and to Canada. Interestingly, the Beamishes were part of a Norman migration to Ireland subsequent to the original Norman invasion of the 12th century. Like that earlier migration of Normans, though, the settlers became so well integrated that they could also have been said to have become 'more Irish than the Irish themselves'. A noted feature of that part of west Cork was the general harmony in which the two main religious communities lived. The first known Beamishes in that part of Cork date from 1642. Interestingly, this was a few years before the massive Cromwellian Plantation, which created such far-reaching tension and animosity in Ireland. The Beamish settlement predated that invasion by several years and was linked more closely to religious strife in France than in England. This could probably explain the relatively 'seamless' nature of the migration.[8]

The original Beamish home town was Beaumais in the famous Calvados department of Normandy, a name which in time evolved into the family surname Beamish. It is a French department swathed in history: from William the Conqueror to the Bayeux tapestry right up to the D-Day landings. Calvados is also famous for the eponymous apple brandy and for its rich cheeses such as Camembert and Pont L'Eveque.[9] Charles de Gaulle must have had Calvados in mind when he said in 1962 and referring to France as a whole: 'How can you govern a country which has two hundred and forty-six varieties of cheese?'[10] Calvados also has the major towns of Caen, Deauville, Cabourg and Bayeux. Over the last fifty years, the population of the Beaumais commune has hovered from between 150 and 200, indicating its very small size. Its beaches were the sites of the Normandy Landings in 1944 and many commemorations of that time remain. One wonders whether George had time to spare a thought for his ancestral homeland while serving in the RAF at the time of the Allied invasion.[11]

The Huguenots were part of the Reformed tradition of Calvin so would have had many issues with the established Anglican Church of Ireland. To gain certain advantages in seventeenth century Ireland, French Huguenots had to accept the Oath of Supremacy, thus allying to the Anglican Church. It is not clear when the Beamishes became Anglicans but by the mid-nineteenth century at least, they were confirmed members of that church. In the seventeenth and eighteenth centuries, relations between local Catholics and Protestants in the Dunmanway area were generally harmonious, despite the many inequities of the Penal Laws. Understandably, their respective populations were more concerned with eking out a living from the land in often straitened times than in political argument. Farming was hard work and often required community co-operation, irrespective of religious affiliation. In the townland outside Dunmanway, a notable topographical feature, known as the 'Beamish Line', has been in place for as long as local residents can remember. It represents the dividing line of land owned by a Beamish in west Cork of many years ago; the Beamishes had thus staked out their presence from very early on and in very definitive terms in west Cork.[12]

While George's father Francis was a school principal, his own family background was farming in a very rural, agricultural part of the country. His father farmed land at 'Four Acres', which was in an area 4 miles outside Dunmanway called Clashnacrona. When Francis got married near the turn of the twentieth century, Protestants made up about 20 per cent of the west Cork population. Yet the *Ne Temere* decrees of the Catholic Church regarding inter-faith marriage were seen as oppressive by minority Protestants fearful of their faith eventually disappearing by force of numbers. While this was an issue of relevance nationally, it would have disproportionately affected an area like west Cork. However, Protestants and Catholics worked the land in close proximity to and in close co-operation with one another, ensuring a degree of harmony. This was far from untypical during an era when agriculture so dominated the economy of the southern part of Ireland. The limited local opportunities available to ambitious people were to play a big part in the eventual decision by Francis to leave west Cork and take his young family northwards. To this day, there remain many Beamishes in the west Cork area generally, all maintaining their proud Church of Ireland traditions. It is from this setting too that the Beamishes of the great brewing company Beamish & Crawford emerged. Although George and his family were not closely related to them, the 'Beer Beamishes' and the 'Flying Beamishes' are part of the wider family group.[13]

Dunmanway is not used to having large spectacles but in 2009, the small town's soccer team, Dunmanway Town played host to the great Liverpool FC in a pre-season friendly. In the process of the visit, the population quintupled to over 15,000. With such popularity, Sam Maguire would surely have been proud, even if it was a 'foreign game'![14]

Dunmanway is in a part of Ireland that suffered considerably as a result of the Great Famine in the 1840s. To this day, many famine graveyards exist all over west Cork as symbols of the human suffering and death of that period. Never an economically dynamic part of the country, Dunmanway and its environs would have continued to be acutely aware of the great hunger and its impact locally. Life was tough for most people and continued to be so throughout most of the twentieth century. Continued emigration from the area to seek opportunities abroad remains a big part of life there.

Although the Beamish family had left the area ten years previously, the 1922 murder of six Protestants by elements of the then IRA sent shockwaves through the local Protestant population. It left a deep mark on relations between the two communities for a long time and disputes remain over the exact details and motives of the attacks, still unresolved.[15] This was in stark contrast with Francis Beamish's and his generation's experience of the area.

Francis Beamish's Ambitions for his Family

Examining the progress of the Beamish family over the remainder of the twentieth century, it becomes clear that the transferable skills of father Francis Beamish, and how he was prepared to develop them outside his own home base, account in large part for the eventual success of his six children, Victor, George, Charles, Cecil, Eileen and Kathleen. Ambition, hard work, modesty, duty and service were all hallmarks of the growing Beamish family. Put bluntly, producing three dentists and three outstanding RAF officers was not a bad achievement for someone of Francis's relatively modest background. His family were from a traditional farming background and had farmed at 'Four Acres' outside Dunmanway since 1792. Francis was teetotal, a Freemason and distinctly Edwardian in his outlook. He also stood out by being a highly educated man, holding an MA from Trinity College, Dublin. His wife, Mary, was placid and practical but with nerves of steel and a strong influence on the young family. After his successful tenure at the Model School, Francis accepted a position in 1912 as a school inspector, first in Dublin, then in Antrim and finally in Derry. These were large distances to traverse in the first decade of the twentieth century when motorised transport was so limited, although a wide rail network was in place. The 'distance' from Dunmanway to Dublin, moreover, was much farther in 1912 than it is now, both physically as well as culturally. On the other hand, it should be remembered that in those years, there was no political distinction between Antrim and Cork: it was all one country at the time so in this respect, Francis's migration was unremarkable. Nevertheless it as a big undertaking and a measure of his ambitions for both himself and his family that Francis was prepared to move to develop his career. Opportunities in Dunmanway for someone seeking to progress materially in life would have been fairly limited, so for the young ambitious Beamish family, the move was entirely logical.

Two Famous Sons of Dunmanway

Another notable son of Dunmanway was Sam Maguire, the GAA man and republican activist who gave his name to the senior All-Ireland Gaelic football trophy. Maguire opted for the 'national' games of football and hurling, while Beamish become a hero in the 'garrison' sport of rugby. Maguire and Beamish were about thirty years apart in age, but their backgrounds were remarkably similar.

George left Dunmanway for Dublin when he was about seven years of age and thus, there is little evidence of them ever having met. That said, however, Maguire would have known Francis Beamish as he attended the Model School during the latter's tenure there. At that time, however, Maguire, was an unexceptional member of his community, long before his migration into republican politics. Like George Beamish, Maguire was of Protestant stock. Thus, on the face of it, it is surprising that Maguire should have joined the republican struggle and to have been so involved in Gaelic games. It is hard to avoid the conclusion that he had the zeal of the convert because of his strong commitment to both the nationalist struggle and Gaelic games.[16] It was while working in London that Maguire became involved in the nationalist politics, strongly influenced there by fellow west Cork man, Michael Collins. Building on that close relationship, he became Collins' chief intelligence officer in London, a position of some influence but with many associated dangers. Maguire's involvement in republican affairs would have undoubtedly distanced him from his religious community in west Cork and after the Civil War, from the new authorities in charge of the Irish Free State. Maguire's end was a sad one, as he died at the relatively young age of forty-nine in 1927 from TB. His last years were spent in penury while George's career as a young man, was in ascendance during those years.[17]

Symbolic of the closeness of the Dunmanway Church of Ireland community, Maguire is buried in the second next plot to that of George's father, Francis, at St Mary's Church, Dunmanway. In 2016 – the centenary of the 1916 Rising – St Mary's installed eight bells in its belfry to be rung in memory of Sam Maguire, their former parishioner. It represented a recognition of a famous former member of their religious community despite his political and sporting interests having been at variance with their own.[18]

Beamish and Maguire would scarcely recognise their respective sports of rugby and Gaelic football today. In their day, there was a firmly entrenched dividing line between the two sports. The GAA banned members of the British security forces from playing, and anyone playing Gaelic games was not permitted to play 'foreign games', code for games such as rugby, cricket and football. This has all changed and now all games are now widely accepted. Beamish and Maguire were creatures of their time, caged into certain prejudices but, in fairness, it is hard to see them rejecting the more inclusive developments of recent decades.[19]

Changing Irish Views on British Servicemen

Sam Maguire has long been revered as a local hero in Dunmanway owing to the tremendous popularity of Gaelic games and by being so directly associated with the annual football championships. It took a lot longer for George Beamish and his siblings to gain that local recognition. This was not surprising in the early part of the twentieth century, the main reasons being the combined issues of national politics and allegiance. It has only been in recent years that Ireland has come fully to terms with the complexity of its history, a history straddling strong British as well as Irish traditions. For many decades, Irish people with family members serving in the British military were often loath to publicly admit to the fact or, at least, tried to play it down. Noting the Beamishes' close relationship with the 'Rebel County' of Cork, any involvement by local inhabitants in the forces of the Crown would have been regarded unfavourably. It is undoubtedly the case, however, that as the Beamishes had left Cork for good in 1912, local animosity would probably have been muted over the activities of a departed family who subsequently maintained little connection with the locale. By the same token, any celebration at their later successes or exploits would have been equally muted. This quiescence would have been supported by the natural desire of the Protestant community of which the Beamishes were part, not to put their heads too far above the parapet in the uncertain years of the early Irish Free State. Fitting in was important and anything that cast them as distinct or 'special' was avoided. This attitude changed gradually, however, towards the end of the twentieth century. In particular, the atmosphere generated by the post-Good Friday Agreement dispensation and the visit by the Queen in 2012 are thought to be among the main factors behind this 'opening up'. A long tribute to that community and the Beamish family was made in the Irish Senate in July 2012 by local Teachta Dála (T.D.) representative from west Cork, Denis O'Donovan. It was in response to an address by the Grand Secretary of the Grand Orange Lodge of Ireland, Drew Nelson, who also happened to be a grand-nephew of George Beamish. It was particularly notable that the tribute to the Beamishes came from a representative of the Fianna Fáil party, a party with a tradition of staunch republicanism – an indication of how far opinion in Ireland had developed. As with Sam Maguire, the local community are proud of the exploits of the Beamishes and in the new spirit of openness, not afraid to express it.[19] An event that also helped boost the profile of the Beamish family among the people of Cork was a conference and air display held in Listowel, Co. Kerry, in 2016, referred to as 'The Flying Beamishes'. This event celebrated the RAF exploits of the four brothers, was widely reported on in local newspapers and brought the family's history to a wider audience.[20]

Beamish & Crawford Brewery
Although Francis and his family were only distantly related to the Beamishes of the famous brewery, Beamish & Crawford, their

roots were similar. They were all part of the seventeenth-century migration of Beaumais families from France to Ireland and west Cork in particular. Over time many Beamishes emigrated to other parts of the British Empire while many remained in familiar circumstances in west Cork. In 1792, William Beamish established the brewery in Cork in partnership with William Crawford and two local Cork brewers, under the name of The Cork Porter Brewery. The Crawford family were to leave an art gallery to the city of Cork, which is popular to this day. Thus the Beamish Brewery family managed to rise from their local circumstances to create a large business and a product with wide appeal. Their stout business thrived during the subsequent French wars as Cork, then a major trading port, provided a provisioning depot for British fleets. The company also managed to secure lucrative markets for its stout in the US, Australia and the Caribbean – one of Ireland's first 'global' companies, you could say. By the end of the eighteenth century, the company's stout was even outselling that of Guinness, a lead the company would eventually surrender to Guinness in the 1830s.[21]

Meanwhile the other Beamish family firmly established its local Cork roots through their close association with the local Model School in Dunmanway. Francis took up his appointment there at the relatively young age of twenty-seven, the year that his first child, Victor was born. Over the years, the school has performed an invaluable service to the area in and around Dunmanway. Its many alumni include three of the 'Flying Beamishes', Sam Maguire and more latterly, Trevor Sargent, former member of the Dáil (Irish parliament) and Irish Green Party leader. For young George, the basic groundings in the principles of education learned there stood him in good stead as time went on. These were also to be significantly built on in his next school, Coleraine Inst.[22] Relations between the Catholic and Protestant communities in the area of Dunmanway had traditionally been good. Few instances of bigotry or direct animosity existed around the time that Francis and his family lived there.

Beamish Connections with Hermann Goering[23]

Another interesting connection between the brewery and the RAF Beamishes is the fact that one of the Beamish family married Herman Goering, top Nazi and future head of the Luftwaffe. Carin Beamish, the great-great-granddaughter of the brewery's co-founder, William Beamish, became the first wife of Goering in 1923. They had met in Sweden and settled in Munich. Carin helped treat Goering after his injuries following the Munich Beer Hall Putsch of 1923, helping to spirit him away to hiding in Austria. Carin had a sad and untimely death from a heart attack in 1931 at forty-three, after a long period affected by TB. Hitler attended her funeral. In her memory, Goering named his palatial estate outside Munich 'Carinhall', where he had her remains re-interred.

Carin died before the full horrors of the Nazi regime became apparent but nevertheless she must have been aware of the Nazis' and her husband's proclivities. Carin and Goering's romantic love story was exploited by Goebbels' propaganda machine, and the couple toured around the nation to boost popularity. Goering, the First World War flying hero and Carin, the Swedish beauty, were cast as the epitome of the model Teutonic couple. But even after death, Carin remained a mascot of the Nazis, who had a booklet printed to commemorate their 'Swedish Saint'. Goering even had a room in his Berlin flat arranged as a shrine to Carin.

Families often throw up anomalies, but few as glaring as these. A family that provided six siblings to the RAF in wartime had a distant cousin who married the head of their deadly enemy's air force. Truth is often stranger than fiction.

The Move Away from Dunmanway

Young George was seven years of age when the family left Dunmanway and he was nine when, in 1914, the family settled in Derry and Antrim. Although young, he would at least have been partly aware of the momentous events enveloping Europe and Britain. When Francis Beamish decided to move his family away from Dunmanway in 1912, it was the year of the 'Solemn Oath and Covenant' in Ulster which committed signatories to resisting Home Rule for Ireland. Ulster and Ireland as a whole were moving into politically incendiary times. Nothing untoward befell the Beamish family during that time, but the potentially explosive atmosphere was palpable and evident to all. George's time in Dunmanway from the time of his birth to the age of seven would have laid down solid foundations for the future: those of hard work, a sense of modesty and the need to progress in life. The following move northwards was also seminal in the development and the successes of George and his siblings. There they received excellent secondary educations, embarked on their RAF careers and developed their notable sporting prowess across a range of sports. Furthermore, due to their move north and with the partition of Ireland in 1920, the Beamishes were to remain British subjects, a factor that contributed critically to determining their future life choices.

Of all the Beamishes, George had the most illustrious sporting career. This included rugby, golf and several other sports while in the RAF – including boxing, athletics, rifle shooting and cricket. His rugby talent was developed in the crucible of schools' rugby in Ulster where, assisted by his large and strong frame, he was a precocious talent. He went on to captain his country and played for the British and Irish Lions.

Importantly too, his time spent living in a religiously tolerant west Cork left George and indeed, the whole Beamish family with none of the religious bigotry evident in other parts of the country. This tolerance impacted positively on the broad range of his friendships during his lifetime. Although the next phase of his life was to lead him to a career in Britain, he was to maintain contact with his Ulster roots regularly throughout his whole life. Although Francis had had little contact with Dunmanway since his departure in 1912, in response to his own wishes, he was buried there after his death in the late 1940s. Being buried in the 'home place' was part of a long Irish tradition. His sons, George and Charles, both senior RAF men, attended the funeral in full uniform. The appearance of two British servicemen in neutral Ireland during the Second World War could have created a stir, or worse, but fortunately matters passed without incident. In the current day, Dunmanway is still relatively untouched. Many Beamishes remain. The area's population is mainly Catholic but with a sizeable Protestant population. Indeed, after Dun-Laoghaire/Rathdown, it has the highest Protestant population of any district in the Irish State. What might have amused or horrified George was the move of a large 'neo-pagan' or 'New Age' community to the area in recent decades, which holds views somewhat at variance with those of local, traditional, religious folk. Given that community's attraction to simple, rural and remote settings, it was not surprising that they chose Dunmanway in which to settle. Rural Ireland is known for its welcome and hospitality and no real issue has arisen from residents over their arrival in the area.

It is important to record the formative influence Cork had on George's early years. Their move north, however, resulted in a whole new canvas and his subsequent RAF career meant that trips to Cork were always going to be less likely. George's rugby international career involved him frequently being in Dublin and his family home in Castlerock provided a further Irish anchor, so that despite his base in England as an RAF man and his membership of Leicester Rugby Club, he managed to maintain solid connections with Ireland.

Many years later a great celebration of all the deceased Beamish brothers was to take place, not in Cork, but in Listowel in the adjacent county of Kerry at the 2016 'Flying Beamishes' air show. The local reception of the exploits of the Beamishes was hearteningly positive and the event was supported by local press interest. Thankfully, gone now are the years of secrecy, evasion and discrimination in these matters.[24] Events such as this marked an opening up to the rich truths and complexities of Ireland's shared histories. The wheel at last seems to have come full circle.

2

CASTLEROCK AND COLERAINE INST. (INSTITUTION)

Castlerock is a small, unassuming seaside village about 7 miles along the north Derry coast, west of the town of Coleraine. Located on the main Belfast–Derry railway line, it is a convenient stopping-off point for visitors. It was probably this key logistical fact that most explains the attraction of Castlerock in the pre-motor car era. It was where Francis Beamish decided to settle his family after a long trek from the southern tip of Ireland and where a local Beamish presence was to remain well into the twenty-first century. Although not on the scale of other Northern Ireland resorts such as Portrush or Bangor, over the years Castlerock has managed to attract a steady number of summer holidaymakers from the larger urban centres of Northern Ireland. Given the inhospitable winters, little happens during the main winter months when most things go into hibernation. According to the 1911 Census, there were 163 residents in Castlerock, a total that rose considerably during the summer months. It also rose in the post-First World War era as more people decided to settle in such a pleasant seaside setting.[1] The Census reveals that established residents included many farmers and several blacksmiths, given the continuation of travel by horse in that era. Summer holidaymakers came from across Ulster, but mainly from Belfast, Derry and Coleraine. In George Beamish's day, its population would never have differed greatly from that number. In recent decades, the town has expanded in size with new housing developments dotted around the perimeter of the town, but it still hovers somewhere between being a large village and a small town.[2]

Before settling in Castlerock, the Beamishes lived briefly in Larne and then Coleraine, two medium-sized towns somewhat lacking in aesthetic charm. The family then decided to move to Castlerock. Conveniently located near good local schools for the children, the setting and aspect alone of Castlerock captured the imagination of Francis and his family. Francis bought a house on the main street of the village beside the Church of Ireland church, where the family became regular members of the congregation. The house was a sizeable two-storey dwelling, necessarily so to cater for two adults and six children. These were the new permanent roots the Beamishes were to set down after their long migration from the south.

The village of Castlerock has also had its fair share of the 'great and the good' pass through it over the years. The nearby castle at Downhill was built by the 4th Earl of Bristol, Sir Hervey Bruce, an English landlord in the early 1770s. Built later was the famous Mussenden Temple, an impressive structure at the cliff edge, which is now maintained by the National Trust; in many current tourist advertisements for Castlerock, Mussenden Temple is prominently displayed as a key attraction. The construction of Downhill House, and the nearby Mussenden Temple, cost an estimated £80,000. During the Second World War, the house was used to billet RAF servicemen and women.[3] In those and subsequent years, the village of Castlerock acted very much as an adjunct to the castle. The Earl even had a house built for his mistress on the Circular Road near the centre of the village. A large red brick house, it was loyally named 'Trafalgar Lodge'.[4] When it was bought by a Catholic family in the early twentieth century, however, it was renamed 'Red House' in reference to the house's brickwork rather than to any social leanings on the part of the new owners. It was said locally that every Twelfth of July, the marching Orange band would beat their Lambeg drum that little bit louder as they passed by the Catholic inhabitants of 'Red House'. The great writer and balladeer Percy French was a regular visitor to Castlerock, as was the Dublin writer, barrister and broadcaster Ulick O'Connor as a young boy. The latter, according to locals, had an assertiveness as a young child that was never to leave him as a grown man. His biographies of Oliver St John Gogarty and of Brendan Behan proved compelling reading. Another writer, C. S. Lewis, often went on holiday to Castlerock and the actor James Nesbitt spent time living there during his teens. One long-term resident in his younger years was Patrick McGilligan who became a government minister in the early years of the Irish Free State. Near-neighbours of the Beamishes on the Main Street, the McGilligans were a Catholic merchant family living in a largely Protestant village yet they were welcomed and firmly integrated into the village. Patrick was a prominent figure in Irish politics and was to take a leading role in Irish government even into the post-Second World War years. As Minister for External Affairs, he was deeply involved in developing policy on the League of Nations and the evolving status of the Dominions within the Empire. In this role, he had regular contact with the British Foreign Secretaries George Curzon, 1st Marquess Curzon, and Sir Joseph Austen Chamberlain, as well as their counterparts in Canada, Australia and New Zealand.[5]

Castlerock's relaxed and tolerant milieu has managed to maintain a harmony between the religions over the years. It was in such an atmosphere of tolerance and acceptance that George grew up. His own views and attitudes perfectly reflected that tolerance during the course of his life. Indeed, one of his closest friends was Patrick McDevitt, a local resident and Catholic businessman from Derry, who was one of George's golf partners. Cases of naked sectarianism were almost non-existent in Castlerock then or at any time, but one incident with sectarian undertones occurred when Sunday golf was first introduced to Castlerock Golf Club in the 1920s. The night before its introduction, a local group of hotheads dug up and scarred many of the greens in protest. It did not stop Sunday golf, however. These isolated incidents aside, relations between the two communities were good.

A broad assortment of legal, judicial and business figures from Belfast made their way down to Castlerock in the summers where they rented houses, swam in the sea and played golf. Resident in Castlerock since the First World War, the Beamish family lived a mere light stroll away from the golf club. Although there have undoubtedly been changes in the interim, the scale and flavour of the village have essentially changed very little since George Beamish's day. For many years after his death in 1967, his house, 'Rocklea', stood on the main street. As a bachelor with no direct descendants, he left its contents to a brother and two nephews based in Scotland. With the exception of one major terrorist incident towards the end of the Troubles period, Castlerock remained untouched by the violence of the era.[6] Peaceful was the village and peaceful it generally remained.

The main attraction that drew in so many visitors was the local golf course. Living in the shadow of the more illustrious Portrush and Portstewart courses, the lesser-known Castlerock thrived by avoiding being overwhelmed by visitors, unlike the two former courses. All three courses were popular with the Beamish family, including George. However, Castlerock held a particular affinity for all the Beamishes, it being the local club and within a short walking distance from 'Rocklea'. Golf played a big part in the Beamishes' recreation time. George was a regular visitor to the fairways; with the village course just on his doorstep, it became a big part of George's life right through to his retirement. The golf course is surrounded by large sand hills and abuts onto the Barmouth at the mouth of the Bann River. The United States has its Mason–Dixon Line and the UK has 'north or south of the Watford Gap'. In Ulster, the key dividing line is 'east and west of the Bann' – the east a majority Protestant, unionist area and the west, majority Catholic and nationalist. Although only a 'notional' line of division, the distinction still manages to retain a powerful psychological significance in Northern Ireland.

Castlerock golf course has some quaintly named holes such as 'Leg o' Mutton' and the 'Postage Stamp' and some very challenging par fours. It attracts regular golf parties from England and Scotland and from south of the border. In layout and terrain, it closely resembles the links courses a short distance across the sea in the west of Scotland.[7]

To the east of Castlerock and prominent on the coastline is another oasis of golf, Royal Portstewart Golf Club. Portstewart was another favourite local course for George and one which gave him the honour of electing him as their president. Portrush is farther along the Antrim coast and unlike Portstewart, not visible from the strand at Castlerock. George was also given the honour of being elected captain at Royal Portrush in the 1950s.[8]

Much farther north on the horizon is Scotland and on a good, clear summer's day, one can see the Isle of Skye, a visible example of the close historic links between Northern Ireland and Scotland. To the west of Castlerock is the coastline of Donegal and the port town of Greencastle. These were all views which George could appreciate from his back garden and they remain unobstructed to this day.

The Beamishes' friendships with the McDevitt family also extended to the golf course. There were four Beamish brothers and two sisters. In the McDevitt family, there were two brothers and three sisters. All were keen golfers and all had an interest in bridge. George Beamish was a regular golf partner of Patrick McDevitt, and Kathleen Beamish a regular golf and bridge partner of Marcella McDevitt. The McDevitts were a merchant family from Derry involved in the linen industry, owning a clothes factory on William Street and a clothes shop on Duke Street in the city. They were to win the contract to supply socks to the RAF during the Second World War, which was considered quite a coup – particularly given their Catholic nationalist origins. George and Kathleen and all four McDevitts were unmarried, which allowed more time for these pursuits. Common interests were the vital cement that forged the friendships between the two families that were to last for a long time.

Coleraine Academical Institution (Inst.)

A fundamental influence in George's development was his attendance at the Coleraine Academical Institution. The school was accessible by train in an era when car and bus transport were rare. The school was colloquially known as 'Inst.' or 'Coleraine Inst.' to distinguish it from the Royal Belfast Academical Institution, also known as 'Inst.'. In fact, the two 'Insts' were to become strong rivals on the schools' rugby field in the post-First World War era, with George playing a major part in some of those encounters. Francis's background as an educator was seminal in the choice of secondary education for his children. He made local enquiries and was given good assurances about the school's headmaster, a Mr Beare, who coincidentally also lived in Castlerock. Beare's tenure at Inst. was from 1915 to 1927. After his death, his son and daughter-in-law lived in Castlerock, only about 200 yards from where George himself settled. Beare was preceded as Inst. headmaster by Thomas Houston who later was elected to the Northern Ireland Senate. In turn, Beare was succeeded in 1927 by the respected but fearsome martinet, Major White, known as 'Chief'.

George's elder brother Victor was the family pathfinder at Inst., followed by the next in line, George, a year later. Two more Beamishes, Charles and Cecil, were to follow in time. The school has a long tradition of excellence, modelled closely along the lines of a British grammar school. The Beamishes were notable alumni but in more recent times, famous former pupils include actor James Nesbitt, golfer Graeme McDowell, newscaster Mark Carruthers and Andrew Trimble, the former Irish rugby international.[9] By contrast, another Inst. 'old boy' was the infamous Eastbourne GP and suspected serial killer, John Bodkin Adams. A total of 162 of Adams' patients died in suspicious circumstances in the 1940s and 1950s but he was acquitted at his trial, as at the time it was hard to scientifically prove that he caused their deaths. With current

DNA forensic technology, he would probably have been found 'bang to rights'. The great irony was that he was convicted only of fraud and was removed from the Medical Register for a mere three years, from 1957 to 1961. Such exaggerated respect for members of the medical profession was to last long after Adams, as the case of Dr Harold Shipman showed. As prolific a killer as was Harold Shipman, Bodkin Adams was about six years older than George and would have departed Inst. just as George arrived. There is nothing to suggest that George knew Bodkin Adams personally, but Bodkin Adams did overlap at Inst. for two years with George's brother, Victor. Owing to his notoriety, it was not surprising that Bodkin Adams did not feature on many subsequent lists of famous Inst. alumni. At the same time, his connection with the school seems not to have had any long-term traumatic effects on succeeding generations of students.[10]

George was a big, strong boy growing up. He was about 6 feet in height at school, growing to 6 feet 2 inches in his early club rugby years. Strong and silent by nature, he had a determined character with a measure of impatience and intolerance of failure. In this respect, excelling at rugby and other sports at Inst. provided a perfect launch pad for his future RAF career and fitted in well with his personal character. Inst. had a strong tradition in rugby in the late nineteenth and early twentieth centuries, winning the Ulster Schools Cup on nine occasions. In 1920, George played for the Inst. cup-winning side which beat Campbell College 3–0. He also played in the following year's final, again versus Campbell, when the result was reversed to an 8–0 win for Campbell. In the first final of 1920, he was only fifteen years of age, indicating a precocious talent that was to grow to display even greater things in the years to come. Campbell was regarded as one of the premier schools in Northern Ireland and were tough competitors on the rugby field, providing many future internationals on the Irish team.[11]

Nowadays Coleraine Inst. is not a school that features too often in the final stages of the Schools' Cup, but its history and traditions are impressive. One exception was the year early in the 2000s when a young Andrew Trimble played in the Schools' Cup for Inst. Representing his province and Ireland at rugby, Trimble was the only other former Inst. boy, along with George and Charles Beamish, to do so. The school is now called Coleraine Grammar School and rugby continues to be a big part of the sports curriculum there. In the history of the Ulster Schools' Cup, Coleraine Inst. is in fourth place among the Cup-winning schools, superseded only by Methodist College, Belfast Inst. and Campbell College. Heroes such as George and Charles Beamish, both commemorated prominently by the school, have acted as role models for many generations of young rugby players. Inst. is now a co-educational school, a fact that may have caused the 'traditionalist' George Beamish some pause for thought, but he would have been proud of the school's overall legacy.[12]

George and elder brother Victor, as young men, were both co-founders of the rugby club in Coleraine and played for the club briefly before joining the RAF and playing with Leicester. The club still exists and provides a lively centre of rugby in the north-west of Ulster.

Although he left Castlerock in 1923 destined for the RAF, George was to maintain strong ties over the years. The family home remained and a sister, Kathleen, continued to live there. There was also the perennial attraction of golf. It was also to Castlerock that he was to retire in 1958, and where he lived out his final years. The next chapter of the Beamish odyssey concerns his entry, career and advancement in the Royal Air Force from 1923.

3

JOINING THE RAF – 'THE EAGLE TAKES FLIGHT'

Like his elder brother Victor, George made the large leap from Coleraine Inst. directly to the Royal Air Force College at Cranwell. Victor – in 1921– and George – in 1923 – were entering an organisation not long in existence, seeking to establish itself alongside the more long-standing institutions of the Royal Military College, Sandhurst (RMC) and Britannia Royal Naval College (BRNC), commonly known as Dartmouth. They joined the RAF very much in its early years; it was only in the dying months of the Great War that the RAF was formally founded. Up until then, aerial warfare remained within the responsibility of the traditional services, the Flying Corps of the Army and Royal Navy. Photographs of the time show shaky, unstable bi-plane aircraft buffeted by the winds, with pilots clad in leather helmets and goggles, while figures such as the 'Red Baron' were part of popular consciousness. These are exciting but rather quaint images reflecting the service's fledgling nature. The potential importance and future impact of a consolidated air force was not missed, however, by the military planners.

George was entering the RAF very much 'on the ground floor' as it gradually established itself as a dedicated service during the 1920s. Many military experts at the time rightly saw air warfare as the means of war of the future. In the light of the monumental waste of human lives in the trench warfare of the Great War, air warfare was seen as more efficient and humane. Few at the time concentrated on the negative side of air warfare – this was a long time before Dresden and Hiroshima. The negative effects, particularly for civilian populations only became glaringly obvious in later conflicts such as the Spanish Civil War. However, in the early 1920s, air warfare and the RAF were then seen as the coming thing.[1]

RAF Cranwell 1923–24

The history of military aviation at Cranwell goes back to November 1915, when the Admiralty requisitioned 2,500 acres of land from the Marquess of Bristol's estate in Lincolnshire. Coincidentally, this was the same aristocratic family, the Hervey Bruces, who were the big landowners in George's home town of Castlerock and Downhill in Co. Derry, so George must have felt at least partially at home as he entered Cranwell as a flight cadet. On 1 April 1916, the Royal Naval Air Service Training Establishment, Cranwell, was officially born. The first commandant was Commodore Godfrey M. Paine. With the establishment of the Royal Air Force as an independent service in 1918, the former RNAS Training Establishment became RAF Cranwell. The first air force academy in the world, Cranwell became the entry point for those wishing to become permanent officers in the RAF. The selection process was extremely stringent, and many applicants came from the Empire and the Commonwealth. Initially, the course took two years, but by the 1950s this had stretched to three.

The main building of RAF College Cranwell is noted for its distinctive dome, visible from most of the surrounding roads.[2] Cranwell, like many of the RAF's installations, is situated in the east of England in the county of Lincolnshire, near the town of Sleaford. In flat countryside and facing in a southeasterly direction on the most likely enemy flight path from the Continent, it was strategically appropriate for the training college to be based there. For this reason, many RAF airfields were established in the east of

England before and during the war. Although the main building was built on a grand scale in the nineteenth century, when George joined in 1923 conditions for cadets were fairly spartan. The Crawnell motto – *Alitum Altrix*, translating roughly to 'Nurture the Winged' – can be found in gold print above the main doors of the College Hall Officers' Mess.[3]

At the time of their entry into Cranwell, the young Beamish men came under the purview of their assertive and over-solicitous aunt Ellen, sister of their father Francis, who lived in London. She was quite a force. George was, in retrospect, probably quite fortunate not to have come under her wing in the same way as his brother Victor. At time of Victor's entry, Nellie took it upon herself to approach the authorities at Cranwell on his behalf to 'smooth his path' into the College. This approach was not entirely welcomed by her military interlocutors and probably less so by Victor himself, a young man wishing to stake out his own independent path. Done, no doubt, with the purest of motives, these overtures by Nellie show how acts of kindness are often seen differently by donor and recipient.[3a]

Both George and Victor went directly from Coleraine Inst. to the RAF without any intervening experience. In their late teens, they were inevitably young and callow. Indeed, many of that era have acknowledged that they were far more naïve than equivalent young people of the current era. It would have been surprising had there not been an element of 'follow the leader' in George's decision to join up, given how all the younger Beamishes looked up to their elder brother. Victor's 'demonstration' effect was certainly to play a role in the decision of the five remaining Beamish siblings to join the RAF. Victor's time as a dashing fighter pilot in the early part of the Second World War, particularly as a surviving participant in the Battle of Britain, gave him a special status within the family.

George and Victor would certainly have been influenced as adolescents by the pictorial publications of the Air Corps' derring-do in the First World War. A number of these *Boy's Own*-type publications were widely read by young men in the burgeoning years of air warfare during the Great War. They were also the precursors of the schoolboy comics of the inter-war years, such as the *Victor* and the *Magnet*. These and other influences would certainly have had an impact on the young Beamish Brothers as they pondered their future careers. The military was a classically 'manly' career choice of the time, and the RAF had that added glamour for young men of being new and exciting. Importantly, the Air Force was also regarded as a world apart from the hellish drudgery and mindless slaughter of the trench warfare of recent years. In a strongly anti-war era, this was quite important.

An RAF figure who would reach the very highest level, Chief of the Air Staff, during the Second World War, Charles Portal was Chief Flying Instructor at Cranwell just before George joined in 1923. Portal held the position from 1919 to 1922, when he was appointed to the Staff College. Portal, like many of the very senior RAF figures in the Second World War, did his initial flight training with the Army Royal Flying Corps during the First World War before Cranwell had been established.[4]

Victor, having joined Cranwell before George, did get the benefit of Portal's instructional skills. He more than repaid Portal's training in his later career as a fighter ace. George, by contrast, was not a noted pilot, but made up for this in leadership, man-management skills and physical endurance. Portal interestingly shared a similar heritage to the Beamishes, being of of Huguenot stock like them. His family settled in England during the seventeenth century, around the same time that the Beamishes settled in Ireland. It is notable that many Huguenots made strong contributions to both countries over the centuries.

As George followed Victor, so Charles and Cecil followed both of them. When all four Beamish brothers had established themselves in the RAF by the 1930s, they had become household names in officers' messes up and down the country.[5] Even though it was only a recently established service, never before had four brothers and two sisters all joined the RAF, a record that still stands to this day.

Once the RAF was founded in 1918, it would have been seen as an attractive career prospect for a fit, active and sporting young man. The force would have faced stiff competition from the more traditional services, the Royal Navy and the Army, and would have been keen to build up its own recruit base. In its early days, the RAF tended to attract young men from the upper middle class, in particular from public schools. George and his brothers would, by the reckoning of the time, probably have been considered 'solid middle class', in so far as these designations have meaning. Yet there was no element of snobbery shown towards them either because of their background or their nationality.[6]

Because of his large physical presence, George did much of his talking on the sports field, which, in turn, would have commanded the respect of colleagues in the RAF. His ability to bend a coin between his thumb and forefinger would have been sufficient to send out all the appropriate signals to potential adversaries!

It is interesting to examine the list of items with which George was required to equip himself before entering Cranwell as a recruit in 1923. The total cost of his kit to his father was a princely £85 for the year. This could be multiplied about 100 times to bring it to current prices – £8,500. Amusingly, blue gaiters cost 5s 9d. Half Wellingtons were £2 2s and mathematical instruments were £1 10s 2d. Chevrons, the badge marking out a recruit, cost George 11 pence.[7]

Although George excelled at several different sports, rugby was his chief interest in these years. He had already shown his prowess at Coleraine Inst. and in the Ulster Schools competition. In the RAF, he was provided with the opportunity to develop that interest in a service which saw the importance of links between sport, military development and leadership. George was an all-round sportsman. He was an RAF champion at golf and boxing.[8] Records from Cranwell show that he represented the College at hockey against

Royal Military College, Sandhurst, in 1923 in which the airmen went down 4–1. His brother Victor as well as two other Irishmen, a Clifford from St Columba's and L. W. Dickens of Clongowes Wood College, two of Ireland's elite schools, played in the same match. A Cranwell report on the match afterwards referred to George as having played at 'outside right'. He was said to have been 'rather clumsy but has a fair idea of the game. Good hands and is fairly fast.'[9] The RAF were clearly not brimming with adulation at George's hockey exploits, and perhaps it was fortuitous that he was later to make his name on the rugby field. Victor played in goal that day and in match reports was said to have 'played well'. In that same year, George played on the Cricket XI along with his fellow hockey player Dickens of Clongowes. After the end of his cadet year at Cranwell, the official College Journal recounted their estimation of him as a rugby player as follows:

> He played consistently well right through the season and has been a source of encouragement to the remainder of the scrum. A very hard worker in the scrum and dangerous in the loose, his physique and fair speed making it difficult to bring him down. Has an excellent knowledge of the game, and uses it to his advantage.[10]

In the early years of the RAF, the Royal Navy objected to the RAF's participation in combined services rugby competition with themselves and the Army. Again, such was the snobbery at the time towards a 'new' service that this 'ban' was instituted. Apparently, King George V got wind of this 'ban' and angrily called for it to be rescinded. Since then, the RAF has competed on an equal basis with the other Services.[11] This ensured that George had a high-profile platform on which he could showcase his rugby skills in his developing career. George made his rugby debut for the RAF versus the Royal Navy in 1925, the 'ban' having recently been lifted. A bad leg injury meant, however, that he was not to play in this fixture again until 1928. This injury also interrupted his international career for Ireland, which began in 1925 and only resumed in 1928. In a rare victory against the Army in that era, in the 1930/31 season, George captained the RAF side. This was when George was at the peak of his rugby career, having recently returned from a Lions Tour, recently selected captain of Ireland and soon to exact a shock defeat on the touring Springboks.

It was not surprising on first setting eyes on George to hear that he was a keen boxer: he had the look of a pugilist which also served him well in close encounters on the rugby field. In 1924, he was the heavyweight champion of the RAF Inter-Squadron Boxing Championship. In one noted RAF bout, he is said to have made short shrift of his elder brother Victor, doing much for fraternal relations with a few swings and swipes.[12] This was the era of the great American boxers Jack Dempsey and Gene Tunney, both heavyweights like George, and role models for keen young boxers. The fact that they were both of Irish-American stock would have heightened their appeal in the eyes of George, his brothers and their friends.

Also skilled at golf like all the Beamish brothers, George won second prize in the Officers v Cadets Golf Competition in 1924 in Sleaford, the nearest sizeable Lincolnshire town to Cranwell. Despite his strong physique, disconcertingly he had a high-pitched voice, also commented upon many years later by a military colleague in the Desert War. Not a particularly charismatic figure, he was more a solid, reliable 'company man'. Acts of great emotional exuberance were not his style. In this respect, he was not too different from his fellow Ulstermen. Not being an Ulsterman by birth or ancestry, however, did allow him to see things through a distinctive prism. In the description of several who knew him, George was definitely a 'man's man'. In the opinion of Air Vice Marshal Tommy Elmhirst, George's close colleague in the Desert War, George was 'as tough as they come'.[13]

Commandants of Cranwell

Cranwell has had a long line of eminent Commandants. Two are worth mentioning in the context of George's life and career: Commandant Borton and Commandant Baldwin. Borton was George's Commandant as a cadet and Baldwin, Commandant about fifteen years later, found his career intersecting with Victor Beamish in quite a dramatic way.

Air Vice Marshal Amyas Borton was the Commandant at Cranwell from 1922 to 1923. He was the second person appointed as Commandant, which indicates how George entered the RAF in its early days. Borton had been a pilot and commander in the Royal Flying Corps during the First World War and a senior commander in the Royal Air Force during the 1920s. He saw active service on the Western Front, in Palestine and in Iraq. He later became Head of Personnel Services of the RAF, a post which George would also hold later in his career. Borton held a considerable number of awards and retired as an Air Vice Marshal.[14] Commandant in the fledgling years of the RAF, much of Borton's responsibility was in building and establishing the cadetships for a new military service. Over time, he succeeded in gaining the respect of the traditional services for the new RAF which soon became a fixed part of the military landscape.[15]

Another Commandant of Cranwell who held the position just before the Second World War was Air Marshal Jack Baldwin. Baldwin was a graduate of Sandhurst, initially serving as a cavalry officer in the First World War and then later as a pilot in the Royal Flying Corps. He served as an ADC to the King in 1931, and was Director of Personnel Services and Commandant of Cranwell from 1936 to 1938. [16] He retired in August 1939 but was recalled to a post in Bomber Command in the early months of the Second World War. He held the position of Head of Bomber Command briefly from January to February 1942 during the period of the German's 'Channel Dash', in which both Victor Beamish and Brendan 'Paddy' Finucane were involved.[17]

George had the knack of being in the right place at the right time and an ability to hitch his wagon to the coming stars of the RAF. His rise through the ranks was, in part, due to these abilities as much as his own innate abilities and qualities as a military man. George also held the distinction of having been the first officer of air rank to pass through the Cranwell training and graduation process as an exclusively 'Cranwell' man.

A number of 'luminaries' passed through Cranwell in and around the time George underwent his training there. T. E. Lawrence, or 'Lawrence of Arabia', is an example of such a 'name' who spent time there after the Great War. Frank Whittle, the inventor of the jet engine, and air ace Douglas Bader both spent time at Cranwell in the 1920s. George would have been quite familiar with the latter two RAF men. It should be remembered that most of the senior RAF officers who distinguished themselves during the Second World War had initially passed through either the Army or Royal Navy Flying Services before the establishment of RAF Cranwell.

Sword of Honour

Training at Cranwell was for a year to eighteen months. In that time, George was able to pack in quite a lot. He excelled on the sports field, particularly in rugby, cricket, hockey and boxing. Photos still exist along the corridors at Cranwell featuring George as a member of the college rugby, football, cricket, athletics and boxing teams, and in them his large physical presence is notable.

George received the Sword of Honour in his graduation year. This was awarded to the most outstanding recruit, which was usually to the student who had achieved the highest marks in his academic studies. As it happened, George only achieved ninth place out of twenty-one, but because of his outstanding sporting prowess and leadership capabilities, he was given the award. As a keenly sought-after honour, George's fellow recruits and superiors would have admired someone with such an achievement. George was officially awarded the Sword of Honour on 17 December

1924, which meant he was a special type of recruit, holding an honour that stood him in good stead in the development of his future career.

Other Distinguished Holders of the Sword of Honour
Wing Commander Andrew Nicolson Combe received his Sword of Honour in 1932, eight years after George received his. After serving in a variety of roles in the Middle East, he returned to the UK during wartime, mainly serving in Bomber Command. He was awarded the US Bronze Star Flying Cross and died in 1978, aged sixty-six.

Group Captain Geoffrey Wallingford entered Cranwell in 1953 and was awarded the Sword of Honour in 1954. His main RAF areas of activity were in the Malayan Emergency 1956–1958, and the Malaysia Confrontation 1964–66. He also fought in Vietnam in a Royal New Zealand Air Force Squadron, 1964–1966. In 1970, he was New Zealand Equerry to Her Majesty the Queen. He was also Defence Adviser, Singapore 1974–1976.

Air Chief Marshal Sir Neville Stack, like George, received the Sword of Honour in 1939 and returned to become Commandant of Cranwell. Like George, later in his career, he was also appointed Commandant of Transport Command. On the cusp of the Second World War, he was first appointed to Coastal Command and later became an Air ADC to the Queen in 1976. From 1976 to 1988, he was Air Secretary and President of the Old Cranwellian Society.

Cranwell and Rugby
A fringe benefit of George's time at Cranwell, and his subsequent RAF postings in the east of England, was its proximity to Leicester Rugby Club. Keen to establish a base to pursue his passion for rugby, George chose Leicester mainly for its reputation but also for its convenience travel-wise. This was an association that was to rebound to the mutual benefit of both parties. For a person of his outstanding abilities and passion for the game, Leicester was the obvious choice.

Famous rugby players who passed through Cranwell over the years were: Rory Underwood (Leicester, England and Lions), Peter Larter (Northampton and England), and Billy Steel (Bedford and Scotland). To the list should be added Charles Beamish, George's younger brother who played for Leicester, Ireland, the Lions and the Barbarians. From being seen as a neophyte service, excluded from the annual services rugby competition in the 1920s, over the years the RAF has firmly gained its spurs.[18]

Goering and Cranwell – A Strange Twist

A further strange twist to the tale of Hermann Goering having been married in 1923 to Carin, a member of the Beamish family, was revealed on a recent research visit to RAF Cranwell. The author noticed a prominent bronze bust in the staff area of the College library. From a distance, I assumed it could have been Winston Churchill, or even a former Commandant of the College. As I got closer, the surreal fact hit me that this was a bust of Hermann Goering. Was this some strange Pythonesque joke? The bust seemed to me a kind of ironic nod in the direction of the enemy. Then a staff member was kind enough to explain its provenance.

Goering had apparently earmarked Cranwell to become his headquarters as he assumed the Germans would be successful in the Battle of Britain. For that reason, he ordered the *Luftwaffe* not to bomb the College during the war. History intervened and he never had the pleasure of taking possession of it, however, his vanity would have been posthumously flattered if he ever knew that he did eventually reach Cranwell, albeit cast in bronze. The British people would certainly have been glad that he reached no further.

In a similar fashion, Hitler had earmarked 'Chatsworth', the home of the Duke and Duchess of Devonshire in Derbyshire, for himself on the assumption that he would be victorious. Hitler's fascination with Chatsworth House was probably because of its sheer grandeur, however, another factor could have been because the Duchess was Deborah, the youngest sister of his great devotee,

Unity Mitford, who eventually shot herself when she heard of Britain's declaration of war against her beloved Nazi Germany. Despite his hatred of Churchill, Hitler had a sneaking regard for Britain, which he saw as another bulwark against the advance of Bolshevism. It also had the trappings of a great empire which Hitler sought to emulate.

In his time as German Ambassador to Britain in the 1930s, Joachim von Ribbentrop, the former champagne salesman, social climber and Hitler devotee, would have been able to report back to Hitler on eligible, attractive redoubts and Chatsworth would have suited Hitler's outsized ego perfectly.

One can only wonder what George's reaction was, as Commandant at Cranwell after the war, whenever he walked past Goering's bust.

Early Commissions

The year George started his training at Cranwell, 1923, was notable for several events. It was the last year of Ireland's Civil War, Hitler carried out his Beer Hall Putsch in Munich, and the Ku Klux Klan continued to gather huge support in the US. Britain was still recovering from the Great War and the public mood was strongly against war in general.[19] The emphasis for those entering the military would have been on 'protecting the peace' and not on waging war. As it turned out, the RAF as the 'new kid on the block' was about to make a huge impact in the coming war and to establish itself securely in the nation's iconography.

After George was commissioned in late 1924, he was posted as a pilot with No. 100 Squadron. This was based in Spitalgate in Lincolnshire, not far from Cranwell. George's career proper began at this point. The squadron had experience in the War of Independence in Ireland and, for a time, was based in Baldonnell, Co. Dublin, which is now the main base of the Irish Air Corps.[20]

George spent a period in 1937 at the RAF Staff College, in Andover. The training programme in 1937 was held at a critical time in terms of Britain's war preparedness in the run-up to the

Second World War. It was widely held that Germany's *Luftwaffe* held a strong numerical superiority in aircraft compared to the number held by the RAF. Even though the strong national mood at the time was to avoid war with Germany, officers such as George Beamish would have noted the key implications for Britain's strategic security due to these deficiencies. In these years, the armed services seemed to be preparing defences for a war that no one wanted but many thought was inevitable.

4

FROM LEICESTER TIGER TO BRITISH AND IRISH LION

When George first entered the stage of senior rugby in the 1920s, the game was a far cry from the commercial and widely marketed game we see today. The game had split in the 1890s between those who went 'professional' and those who wished to retain the game's amateur status. Players who left the amateur game were eternally shunned, such was the animosity between the two codes – an animosity laced with social class frictions. Players switching to professional status were regularly said to be 'heading North' as most of the new rugby league clubs were in the north of England.

In 1922, England and Wales used player numbers for the first time in a home nations match. However, George's club, Leicester, decided to buck the trend by having letters for its forwards. It was not until 1950 that all the home nations played with numbers.[1]

In George's first year at Cranwell, in 1923, the Centenary Match commemorating the founding of the amateur game by William Webb Ellis was played between a selection of English, Scottish, Irish and Welsh players.[2] In 1924, George Beamish first togged out for Leicester and the following year, he won his first international cap for Ireland. That was the 'status quo' for George Beamish in the 1920s. His evident rugby prowess was a skill and quality that stood on its own merits and was also to complement his developing prowess as an airman. In such a 'macho' world as the military, being an eminent sportsman undoubtedly added to an individual's allure. George and his brothers fitted that bill perfectly.

In 1927, the BBC broadcast its first rugby international by radio between England and Wales.[3]

Leicester – Club of Choice

The city of Leicester's 'Jewel in the Crown' is undoubtedly its rugby union team, based at Welford Road. While its football team may have caused some excitement in recent years, its record does not compare with the longevity and consistency of its outstanding rugby team, the most successful team in England with a veritable 'Who's Who' of past players. Leicester Football Club (the rugby club) has had a long tradition of success. It has also had a long history of welcoming many Irish players through its portals over the decades.

Central to the club's development was the figure of Tom Crumbie who steered the progress of the club in the late nineteenth and early twentieth centuries.[4] He was appointed club secretary in 1895, a post he held until 1928, and he is credited with bringing the club to national prominence. During his time, the All Blacks played twice at Welford Road and the annual Barbarians fixture there was established in 1909, a fixture to last into the 1990s. At the time of George's arrival at the club in 1924, Crumbie was a towering figure of respect.

George was one of the first few Irishmen and non-Englishmen to blaze a trail at Leicester. After him, the list includes a whole host of Irish rugby talent, including Tony O'Reilly, Andy Mulligan, Charles Beamish, Cecil Beamish, Leo Cullen, Eric Miller, Geordan Murphy, Shane Jennings, Jeremy Staunton and Tom Tierney, all of whom were Irish internationals.[5] While London Irish was the main destination for the Irish living in London and the south-east of England in that era, a team like Leicester provided an alternative choice for many. Its traditions and its consistently high standards of performance made it an attractive option. Based as he was with the RAF in the English Midlands, for George it was the obvious choice and he was certainly conscious of joining one of the major clubs in Britain at the time. In retrospect, he had joined a club which was to have the most illustrious track record in the English game.

George arrived at Leicester with a notable record, forged first at Coleraine Inst. and then at RAF Cranwell. His size, at 6 feet 2 inches tall, made him strong forward material. He was to play mainly at No. 8 or occasionally at wing-forward in his subsequent career. His physical strength, combined with his RAF training and bearing, ensured that George came to Leicester with much to offer. He did not disappoint.

It was in the year following his arrival in England that George signed up with Leicester. He made his debut in a home match against Heriotonians, the Edinburgh club, on the day after Boxing Day, 27 December 1924. Two days later, he played for Leicester in the annual match against the Barbarians. All in all, he played for the Tigers on 118 occasions over the course of his career.[6] George had not yet joined the club in time for the arrival of the All Blacks on their 1924 Tour; Leicester lost by 27–0. However, he was a member of the team that won the County Championship in 1925, becoming, it is said, quite a crowd favourite at Welford Road thereafter.[7]

From 1926 to 1927, the jerseys of Leicester forwards had letters instead of numbers on their backs, from A to G, to distinguish them from the backs. A club of Leicester's stature probably gave it licence for such individualistic gestures. It was in George's third season with Leicester that the club made the transition from numbers to letters, which was to be the policy until the late 1990s.[8]

When George arrived at the club, Tom Crumbie continued to be its leading light. It had established itself as one of the leading clubs in Britain and had a fixture list that included the main clubs in England and Wales and a smaller number in Scotland.[9] Leicester's main opponents in those years were: Mosley, Blackheath, Bristol, Bath, Harlequins, Northampton, Cardiff, Llanelli, Swansea and Heriots FP. As part of the amateur game, matches were generally contended as 'friendlies' and with fewer competitive events than in the modern era.

Another man was also to rise to the very heights of the RAF played for Leicester during the 1923/24 season.[10] That individual was Charles Medhurst in the season immediately preceding the year of George's debut for the club. He was to eventually reach the rank of Air Chief Marshal and was appointed Head of RAF Intelligence, the Commander-in-Chief of Mediterranean and Middle East Command and Vice-Chief of the Air Staff. Highlighting the closeness of the RAF family at the time, Medhurst's wartime position as Head of RAF Intelligence was held a number of years later by George's close associate in North Africa, Tommy Elmhirst. Medhurst's association with Leicester was one of several examples of close regional links between Cranwell, the RAF and the club.[11]

Leicester's Ground at Welford Road

Leicester's ground at Welford Road has witnessed many bruising encounters over the years. It was first opened in 1892 and through time it has seen many alterations and developments. In rugby terms, it has gained the just reputation of being a 'fortress' for visiting teams. In these islands, very few club grounds hold such a reputation, with the exception, perhaps, of Gloucester's Kingsholm or Munster's Thomond Park. One year before George joined Leicester and two years before his first international cap, Ireland played England in Welford Road during the 1923 Five Nations series. Ireland lost by a convincing 23–5. On two other previous occasions, Ireland played England at Welford Road. In 1902, they lost by 6–3 but in the 1906 fixture, they won by 16–6. The Irish match was the last time that Welford Road hosted an international until the 1991 World Cup. However, the club did host international visitors – on 24 October 1924, a record attendance of 24,000 at the ground saw Leicester play the touring All Blacks.[12]

George's early performances for Leicester caught the attention of the Irish selectors and he was rewarded with being selected to make his debut against England in February 1925.[13] This was quite an achievement as he first played for Leicester the previous Boxing Day.

Much has been written about how much the game has changed during the professional era. The changes since George Beamish played in the 1920s and 1930s are even starker. Forwards in the Beamish era, for example, were not expected to be as versatile and fleet of foot as nowadays. Scoring tries was not top of their agenda in those days. While the game may have lost its raffish amateur charm, most fans would probably agree that the game has advanced positively over the years. Players now tend to be fitter, they are scientifically trained, fed and watered, and they are all built like tanks.

Leicester has an impressive tradition of producing top class players. Doug Prentice, Dean Richards, Martin Johnson, Neil Back, Rory Underwood, Clive Woodward, Will Greenwood, Bernard Gadney, Richard Cockerill, Paul Dodge, Graham Rowntree, Peter Wheeler are a list of only the very best of them. All are internationals and ex-Lions. Very few if any clubs can command such an impressive list of top players. Its foreign players included Tony O'Reilly (IRE), Paul Howard (AUS), the Tuilagi brothers (NZ). Geordan Murphy (IRE), Leo Cullen (IRE), the Beamish brothers (IRE), Josh Kronfeld, Brad Thorn (NZ), Roger Arniel (SCO), Joel Stransky, Jacob van der Westhuizen (SA) and many others.[14] The club also has a strong tradition of producing big, powerful leader figures like George Beamish. In recent decades, three such figures stand out: Dean Richards, Martin Johnson and Martin Corry. Like George, these three were also English internationals and Lions with very deep and long-standing links with Leicester. The club appeared to churn out such players as if off a production line!

One of the greatest honours George achieved was to have been selected for Leicester's 'Team of the Century'. On that team, he rubbed shoulders with the esteemed company of, amongst others, Martin Johnson, his former colleagues, Doug Prentice and Bernard Gadney, ex-RAF man Rory Underwood, Dean Richards, Clive

Woodward, Peter Wheeler and Neil Back.[15] George was selected in his second position of lock which would have involved him scrumming down beside Martin Johnson! He and Ken Scotland were the only two non-English internationals chosen for the notional team. George's long career with Leicester, his many selections for and captaining of Ireland, his Lions selection and his sheer talent, moreover, all made him a worthy choice.

George's Debut for Ireland

In his debut for Ireland in 1925, he was only nineteen years of age. Despite his relative youth, he was a broad, towering figure who had been blooded in the school of Leicester rugby. His first match was against England which ended in a 6–6 draw. Such was his performance that the selectors decided to retain him for all the remaining matches of the championship that year. After a break of more than two years due to an injured leg, George was recalled to play for Ireland in the 1928 season. It was a great boost to George to be back in favour with the selectors after such a long break. From that year until his retirement in 1933, George was rarely out of the Irish team, receiving the honour of the team captaincy during the final period of his career. The only other acting serviceman to captain Ireland was more than fifty years later with the appointment of Captain Ciaran Fitzgerald in 1982. In that year, Fitzgerald led Ireland to its first Triple Crown since 1949. Fifty years separated the Irish captaincy of a British air force officer and that of an Irish army officer – just another example of Ireland's quirky historical landscape. Like Beamish, Fitzgerald also played with the Lions whom he captained in 1983 on their tour to New Zealand.

George's Irish teammates included the legendary Eugene Davy, outside half for the Dublin club Lansdowne; Mick Dunne, also a Lansdowne man and a member of the 1930 Lions tour; as well as the renowned flanker and medic, Jamie 'Jammie' Clinch. Mark Sugden of Wanderers played scrum-half on several Irish teams with George, and he was regarded as one of the best in the world in that position. Two more of George's fellow internationals also worth mentioning are Morgan Crowe of Lansdowne, scion of the famous sporting Crowe family, and Noel Murphy, supremo in his own right and father of Noel Murphy of Cork Constitution, of Ireland and of Lions fame, and one-time manager of Ireland.[16]

During his first international season, George gained three caps against all the Triple Crown teams, playing in his preferred No. 8 position. In 1925, he also played on the all-Leicestershire side that won the County Championships for the first time, beating Gloucestershire in the final. After a brief absence from the Irish team, George returned in 1928, playing almost uninterrupted until his retirement in 1933. It was during that period that he toured with the Lions in Australasia and captained a provincial English side to a heroic victory over the 1931 touring Springboks. From 1931 to 1933, he was chosen to captain the Ireland side. At his retirement, he became the most capped No. 8 in rugby history.[17]

It was an era in world rugby when Ireland's record was very 'middle of the road' despite the calibre of its international players. In the 26 matches George played for Ireland from 1925 to 1933, he was on the winning side on 13 occasions, lost on 11 occasions and drew 2 matches. Notable in those days was how matches tended to have fewer scores than nowadays. In 1926 and 1927, Ireland and Scotland shared the Five Nations title. In 1928, England won the Triple Crown and the Grand Slam and in 1932, there was a three-way tie for the title between England, Ireland and Wales. France didn't feature prominently in those years until it became a major force from the mid-1950s onwards. England probably held a slight advantage against the other Five Nations teams during those years by dint of the strength in depth of its game and its larger number of clubs.[18]

On a lighter note, George became one of several 'poster boys' for international rugby by being chosen as one of the figures on tobacco manufacturer H. D. and W. O. Wills's 1929 Rugby Card series. The series encouraged a thriving trade of cards among enthusiasts at the time. Recently, one of that series went on sale on Amazon for the 'grand' price of £2.95! In that year, fifty of the top international players appeared on a card, including George's Irish international colleague Mark Sugden and a number of his fellow Lions Tour members in 1930. In that era, odd as it may seem now, it was not uncommon for cigarette companies to sponsor and promote sports events and sportsmen in such ways.[19]

In the 1927/28 season, George was also asked to become a member of a Barbarians touring side, a further sign that he was in favour with rugby's 'powers that be'. He is one of 92 Leicester players to have been selected for the Barbarians since their inception. This included his brothers, Charles and Cecil. Fellow Irishman, Tony O'Reilly holds the record of most appearances for the Barbarians (30) and most tries (38).[20] George had already entered the fold of respectability by gaining international honours for Ireland and Barbarian selection. He was soon to gain the ultimate honour of being selected for the Lions.

1930 Lions Tour

In 1930, Beamish was one of three Leicester players to be selected for the Lions tour to Australia and New Zealand. The other two were Doug Prentice as captain and a nineteen-year-old prop, Doug Kendrew.[21] Like George, Kendrew had a distinguished record in the Second World War, in his case with the Army. He later became a distinguished High Court judge.

From a New Zealand perspective, the tour was seen as business as usual. The Lions had never won in New Zealand and the Kiwis were determined not to let it happen this time. Their press pundits praised the quality of the Lions' backline but were rather dismissive (unfairly) of their forwards.

The 1930 tour was the first time when the party were officially referred to as the Lions. The iconic four-quartered crest had first been adopted in 1924. Beamish made a huge impact on the 1930 tour, playing in twenty-one matches, also captaining the side on three occasions in Prentice's absence. He managed to score a try against Otago. George was building towards being a real leader of men through his rugby and his role in the RAF.[22]

The invitation from Lions management in 1930 to prospective tour players makes amusing reading. A transcription of its contents is set out below. It has a very 'top down' tone and is heavy on the sense of duty expected of all players participating on the tour. The ingrained amateur ethos comes through strongly in the letter's reference to personal pocket money required by tour players. An equivalent letter in the professional era of 2018 would adopt a less magisterial tone.

> Dear Sir
> You have been provisionally selected to take part in the above tour. The final selection will not, however, be made until two or three months before the Team sails.
>
> The Team will leave England about the second week in April 1930 and arrive back about the second week in October. Each player should be in possession of about £50 to £75 for incidental expenses.
>
> We hope that the team eventually chosen will represent the full playing strength of the Home Nations, in order that we may give New Zealand and Australia a true idea of our standard of play, and we hope you will make every effort to take part in the Tour.
>
> Will you please inform the Secretary of the Rugby Football Union, Twickenham, whether you would be able to take part in the Tour.

The 1930 excursion is widely believed to be the first to properly represent a British team and the first to be properly called 'the Lions' after the name first crept into usage in South Africa, six years before.[22a] As a Lion, George was now a member of a select club. Whereas the tours of that era lacked the high octane of nowadays, more focus would have been placed then on the honour and representative aspects of a tour. When tours could last as long as six months, special qualities were required of touring players: endurance, tolerance and forbearance being chief among them. A Lions Tour also highlighted the links between the then British Empire and the sport of rugby. The international game at that time was essentially a sport played in the 'kith and kin' empire, the home nations, and France. Not only did the sport cement individual sporting relations but those between nations. The fact that the team was known as the British and Irish Lions marked this inclusivity and even-handedness.

Other Irishmen on the 1930 tour were Mick Dunne of Lansdowne, Jimmy Farrell of Bective Rangers, Henry O'Neill of Queen's University, Belfast, and Paul Murray of Wanderers – all figures George played with for Ireland. Mick Dunne acquitted himself well on the field of play but was to leave his mark on the tour for another reason: a celebrated romance with a New Zealand woman. Dunne gave up his job in Dublin before embarking on the months-long tour of 1930. While in New Zealand, he had a romance with a local girl, Rau, to whom he gave his Lions jersey. In those days, the Lions jersey was navy blue and it was not until the 1950 Tour that the colour was changed to red. Both Mick and Rau eventually married separate partners and the jersey seemed to get forgotten. In 2013, eighty-three years after the tour, the jersey was returned to Ireland and Dunne's surviving family by Rau's daughter, Robyn Opie. Much media interest followed this story which highlighted the often-forgotten 'human dimension' of rugby tours.[22b]

Brendan Gallagher of the *The Rugby Paper* (16 September 2016) in a not entirely unbiased account of both the tour and the Lions team, noted how the Lions party was hugely popular socially and indeed, rather distinguished. For example, he refers to George and his future wartime exploits, to Carl Aarvold and his future elevation to the English High Court bench and to another tourist, Doug Kendrew, who had a distinguished army record in the Second World War.[22c]

The Lions committee picked a provisional party in April 1929, giving those selected twelve months to arrange six months leave and accumulate the £80 each player was required to bank with the Lions to cover their incidental expenses. All those making the trip also had to provide their own dinner jacket, which was to be worn nightly when dining on the voyage to New Zealand. As an RAF officer, George had to seek permission up the chain of command to join the tour. He was understandably put on half-pay for the period of the six-month tour.

Another fascinating individual on the tour was Blackheath's South African-born forward Bryan Black who arrived in Britain as a Rhodes Scholar at Oxford. Black served in the RAF during the war and was to be killed in action, flying over Wiltshire in July 1940.

Gallagher also refers unflatteringly to James Baxter, the Lions Manager as 'a crusty old former England international who had also won an Olympic silver medal for sailing at the 1908 Olympics'. Although Gallagher was writing more than three-quarters of a century after the tour, he shows the same facility at needling the Lions which his Kiwi predecessors showed in 1930. In truth, most New Zealanders saw the Lions as little match for their beloved All Blacks and relished pointing out their deficiencies.[22d]

Perhaps, the most noteworthy aspect of the 1930 Tour for George was his role in reshaping the Lions' uniform. At that time, the strip had a jersey of Scottish blue, English white for the shorts and the red of Wales for the socks. However, there was no green of Ireland. George bravely approached the tour authorities about this anomaly and won their agreement for having a green flash at the top of the team socks. A green turnover on blue socks was instituted for the next tour in 1936. Although it was a small innovation, the inclusion of Irish green cemented the four-nation element of the Lions and reinforced the fact that the team was very much the British and Irish Lions. One could say that this was George Beamish's gesture towards rugby inclusiveness and equality. As anyone who has played sport knows, your kit is important as an expression of identity.

A more intense controversy during the tour involved the team strip of the All Blacks. Their all-black colours clashed with the

Lions' navy blue jersey. All Black aficionados were aghast at the thought of their national team not wearing the traditional black in a Test match. However, the established norm was to allow the visiting side to retain their strip in the event of a clash of colours. A solution had to be found. Eventually, the All Blacks agreed to wear white in the Tests and the matter was resolved, not without some Kiwi gnashing of teeth. With the Lions' jersey eventually changing to red in 1950, this avoided any future controversy in New Zealand. Over the years, the Springboks have occasionally worn white jerseys to avoid colour clashes but never with the same impact as the 1930 All Whites!

Coming on the back of the 1924 All Black Tour of Britain and Ireland, which showcased the skills of such players as George Nepia, it was important for the Lions to stamp their mark on the 1930 tour. They won 15 and lost 6 matches and lost the Test series by 3–1. Their 3 further losses were to the great sides from Auckland, Canterbury and Wellington – provincial teams that continue to hold top positions in New Zealand rugby.[23] The one Test match the Lions won, ironically, was at Dunedin's Carisbrook, notorious for its weather and so often the graveyard of Lions sides in previous and subsequent tours. It is the home ground of Otago and locals proudly refer to it as 'The House of Pain'.

In rugby circles, they say 'what goes on on tour stays on tour'. Participants' lips are sealed forever like a form of Mafia *omertà*. That is not to say that anything nefarious took place on the 1930 Tour. However, even the perennially serious George Beamish was not beyond 'showing a bit of ankle'; during a team celebration involving a visit to a Maori community, George was photographed dancing in a grass skirt.[24] For the ultimate macho individual, this showed a 'new side' of George in a harmless explosion of high spirits typical of rugby tours.

Such were the many challenges of a tour to New Zealand that it wasn't until 1971 that the Lions, coached by Carwyn James and captained by John Dawes, managed to beat the All Blacks in a Test series on their own home soil. This team has often been hailed as the most talented Lions combination ever to leave these islands. George managed to score two tries during the 1930 tour: one against Otago and one against Marlborough/Nelson. The Otago match was played at the fearsome Dunedin, a proud victory for the Lions.[25]

New Zealand Rugby Museum director Stephen Berg is quoted as saying about the 1930 tour:

> The 1930 tour followed on [from the 1924 Invincibles] and we wanted to make the statement that we were the best rugby nation in the world.
>
> The series proved to be the swansong for one of our most famous and beloved All Blacks, the great George Nepia.[26]

The above quotation highlights one key point: the All Blacks have been at the very top of world rugby for almost a century. Over that period, their tradition of winning has almost become part of their DNA. When an All Black team takes the field, you sense the ghosts of former All Blacks hovering in the background. They and their supporters were not in the habit of losing. George and his fellow tourists faced that pressure on the 1930 Tour. It took another forty years for the hoodoo to be dispelled.

The 1930 Tour also included a visit to Australia where the Lions lost 2 of their 6 matches, against Australia and New South Wales respectively. This leg of the tour did not attract the same attention, as Australian sides then stood very much in the shadow of their Kiwi neighbours. Unlike today, the exigencies of long-distance travel in the 1930s required the Lions party to take in Australia and New Zealand in the same year.

The trip back to Britain by sea took several weeks and involved a stopover in Ceylon (now Sri Lanka) where the Lions played a match. Due to the fact that commercial air travel was in its infancy, sea travel meant these trips took a long time. It also meant that a tour was much longer than a typical tour nowadays. It must also have involved very tolerant and understanding employers. In George Beamish's case, the RAF's positive view of sporting representation worked in his favour. Yet, he was put on RAF half-pay scales for 1930 as he was away on tour for about six months during that year. One of the most challenging jobs on the boat over must have been that of 'Deck Entertainment Manager' who was tasked with keeping 30-odd rugby players amused within a confined space for many weeks. Harry Bowcott, a Welsh member of the 1930 Lions had the following interesting observations on the tour many years after, in an interview in 1980:

> Packed on the Monday, down to Southampton and away to New Zealand via Panama. It was typically ship's life.
>
> Good-quality food, as good as any London hotel. Nice four-course lunch and if you wanted it a seven- or eight-course dinner.
>
> Many of us, of course, were not used to having more than perhaps two meals a day. We all turned out in our dinner jackets, some, I'm certain, for the first time.
>
> It added something to the tour – a sense of importance.[27]

With the Second World War intervening, the next Lions Tour to the Antipodes was not until 1950, then captained by Ireland's Karl Mullen. As usual, that tour had its fair share of frothy high jinks. Not far from such activity could regularly be found one Tom Clifford, a prop and butcher from Limerick. It was said that Clifford's mother was so concerned for her son's well-being on the sea journey from Southampton that she filled a whole travelling trunk with pies and cakes as sustenance. By all accounts, Clifford shared the grub among his teammates, with the trove lasting not long after their departure from Southampton! Although that Lions party performed creditably on that tour, they again failed to crack the New Zealand nut.

Victory over 1931 Springboks

George and his fellow Lions tourists could be forgiven for finding life back in Britain and Ireland after a six-month tour 'down under' a little underwhelming. Work and local rugby had a way of bringing reality home again, however, and it was not long after their return that they were preparing for the arrival of the 1931 Springboks. Probably George's biggest career success was his captaining of a Leicestershire and East Midlands XV to a stunning victory against the touring Springboks team. George not only captained the side but scored a try on the day. According to Stuart Farmer and David Hands, the authors of *The Tigers Tale*, as captain George delivered a speech after the match to the crowd before they dispersed, such was the historic occasion.[28] In recognition of the Counties being the first team to beat the Springboks on tour, four days later the South Africans presented the team with a head of a dead springbok.[29]

Such was the reverence towards the touring Springboks that this victory would have been on a par with later 'giant killer' victories such as Llanelli beating the All Blacks in 1973 and Munster's victory against the All Blacks in 1978. A week before the match, George also participated in a Combined Services side that went down to the tourists at Twickenham by 23–0.

On tour, the Springboks were led by Bernie Osler, fly half and half-back partner of Danie Craven. Although a well-regarded player, Osler's decision to play ten-man rugby took much of the flair out of the Springbok game, which had previously been their hallmark. Although blessed with good backs, this ten-man strategy making use of the firepower of large forward packs, was to become a feature of future Springbok sides. As a fly half, Osler would have been a clear target of special attention of George Beamish.

Another member of that Springbok touring party was a figure who was to have a major impact in international rugby years later as an official of the South African Rugby Board. That man was Danie Craven, who gained his first cap for South Africa at scrum-half at the age of twenty-one against Wales on the famous 1931 Tour. He was a third-year student at Stellenbosch University, a proud rugby bastion a few kilometres north of Cape Town, and at the time he was no doubt buoyed up by this international rugby opportunity. His second cap was a week later against Ireland. South Africa won both matches. Craven, the tough-nut Boer, as the South African scrum-half had many close physical encounters with George, the equally tough Irishman, during the three matches they played against one another. After his retirement, Craven became Chairman of the South African Rugby Board through most of the period of the anti-apartheid boycotts of South Africa. Though a traditional South African, to his credit he tried to keep the lines of communication open with his international counterparts in seeking solutions. Multiracial rugby was on its way by the time he died in 1993. He passed away two years before the advent of professional rugby and before the emotional appearance of Nelson Mandela in a Springbok jersey at the final of the World Cup in South Africa in 1995.[30]

Final Years at Leicester

George was also given a third bite of the South African cherry during their 1931 tour when he was selected to captain Ireland against the Springboks. Ireland lost the encounter by 8–3, but Ireland performed creditably.[31] Indeed, all the home international sides fell to the Springboks that year. South Africa's only loss on that tour was to the Beamish-captained Leicestershire and East Midlands side.[32] Both Craven and Beamish were near contemporaries in age, with George just four years older. Both had had a 'good war' during the Second World War. When they both retired from the game, George, with the exception of his membership of the RAF Rugby Selection Board, went into discreet retirement, while Craven became one of the most well-known and controversial officials in world rugby.

Nearer to home, George's next youngest brother, Charles, followed George to Leicester, playing there in the position of prop. Like George, he also played for Ireland and the Lions, travelling on their 1936 Tour to Argentina, captained by fellow Leicester man Bernard Gadney.[33] By 1934, George and Charles played together on the same team at Leicester. Victor had also played briefly for the club and when youngest brother Cecil played some years later, the four brothers set a record for brothers who played for the club. This record was only surpassed seventy years later when the sixth of the six Tuilagi brothers togged out for Leicester in 2009. As in the RAF, the Beamishes were also setting early records in one of Britain's most illustrious rugby clubs.[34]

George's time at Leicester was an invaluable experience for him. It was his first exposure to club rugby at the highest level among players who played or aspired to play at international level. Among his team mates were players like Doug Prentice and Bernard Gadney, both future captains of the Lions. Indeed, George himself was called upon in the tour to New Zealand to take on the role of captain on a couple of occasions. Unlike some of the bigger city clubs, at the time Leicester drew many of its players from the rural and agricultural parts of the east Midlands.[35] This produced a hardy, strong prototype player, not unlike the sort of player selected for the All Blacks. All Black legend and farmer Colin Meads, for example, would have fitted the bill perfectly at Leicester. George too would have been in his element among the burly farmers of Leicestershire who played in large numbers for the Leicester club. Although farming is a fading occupation in the twenty-first century, as recently as the 1980s, Leicester had a farmer at fullback, one Dusty Hare, who also went on to play for England.

A memorable match which George competed in was the 1929 Rowland Hill Memorial match, played in memory of a famed administrator of the game from the nineteenth century, George Rowland Hill.[36] Rowland Hill was President of the Rugby Football Union between 1904 and 1907 and was its secretary for twenty years. He also presided over the split in the game between rugby union and rugby league, a rift that while not so intense now has never finally been resolved.[36a]

It was decided to field two teams from the best of England/Wales vs Ireland/Scotland. Many of the players in the Rowland Hill match were also colleagues from the 1930 Tour. Ireland/Scotland were the winning side on the day with Irishman Eugene Davy one of the try scorers. The teams included such stars as J. Bassett, C. D. Aarvold, W. G. Morgan and J. S. Tucker for England/Wales, while the Scotland/Ireland team included I. S. Smith, G. P. S. Macpherson (Captain), M. Sugden, G. R. Beamish, M. J. Dunne.[37] Matches with similar formats to the Rowland Hill Match were held in the 1970s and 1980s for the centenaries of the rugby unions of England, Wales, Scotland and Ireland respectively – in all cases, great spectacles.

RAF Rugby

> The RAF has a long and distinguished history of supporting personnel in the playing and organising of sport
>   – RAF Sports Federation.

The Royal Air Force Sports Federation encapsulates the philosophy as follows: 'NOW'.

Historically, sport has played a major part in the military. From being a factor in recruitment, to enabling promotion through the rank structure, military life has been underpinned by competitive sports. The Royal Air Force places sport at the very heart of its activities.[38]

It was against this philosophical background that George embarked on and developed his rugby career while in the RAF. Great encouragement was given to him in progressing his participation with nearby Leicester and ultimately with Ireland and the Lions – all requiring some flexibility regarding leave arrangements. George also had an impressive record playing with the RAF rugby side, which he eventually captained. He was also selected to play for the Combined Services against the touring Springboks side of 1931. Along the corridors of RAF Cranwell, there are many photos of teams George had played with. He captained the RAF rugby team and later in in his career, he became an RAF rugby selector.

At 6 feet 2 inches tall and 17 stone in weight, he was known as the 'Irish Hercules'. Later photographs of George when he was a high-ranking RAF officer depict a slightly portly, full-faced man. One of the drawbacks of aging, particularly for former rugby players is that they can gain large amounts of weight when they give up intensive training following the end of their careers. This was the case with George and is quite common up to the present day.

From the foundation of the RAF in 1918, the airmen were keen to have the opportunity to play high-level rugby and to compete against the soldiers and sailors on the rugby field at the earliest opportunity. However, when the young RAF Rugby Union's Honorary Secretary William Wavell Wakefield (England and Harlequins) tried to arrange fixtures against the other two Services, the Army agreed but initially the Royal Navy did not.[39] After discussions, the Royal Navy acquiesced but refused to award caps for the encounter, although they did for their annual game with the Army. When the Chief of the Air Staff, Marshal of the Royal Air Force Sir Hugh (later Lord) Trenchard got to hear about this, he mentioned it to the pro-RAF King George V. The King then summoned the First Sea Lord and put him on the spot by saying: 'I would like to know more about this insult to my Royal Air Force'. Needless to say, the issue was rapidly resolved and the Tri-Service tournament came in to being in 1920. The RAF took its first Inter-Services title in 1922.[40]

During his time in the RAF, George played for RAF teams with the famous air ace Douglas Bader. Two more different characters could not have been imagined. George was robust, stolid and a team player, while Bader was mercurial, prickly and an individualist. George played No. 8 and Bader played fly half or wing.[41] George's future RAF career was a 'slow burn', while Bader had a dramatic career, losing both legs following an air accident. After many rejections, Bader persisted in asking the RAF authorities to allow him to return to flying. Eventually they relented and allowed the disabled Bader fly with the RAF. His role and history are depicted in the 1956 film *Reach for the Stars*, with the actor Kenneth More playing Bader. Although Bader was undoubtedly heroic, not a lot people warmed to such an outspoken maverick and many have said that More's portrayal of Bader was 'flattering'. The RAF afforded much tolerance to those wishing to develop their sporting skills and Beamish and Bader were two among many who were to avail themselves of such tolerance. In 1931 at the height of George's air force career, George was also captain of the RAF rugby side with Bader as his star fly half.[42]

In the Second World War, many former Five Nations internationals joined the RAF. This was also the case in peacetime. Probably the most outstanding player to emerge from the RAF in peacetime was Rory Underwood of Leicester and England in the 1980s and 1990s. Underwood was capped 85 times for England, and holds the English record of 49 tries. Other notable internationals who also served with the RAF were Welshmen – Bleddyn Williams, Ken Rees and William Wavell Wakefield. The Scot, Billy Steel, and Englishman, Peter Larter, were also both RAF men and internationals in the 1980s, and the 1960s–70s, respectively. Prince Alexander Obolensky also played for Leicester and England in the 1930s as well as being an RAF pilot. [43]

From the end of the Second World War, George was an RAF Rugby Selector and effectively in charge of RAF rugby. An incident occurred involving George and his brother Cecil which led to a long rift between the two. George called Cecil saying he had been selected to play in an RAF rugby team. Cecil said he was due to play golf for the RAF at that time and had to decline. George, the 'senior officer', dug his heels in over the matter and arising from the animosity, the two never talked for twenty years. The story highlights why Irish family feuds are said to be among the most intense anywhere.

The Barbarians
This club was founded in 1890 by a player from Blackheath, in London, Percy Carpmael. His dream was to spread good fellowship among all rugby football players and that dream became reality on 27 December at Friary Field, Hartlepool. At the founding of the

club in a restaurant in Bradford, the Right Reverend W. J. Carvey declared: 'Rugby Football is a game for gentlemen in all classes, but for no bad sportsman in any class.' This ethos ensured that the Barbarians did not discriminate in terms of class, race, creed or colour and the only qualification to be invited to become a member was that you were a good rugby player and a good sportsman.[44]

For those of a certain age, the enduring image of Barbarians rugby is of Gareth Edwards scoring a memorable team-effort try during the 1973 fixture against the All Blacks. It has always been a feature of the Barbarians to throw caution to the wind by playing open passing rugby, in the way that Edwards and his teammates demonstrated in that 1973 match. The club also liked to select players who could accommodate to such a mindset. Another tradition is the selection of one non-international player for each match, usually an up-and-coming club player. A unique feature of their team strip is the fact that players wear their own club socks.

Along with other Leicester and Ireland players, George was a fairly regular player with the Barbarians club. On 27 December each year, the tradition has grown up of a match between the Barbarians and Leicester. Leicester also regularly played a match against each of the touring Australian, New Zealand and South African sides, reflecting the club's status in British rugby. All three hold a winning record in their matches against the Barbarians. The Barbarians also play against other international sides, the Combined Services and on their Easter tour, several Welsh clubs.[45] George was, in many ways, the classic Barbarian – good at rugby and a keen sportsman with a team player's focus. His membership of the club was yet another feather in his cap on his rugby career journey.

The Best Five Nations Players of the 1920s/Early 1930s Era
The RAF and rugby were the two biggest parts of George's life. Most sport was amateur in that era, rugby being no different. A great team player, George was conscious of the skills and character attributes needed to excel both in sport and in the

services. On the rugby field, he played with and against the very best of his era. This was one of the huge benefits of playing on a Lions tour: the chance of playing with, training with and living close by with so many of the best players in the world. Accounts of these individuals' careers help to flesh out the context of the rugby era and in the process, to add some colour to it. During the years of George's international career in the 1920s and 1930s, the Home Nations competition was known as the Five Nations involving England, Scotland, Ireland, Wales and France, until Italy joined in 2000. To give a slight flavour of the era in which George played the game, the details of some of these characters are worth recounting. They are listed in Appendix 1.

George Beamish's career was very much anchored in the amateur era, with all the adherence to Corinthian values which that entailed. Those who wished to play professionally, 'headed north' to the rugby league clubs of Northern England. It meant eternal banishment from the groves of rugby union, such was the enmity between the two codes in those years. It was drilled into players at the time that they were 'playing for the jersey', that representing your country was the highest honour, and that money was of no consideration. This view ironically sat side by side with the informal practice of paying 'boot money' (essentially, professional backhanders) – a practice that was 'officially' denied. These values might seem quaint to us now in the professional era, but they were very much the driving values of the time. For someone like George Beamish, also trained in the values of service to the RAF, they were central to the man he was.

Irishness and Britishness – Rugby in a Political/ Cultural Context

Had George and his fellow serviceman been living and playing in the 1968–1997 period, they would have encountered quite a different atmosphere from that which existed in the 1920s and 1930s. During the years of the Northern Ireland Troubles with the constant threat of paramilitary attack, anyone serving with the

British forces was a potential target. During that time, members of the security forces based in Northern Ireland selected to play for Ireland, for example, were given a police escort down to Dublin for training sessions and matches. The references to them in match programme biographies made use of an anodyne title such as 'civil servant' in order to protect them. These were no idle fears as witnessed by the injuries sustained by internationals from Ulster, Nigel Carr and David Irwin, following a bomb blast that killed a Northern Ireland judge, Judge Gibson, on the main Dublin–Belfast road in 1987. Horrible though such incidents were, those kinds of events are now very much in the past, thanks in the main to the more open and inclusive attitudes generated by the Good Friday Agreement in 1998 and the end to paramilitary violence. Not to be underestimated too was the positive impact in rugby circles, and the country as a whole, of England playing Ireland in Croke Park in 2002 and the Queen's visit to Ireland in 2012. A new chapter in Anglo-Irish relations was opened up. Rugby, moreover, has never been more secure as an inclusive all-Ireland sport in which divisive politics plays no part.

George was equally proud to be British as he was to declare his Irishness. Even in today's era, many others also have this dual allegiance. It must be remembered that George came of age shortly after Partition so for most of his life up until then, Ireland was one entity. This dual allegiance was particularly important in the context of his rugby career. Firstly, he could play, as an Irishman, for a club like Leicester as if it was one of his own local clubs. More significantly, he was able to play rugby for Ireland while standing to attention to 'The Soldier's Song', Ireland's national anthem, while also being a dedicated RAF man.

In the early part of George's international career, it was the Irish Rugby Football Union (IRFU) flag that flew at Lansdowne Road. It was only from 1932 that the Irish Tricolour flew alongside it. This was all a sensitive issue at the time but, to their credit, the IRFU and the majority of the wider Irish public succeeded in keeping politics out of the sport. Of course, these challenges were not peculiar to George. Most of the Ulster players selected for Ireland and those who served the Crown in the post-Independence era experienced the same dilemmas. Not wishing to 'stir up a hornet's nest, most simply lived with the anomaly.

One of the aspects of life enjoyed by amateurs was how they, unlike professionals, could lead interesting and varied lives outside their sport. One could put it all down to money: professionals often didn't have the luxury of the amateurs' ability to lead such varied lives. One is reminded of the great Irish sportsman of the 1920s and 1930s, T. G. McVeagh, who managed to combine playing international tennis, squash, cricket and hockey – something unheard of today. The fact remains, however, that amateur rugby threw up many interesting characters and incidents. Compared with the professionals of today, they had the freedom to lead more rounded, multi-dimensional lives.

Irish Rugby Internationals Who Served in the Second World War

As mentioned, many Irishmen served with the British forces in both the First and Second World Wars. Playing rugby during the 1920s and 1930s, George would have encountered and played with both groups of men. This joint connection of rugby and military service was very important to him in forming a strong bond of identity. A few of those who died in the Second World War are identified in Appendix 2. Proportionate to population, there was quite a sizeable list of Irish rugby internationals involved in the Second World War.

Reviewing George's rugby career, he was the most illustrious rugby player of his era in the British armed forces and certainly in the RAF. No other serviceman can compare with George's tally of internationals, his captaining of his country, and his selection for and occasional captaining of the Lions. It is a rare person who can bring a sense of command to an occasion simply through their physical presence. George could use his physical dominance to his advantage, although he did not have to rely completely on it, having many other arrows in his quiver. In terms of his longevity, his career was cut short when he broke his leg in 1926, which put him out of international rugby until 1928. This was quite a blow in the middle of a stellar international career. The fact that he 'bounced back' owes much to George's huge reserves of character. It was the proper swansong to his career that he was selected captain of Ireland after his return. As a man of Ulster, he set a great precedent for other Ulster captains to follow: Robin Thompson, Jack Kyle, Syd Millar, Willie John McBride, Mike Gibson, Phillip Mathews, David Humphreys, Paddy Johns, Willie Anderson, Rory Best, all proud captains of Ireland.[47]

On a lighter note but still on a health theme, Beamish family lore relates how George would often decide to give up his pipe three weeks before the international season to boost his fitness.[45a] His pipe, however, was to remain a regular feature for the rest of his life. Even around the time of El Alamein, where he served with the Western Desert Air Force, his fondness for tobacco was noted.[46]

On a more serious note, his knees also took huge punishment through playing rugby. With his cartilages removed, he found it difficult to walk in later life.

At his retirement from international rugby in 1933, he was the most capped No. 8 in world rugby. In recognition of these achievements, he was later appointed RAF Rugby Selector and Chairman of the RAF Rugby Union. By the time of the outbreak of the war, he had left the international rugby scene behind and his focus was now on his career.

George's Rugby Years in an International Context

To set the years of George's rugby career in an international context, the 1920s and 1930s saw the gathering of storm clouds in international relations. The first year of the Great Depression was 1930, Franklin Delano Roosevelt was elected US President in 1932 and Adolf Hitler took power in 1933. Although few believed it at the time, in these years the world was on a path towards war, the war that everyone sought to avoid. As we shall see, George Beamish was one of many young men prepared to play their role in the war to come.

As a response to those worrisome times, games like rugby also performed a role as public entertainment. The ancient Romans had discovered that the public could be pacified by 'bread and circuses' and so it was in the twentieth century. Sport and the cinema in the inter-war years, to some degree, performed this function as the Great Depression bit deep into many people's lives. For every Clark Gable, there was a Joe Louis; for every Douglas Fairbanks, a Jesse Owens.

From the time of George's appointment to the Staff College in 1937, the storm clouds had been accumulating rapidly in a war-bound Europe. Attending the College in Andover as an officer with potential, he was to learn more about Intelligence and the role it played in warfare. By the late 1930s, the international political climate was changing. In this climate, George and his colleagues were set to abandon any role they had as entertainers and to take on the roles of warrior and defender. International rugby provided strong bonds of identity and loyalty for George and many others as trouble loomed on the horizon. He had played against the best of England, Scotland, Wales, South Africa, Australia and New Zealand as these countries also prepared to participate in the Second World War. Many players became illustrious participants in that conflict, their shared histories on the sporting field providing the key linking point.

5

EARLY YEARS OF RAF SERVICE

Cranwell provided the training; the real thing was to follow. George's period as a cadet, as was the norm, was relatively short at just eighteen months. The transition from Cranwell cadet to working RAF officer was relatively smooth and seamless as training took place in a strong RAF environment. George was not yet twenty years old when he graduated into the world of RAF service, but for the first fifteen years of his RAF career he was in peacetime service. Over time, that period proved to be useful 'money in the bank' in terms of training and experience. His wartime service, by comparison, was six years long, yet as dangerous and exciting as it was for most servicemen. From his first major appointment with the enemy in Crete in 1941, through to the Desert Campaign and Sicily, George saw action in some of the most intense theatres of the Second World War. He had what was conventionally known as a 'good war'. This did not go unrecognised by his superiors. As has been the case in war since the very beginning, to the victors go the spoils. George was no exception and made use of his advantages.

It was in late 1924 that George was appointed to his first squadron, No. 100. It had been in existence since February 1917 under the Royal Army Flying Corps, shortly before the RAF was founded, and remained as a squadron on active duty until 1942. Its motto, the original of which was in Malay, is translated as 'Never stir up a hornet's nest'. Looking at George's steady movement up the ranks of the RAF over the years, one could say that he was loyal to the Squadron's motto.[1]

The squadron was noted for the bombing of industrial sites in Germany towards the end of the First World War, thus succeeding in weakening the resistance of the enemy. In one sortie near the Western Front towards the end of that war, No. 100 Squadron managed to exact considerable damage on an encampment occupied by the famous 'Red Baron', Manfred von Richthofen, yet the Red Baron survived.[2] After the First World War, the squadron remained on the Continent until September 1919 when it was transferred to Baldonnell Aerodrome, just outside Dublin. There it provided close air support to British troops during the Irish War of Independence, and at the end of hostilities in 1922 it was transferred to Lincolnshire. With George graduating in 1924, he avoided having to serve in Ireland and had to move only a short distance within Lincolnshire to RAF Spitalgate for his first posting. George was joining a squadron with a notable track record.[3]

National and International Turmoil

The squadron was active during the 1926 General Strike in aid of the civil powers, delivering post by air. The country was inevitably quite divided along class lines between those who supported the military's activities in an industrial strike and those who didn't. Indeed, many trade unionists and Labour politicians never forgave the Home Secretary, Winston Churchill, for his 'gung-ho' strike-busting methods during the period. Between 1926 and 1934, George bided his time as a junior officer, attending several key courses to enhance his skills. He transferred to No. 45 Squadron in 1934.

The Great Depression occurred at a time when the United Kingdom and Ireland had still not recovered from the effects of the First World War. Reflecting the increasing interdependence in the world economy, the effects of the Depression in Britain were accelerated by the 1929 Wall Street Crash. The worst years of the Depression actually took place when George was at the height of his rugby career from 1930 to '33. Fortunately, for many people sports such as rugby and soccer acted as diversions from the awful economic situation, and the cinema performed the same escapist role in those years. As the Second World War approached, the main economies began to pick up. Britain's economy was eventually commissioned into a full wartime economy to meet the challenges of the battles ahead.

In 1930, George was put on the RAF's half-pay list as a relatively inexperienced Flight Lieutenant.[4] That was the year of the Lions tour to Australia and New Zealand that was to keep George away from his RAF duties for a full six-month period. From the view of the beleaguered taxpayer, it is comforting to know that strict financial rectitude was adopted by the RAF as far back as the 1930s!

Formed in 1916, No. 45 Squadron, George's squadron from 1934, also had a good track record in the Great War. It initially fought in northern France and then was transferred to the Austro-Italian front in September 1917. Towards the end of the war, it provided long-range bomber escorts.

Some thirty flying aces passed through No. 45's portals. Chief among these was Arthur Harris, later famous as RAF Head of Bomber Command. Harris was Squadron Leader between 1922 and 1924 – before George Beamish had even graduated from Cranwell.[5]

The squadron's motto was 'Through difficulties, I arise'. It spent a significant amount of time in the Middle East in support of Britain's responsibilities in Egypt, Palestine, Iraq and Transjordan. George was appointed Squadron Leader of No. 45 in 1936.

At the start of the Second World War, No. 45 Squadron was given Bristol Blenheims and assigned to the Western Desert Campaign. By that time, George had left the squadron to be appointed to Middle East HQ in Cairo. On 11 June 1940, No. 45 Squadron participated in the first attack by the RAF on the Italian Air Force base at El Adem, where 18 aircraft were destroyed or damaged on the ground, against the loss of 3 British aircraft from three squadrons.[6]

It would have been unsurprising if George had not felt in the shadow of his illustrious elder brother in those years. Victor showed exceptional talent as a fighter pilot early on in his career and had that dashing, charismatic quality so typical of the fighter pilot. George, by contrast, was more the 'organisation' man who, although very talented, was more likely to make his impact over the longer term. Without the style and finesse of Victor, George's solidity and reliability were quickly recognised as key qualities in wartime, when co-operation and teamwork are so vital. As the example of Field Marshal Montgomery demonstrated, individual talent was not necessarily a guarantee of military harmony and co-operation. Often, it was the mild-mannered 'people's persons' who came through in the end: the Alexanders, the Bradleys, the Eisenhowers.

Staff College Appointment – 1937
In 1937, George was selected to attend the RAF Staff College. This was usually reserved for those younger officers seen to 'have a future ahead of them'. Since George's Sword of Honour and his international rugby honours, he was lucky to have had the 'halo effect' which positively affected people's perceptions of him. Having the reputation for being a 'strong man' was to work in George's favour many times in his future career.[7]

In 1942, after a further period of training which led to his appointment as Air Vice Commodore, he was to hold the distinction of being the first full RAF man of air rank to pass out from the College, other than airmen from other services. After a few months there, he was transferred to the Directorate of Intelligence of the Air Staff, suggesting that his Staff College time concerned matters of some operational importance.

Reading the runes, it appears that George's career started to take off from this point onwards. Perhaps he had caught the eye of some senior figure who championed his cause. During the Second World War, George proved quite adept at being in the right place at the right time and of associating with key figures. Although there is no direct evidence of this at this stage of his career, it cannot be ruled out. He would not have been the only person to progress in his career as a result of support from a powerful patron. What is certain is that the RAF was determined to provide a wide range of diverse forms of training for its aspiring leaders. George Beamish was to derive much benefit from this strategy.

Following the foundation of the RAF in April 1918 and the end of the First World War, there was a determination to maintain the Air Force as a service independent from the Army and Royal Navy. Therefore, the creation of an RAF Staff College to parallel the Army Staff College and the Royal Naval Staff College was an important element in fully establishing the RAF. It was initially situated in Andover.[8] On 2 April 1922, the new RAF Staff College came into being. with Air Commodore Robert Brooke-Popham as its first commandant. He had held the position of Air Officer Commanding (AOC) in Iraq, an appointment which George himself would take up in the early 1950s. From its foundation, the Staff College provided training to selected officers to prepare them for staff duties at the Air Ministry or at Command or Group headquarters. In 1970, it was absorbed into the RAF Staff College at Bracknell.

RAF Intelligence

After the Staff College, George was appointed to the Directorate of Intelligence; understandably there is scant information on the public record about this institution. This period, however, was in the run-up to the outbreak of war with Germany and George would doubtless have been involved in developing a knowledge of the disposition of German air power. This certainly stood him in good stead for Crete and, later, the Desert War. It is a little difficult to piece together George's time in RAF Intelligence, partly because the secret nature of the work, and also due to the fact that the RAF Intelligence Branch had not been formally established by the time of George's appointment. It was possible to glean some information, however, from several sources.

The RAF Intelligence Branch formally dates back to 1939, following the outbreak of the Second World War, but intelligence duties were part of the RAF's activities since its foundation in 1918. Additionally, in 1939 the Secret Intelligence Service (SIS) established a dedicated Air Intelligence Section under the command of Group Captain F. W. Winterbotham (Chief of Air Intelligence, MI6). During the Second World War, the Intelligence Branch became larger to encompass the Signals Intelligence staff at Bletchley Park and the Imagery Intelligence staff at RAF Medmenham.[9]

At the outbreak of war, the Air Ministry recognised the requirement for formalised intelligence training and established a number of fairly rudimentary courses to teach Volunteer Reserve Officers the art of intelligence analysis. In 1943, the Unit was transferred to RAF Technical Training Command.[10] From the end of the war in August 1945, George Beamish's close colleague in the Desert War, Sir Thomas Elmhirst, was appointed Head of RAF Intelligence; he remained in this post until 1947. Despite the end of the war, intelligence remained a key activity for the RAF, particularly with the oncoming Cold War, requiring people of the calibre and experience of Elmhirst.[11]

A number of notable public figures spent time in RAF Intelligence during the Second World War.[12] Some even came within the orbit of George Beamish during the Desert War. George himself had privileged access to *Ultra* intelligence intercepts owing to his support role to Air Marshal Arthur Coningham. (*Ultra* was the designation adopted by British military intelligence in June 1941 for wartime signals intelligence obtained by breaking high-level encrypted enemy radio and teleprinter communications at the Government Code and Cypher School, GC&CS, at Bletchley Park.) These contacts included Sarah Churchill, daughter of Sir Winston; Michael Bentine, the comedian with *The Goon Show*; Christopher Lee, the actor; and Denis Wheatley, the writer. It is worth describing in more detail the roles of this colourful crew, so more detailed information on these individuals is set out in Appendix 3.

Ultra

The fact that British Intelligence had access to Germany's communication codes was one of the most closely guarded secrets of the war. Information from *Ultra* intercepts was sparingly and carefully disseminated to avoid exposure. It was F. W. Winterbotham who decided when and who received it (as a top-ranking member of MI6, he reported directly to its head, Sir Hugh Sinclair). One of the key recipients was Arthur Coningham in the Western Desert, and by extension his Senior Air Staff Officer (SASO), George Beamish. *Ultra* intercepts also played a controversial role in the Battle for Crete when the commander of British and Commonwealth forces there, General Freyberg, was said to have ignored vital information about the German information contained in them.

Fred Winterbotham had quite a colourful career before and during the Second World War. In 1929 he joined the Air Section of the Secret Intelligence Service (MI6), and in the 1930s he travelled through Germany developing relations with many of the top leaders in the Nazi regime. He put these connections to good use in his work at SIS.[13] With the publication of *The Ultra Secret* by Winterbotham in 1974, the secrets about *Ultra* were finally revealed after having been kept under cover since the war. Hitler's invasion of Russia, the Battle of Crete, the Desert War, the Sicilian Campaign and the war in the Far East were all impacted upon by the receipt of *Ultra* intelligence.[14]

Continued Service

In April 1939, George was appointed Senior Operations Officer in HQ Palestine and Transjordan at the rank of Squadron Leader. When war broke out in September of that year, he was still based in the Middle East and in January 1940 he joined the Air Staff HQ Middle East. [27] Away from the key war theatre of north-west Europe, although that front was far from active during the months of the 'phoney war', George remained in the Mediterranean and Middle East theatre. It was from this time that his career began to involve participation in some notable action which had significant implications for the war. Things were to heat up in that theatre before long and George was to play a large part in it.

Irish RAF Heroes in the Second World War

George Beamish was extremely proud of both his Ulster and Irish backgrounds, the latter of which he saw as being in no way in conflict with his service to the Crown in war. In this, he was in the distinguished company of many Irishmen who excelled themselves in the Second World War. Many of these fought with the RAF. The involvement of many thousands of Irishmen as servicemen in the Second World War has often been overshadowed by friction between the two islands over the neutral status of the Irish State during that war. Whatever the official policy of the Irish government at the time, many Irishmen served and died in the war, enlisting for a wide variety of reasons. Indeed, among all the services at the very top were Irishmen or Anglo-Irish such as Alanbrooke, Alexander, Montgomery, Dill, Auchinleck, Boyle, Bandon and others.

While service with British military forces has been a fraught issue in Ireland for a long time, much change in a more tolerant direction has taken place in recent years. Highlighting those Irishmen from North and South who distinguished themselves in the service of the RAF has helped in demystifying and 'normalising' these situations. For example, Dermot Boyle, from Rathdowney, Co. Laois in Ireland, attended Cranwell with George, joining the RAF in 1922. After commendable service in the Second World War, he became Chief of the Air Staff in 1956, commanding air activity in the Suez Crisis. In June 1940, he joined HQ of Bomber Command and in 1944 was appointed Air ADC to George VI, a position also held by George Beamish around that time. After a series of honours, he was made Marshal of the Air Force, the highest rank in the service, in 1958. He retired in 1960 and died in 1993, aged eighty-eight.[15]

Eugene Esmonde, an Irishman with roots in Co. Tipperary, was a posthumous recipient of the Victoria Cross, the highest award for gallantry awarded to members of Commonwealth forces. Esmonde earned his VC while in command of a torpedo bomber squadron in the Channel that attacked the grand German battleships *Scharnhorst*, *Gneisenau* and *Prince Eugen* in February 1942 during the 'Channel Dash'. The Royal Navy's Fleet Air Arm Museum's website says:

> The German battle group of 66 ships, with continuous air cover provided by 250 day and night fighter aircraft, left Brest at night on 11 February 1942 and reached the Dover Straits, virtually undetected, at about 11.00am on 12 February. The Fleet Air Arm's 825 Squadron, led by Lieutenant Commander Eugene Esmonde and comprising six Swordfish aircraft and aircrews ... had been preparing for a night attack on the German ships. Promised fighter cover of five squadrons of Spitfires, Esmonde agreed to lead his squadron in a daylight attack. Just one squadron, No. 72 Squadron RAF led by Squadron Leader Brian Kingcombe, rendezvoused with Esmonde's squadron and so with fighter cover of only 10 Spitfires, 825 Squadron attacked the mighty Germany battle group. Against the guns of the big ships and the power of the Luftwaffe, the slow, out-dated Swordfish stood little chance. All the Swordfish were shot down and only five of the eighteen men who set out survived.

Esmonde first served in the RAF in the 1930s and then joined the Fleet Air Arm, part of the Royal Navy. He earned his DSO following an attack early in the war on the German battleship *Bismarck*. He died in his attack on the three German battleships after his Swordfish was hit by a Focke-Wulf 190. His body was eventually washed up on the Thames Estuary near the River Medway three days later.[16] George VI awarded him the posthumous VC in March of that year. In a famous broadcast at the end of the war seen to be a conciliatory gesture to the Irish nation, Winston Churchill mentioned him with a number of other Irishmen for their bravery during the war.[17]

Both Esmonde and Victor Beamish died within a short time of one another, both in air engagements on which official records are hazy and confusing. The sinking of the three major 'capital' ships of the Germans in the 'Channel Dash' would have been a major 'feather in the cap' for either Esmonde or Beamish and their colleagues. There were many more illustrious pilots in the Second World War, but few who came so near such 'prizes' as the three German capital ships as had Esmonde.[18]

Brendan 'Paddy' Finucane, from Dublin, was one of the most decorated flying aces in the RAF during the Second World War. Born in Dublin in 1920, he was christened in the most impeccably Irish fashion with the name Brendan Eamon Fergus Finucane. 'Paddy' was the nickname given to him by his colleagues in the RAF. In honour of his ancestry, he also painted a shamrock on the side of his aircraft. He continues to be the youngest person in the history of the RAF to reach the rank of Wing Commander, which he did at the age of twenty-one. Interestingly, Finucane family members participated in the Independence struggle in the early part of the twentieth century. His father, Thomas, fought with Eamon de Valera in Boland's Mill in the 1916 Rising, which makes Brendan's RAF recruitment all the more intriguing. He applied and joined in April 1938. In the early months of the war he built up his flying hours before he was posted to RAF No. 65 at Hornchurch at the beginning of the Battle of Britain in July 1940.[19]

Brendan and Victor came across one another in January 1942, when Victor was appointed Group Captain and Station Commander of No. 602 Squadron at RAF Redhill in Sussex where Finucane was based as a flyer. Immediately, Victor appointed Paddy as squadron leader. Like Finucane, Victor Beamish had flown in the Battle of Britain and was posted to Group Captain Operations Headquarters at No. 11 Group in 1941. Beamish was ordered by Leigh-Mallory not to fly on operations but nevertheless usually flew whenever he felt like it. Beamish was killed on operations just two months after he had promoted Paddy.

The British counter-plan to the German plan to move battleships through the English Channel, Operation *Fuller*, was put into action after Beamish had landed and reported the enemy position. Finucane was ordered to take-off with 602 Squadron, firing on warships and catching the images on a gun camera. The Germans broke the blockade. On 19 February 1942, Finucane was ordered with his former squadron mate Keith Truscott to give evidence before the Operation *Fuller* Inquiry, which reported on the failure to prevent the breakout.[20]

By the time of his death near Pointe du Touquet, France, on 15 July 1942, Paddy had shot down at least thirty-two enemy planes and had been awarded the DSO and DFC and two bars. According to the report in the *Daily Telegraph* of 18 July 1942, his last words were 'This is it, chaps'. Finucane's name is inscribed on the Air Force Memorial at Runnymede in England. The memorial commemorates airmen who were lost in the Second World War and who have no known grave. Nearby in Runnymede is another iconic site, this one commemorating the signature of Magna Carta.[21] Because of ambiguous attitudes in Ireland over the war, Finucane only received belated recognition in his native country, but few could deny the magnitude of his achievements.[22]

Percy Ronald Gardner Bernard, 5th Earl of Bandon, was an Anglo-Irish aristocrat who served as a senior commander in the RAF in the mid-twentieth century. He was a squadron, station and group commander during the Second World War. In 1924, while still a cadet in B Squadron at Cranwell, Bernard succeeded to the title of Earl of Bandon. The centre of his earldom coincidentally stood in the townland area in County Cork from which George and his family had migrated northwards in 1912. A year older than George, the two graduated from RAF Cranwell in the same year, 1924. Seen as a slightly 'Bertie Wooster'-type figure who never encountered a rule he didn't want to break, the Earl was said to have come through some difficult scrapes during his career – but this did not prevent him from becoming an Air Chief Marshal. During the Second World War, he was a station commander in several mainland RAF stations and served most of the rest of the war in India and Burma. In 1956, he was promoted to Air Marshal and in 1959 to Air Chief Marshal. His crowning achievement was to have been appointed, in 1961, the Commander of NATO Air Forces in Central Europe.[23]

Air Chief Marshal Sir Edgar Ludlow-Hewitt was born in 1886. He spent his early life in County Cork and was commissioned into the Royal Irish Rifles in 1905. He was appointed to the Royal Flying Corps in August 1914. The following year he joined No. 1 Squadron, serving in France, where he saw much action during the rest of the war. Between the wars, his career developed quickly with appointments as Commandant of the RAF Staff College (1926–30), Director of Operations and Intelligence at the Air Ministry, and Deputy Chief of Staff (1933–5), AOC India (1935–7), followed in 1937 by appointment as C-in-C Bomber Command.[24] Ludlow-Hewitt steered Bomber Command through the difficult pre-war expansion period but recognised the deficiencies of the Command and its unreadiness for combat as war approached in September 1939. In early 1940, Ludlow-Hewitt was posted away from Bomber Command, an act seen as a fit of pique by the Air Ministry. He was to hold the position of Inspector-General of the RAF until 1945. He interacted closely with Tedder and Coningham in that role when he was sent in 1942 to review air activities in the Middle East and North Africa.[25] Bomber Harris credited Ludlow-Hewitt for a considerable contribution to the winning of the war. He was also a member of the Operation *Fuller* Inquiry, which interviewed over 100 RAF officers, including Victor Beamish. Air Chief Marshal Arthur Tedder was quite pleased with Ludlow-Hewitt in his role as Inspector-General visiting Egypt in 1941: 'I was deeply impressed by his wide and detailed knowledge … and his desire to be of practical help.'[26]

Wing Commander Harry Clarke was the last surviving Battle of Britain airman from Northern Ireland when he died aged ninety-two in July 2010. He was a private man and did not speak much about his time in the war. Clarke flew Spitfires with RAF No. 610 Squadron until a training accident in 1940 brought his flying career to an end.

Kenneth William Mackenzie DFC was one of the most renowned of Northern Ireland's Battle of Britain heroes. By the end of the battle, he was an RAF hero with seven combat victories. His most famous exploits came on 7 October 1940 when he brought down three *Luftwaffe* Me 109 planes. Feigning insanity as a POW in 1944, he was able to gain repatriation.

Squadron Leader Noel Corry was one of the ten Northern Irishmen of Battle of Britain fame to survive the war. Described as modest, he was not one to spin tales of his heroics. He enlisted in 1939 at the age of eighteen with friends Sydney Ireland and George Calwell. Noel flew Bristol Blenheim light bombers in the 1940 campaign. He was awarded the DFC in 1944.

Sydney Ireland was the first of Northern Ireland's Battle of Britain heroes to be killed during the battle. His plane was shot down on 12 July 1940. He was part of the 'Gang of Three' grammar school boys who enlisted in 1939 at the age of eighteen with dreams of flying modern aircraft and escaping a nine-to-five career.

George Calwell survived the Battle of Britain and came through the Second World War. A friend of both Noel Corry and Sydney Ireland, he would lose one of those friends in the first days of the Battle of Britain. Undeterred, the nineteen-year-old from Belfast fought on, serving his country and becoming one of the lucky few to return home after the battle.[28]

6

BATTLE OF CRETE (1941)

By the Declaration of 1939, Britain was obliged to assist Greece in the event of a threat to Greek or Romanian independence: 'His Majesty's Government would feel themselves bound at once to lend the Greek or Romanian Government all the support in their power.'[1] Winston Churchill believed it was vital for Britain to take every measure possible to support Greece.

George spent a period in Greece before the German invasion of Crete, so a brief summary of events is worthwhile. The German plan was to attack on both the Greece and Yugoslavian fronts and the long-expected operation began on 6 April 1941. Meanwhile, the British had sent units to Greece in preparation for battle; the first British effort was the deployment of RAF squadrons commanded by Air Commodore John D'Albiac which arrived in November 1940, and ground troops in March 1941. A total of 62,000 British and Commonwealth troops arrived in Greece, a substantial force reflecting the importance attached by Churchill to saving Greece.[2] Many said it was desire for atonement for the Gallipoli disaster of the First World War that motivated him, but protection of British imperial possessions to the south and east was also critically important.

On 25 April 1941, King George II and his government left the Greek mainland. After a series of Axis victories, in April the British decided to withdraw to Crete and Egypt. On 27 April, the

Germans entered Athens and the Battle for Greece was effectively over. Crete was attacked by Nazi forces on 20 May, 1941. With Greek government consent, British forces were also dispatched to Crete on 31 October to guard Souda Bay. The Greek Navy and Merchant Marine played an important part in the evacuation of the Allied forces to Crete and suffered heavy losses as a result. [3] In the defence of Greece against the Axis, the British lost 903 soldiers, with another 1,250 wounded and over 13,900 captured; the Greeks on the other hand lost over 13,300, had another 62,660 wounded and 1,290 missing. Germany, Italy and Bulgaria all seized parts of Greece following its surrender.[4] During the Allied evacuations, the German troops managed to capture 7–8,000 of their soldiers. At the end of the evacuation, the British escaped with some 50,000 men.

The victories in Yugoslavia, Greece and Crete, however, would come at a price for the Germans. The Battle of Greece and other battles in the Balkans meant that the invasion of the Soviet Union had to be delayed with the prospect of having to fight in the Russian winter. On such matters hinged the eventual outcome of the Second World War.

The Fall and Evacuation of Crete

The only Greek territory remaining free from Nazi domination by May 1941 was the large and strategically important island of Crete, which was held by a strong Allied garrison. Critically, this was not replicated in the levels of air defence on the island, a factor that ultimately proved to be crucial. To conquer Crete, the German High Command prepared Operation *Mercury*, the largest airborne attack seen to date.[5]

The Second New Zealand Expeditionary Force, under the overall command of General Bernard Freyberg, had been forced off the Greek mainland to Crete in April 1941 by invading German forces. Freyberg was the seventh commander on Crete since the previous November, suggesting a large degree of volatility at the upper end of command.[6] Freyberg, a British-born New Zealander, was a holder of the Victoria Cross from the First World War but had a mixed Second World War. He became associated with two key defeats, the first in mainland Greece and following that, the loss of Crete. He performed well in the North African campaign, however, including at El Alamein and later in Italy. He had a troubled relationship in North Africa with his then superior Auchinleck, but later, had a more positive one with Montgomery. Although there was a big gap in rank and experience, he was to work closely with George Beamish on the evacuation of Crete, realising that RAF support was vital.[7]

Adolf Hitler agreed to Operation *Mercury* to give his forces a base in the eastern Mediterranean. Before the invasion, he sought assurances that plans for the invasion of the Soviet Union would not be disrupted. He also noted the proximity of Crete's three airfields to the oilfields at Ploesti in Romania – a vital source for oil for the German campaign in the Soviet Union. Most of the evacuated British troops from Greece withdrew to Crete, planning to use it as a base from which to attack the oilfields at Ploesti.[8]

After the fall of mainland Greece to the Nazis, George was appointed, in April 1941, as Senior Air Officer to Crete. This was his first command of real significance. To protect British possessions in the Mediterranean including Malta and Cyprus and its North African and Middle Eastern territories, holding Crete was of vital strategic importance. This was an appointment which could either make or break a young man's career. The war was not going well for Britain, the 'game changing' Battle of El Alamein was still some time away and British imperial possessions were severely under threat.

The situation facing Beamish on 17 April when he arrived to take command of the RAF on the island was far from reassuring. There was only one squadron, 805 FAA Squadron. Their primary role was to provide fighter defence for Souda Bay. But the squadron was operating at a reduced strength and consisted of a mixed force of Fulmars, Gladiators and Brewsters, of which the last could be flown only in an emergency.[9] George was tasked with overseeing the reception of units following their withdrawal and evacuation from Greece. For this purpose, he was then allocated two squadrons (30 and 203) from Egypt and the fighter squadrons which until recently had been operating in Greece itself. However, due to the German decision to invade Crete, he found himself conducting the defence of the island. He was totally unable to convince Freyberg that the best means of destroying the invaders was in the air before landing. One commentator later referred to the descending German paratroopers as 'sitting ducks.' This was another major defect in British strategy in Crete.[10]

On 21 April 1941, the German Paratroop Division leader, General Kurt Student devised plans to take Crete by an airborne invasion involving two divisions. He believed that only 5,000 Allied troops were on the island, while there were actually 42,000. The German 7th Parachute Division was sent to seize the Cretan airfields at Maleme, Retimo, and Heraklion as well as the harbour of Souda Bay, while the German 5th Mountain Division was to be flown to the secured airfields as reinforcements for the paratroopers. This was the first use of paratroopers in an airborne offensive and one that was to cause much subsequent soul-searching.[11]

Freyberg was convinced that the main assault would come from the sea and not from the air. His misreading of *Ultra* intercepts was to be a costly error in this regard. On 28 April, a resume of *Ultra* intercepts was sent to George Beamish and then to Freyberg about *Luftwaffe* intentions to invade by air.[12] Freyberg was found to have paid scant attention to this vital piece of intelligence. Only 6 Hurricanes and 17 obsolete aircraft remained on the island, reflecting the ill-judged low priority accorded to the defence of Crete.[13] Freyberg contacted General Archibald Wavell, Commander-in-Chief Middle East, to get more fighters and naval forces given the inadequate defences on Crete. Tedder, overall RAF Commander for the Middle East and Mediterranean, later said: 'It made my blood curdle that we could provide from Egypt no fighter opposition whatever.'[14] The RAF refused to reinforce the

25 obsolete fighters on the island due to German air superiority in Greece. In such circumstances, Freyberg and his forces were in a highly vulnerable position.

On 13 May 1941, the *Luftwaffe* began to attack Crete and the surviving British planes were withdrawn on 19 May 1941, depriving the island of air cover. On 20 May, the German invasion began, but 2,000 paratroopers were killed shortly after landing. Historian Antony Beevor notes that on 7 May the last RAF fighters left Crete, but Cairo HQ rejected the idea to mine or block runways because the Air Ministry demanded that the landing grounds should be kept operational in case of a sudden deployment from Egypt.[15] As a result, the success of the German airborne assault soon overwhelmed the British forces and George was forced to order the last RAF aircraft to withdraw back to Egypt on 19 May 1941.

Watching the first German attacks, David Hunt, Army staff intelligence officer, recalls standing beside George Beamish who murmured: 'What a remarkable sight. Looks like the end of the world'. Hunt and Beamish could see puffs of smoke rising above the olive groves and the odd patch of white where a parachute had caught in a tree or snagged on a telegraph pole, according to Beevor. So strange a sight was it that it seemed to George to be some kind of pyrotechnic display.[16] George's colleague on that occasion later became a trusted member of General Alexander's staff, an Oxford don and a diplomat after the war and notably, Private Secretary to both Clement Atlee and Winston Churchill. He went on to hold the positions of High Commissioner to Uganda, Nigeria and Cyprus and Ambassador to Brazil. In 1967, he was knighted and after his retirement in 1973, became a winner of *BBC Mastermind* in 1977. He wrote a noted account of the Italian Campaign in the Second World War and is said to have been the official who drafted Harold MacMillan's famous 'Winds of Change' speech on the retreat from Empire.[17][18]

The task George faced as head of the evacuation was monumental. Firstly, he was severely under-resourced for such a major initiative.

Limited air facilities worked against a smooth evacuation. He was also facing the most powerful military and aerial power in the world and one that had never experienced a major defeat. With such little strategic priority given to the air defence of the island by Middle East HQ before and after the fall of Greece, George can be forgiven for feeling he may have been handed the poisoned chalice. Again, the evacuation's comparison with Dunkirk seems apposite – tactically astute if somewhat embarrassing.[19] It has to be acknowledged, however, that many men and much equipment and aircraft were saved as a result of George Beamish's handling of the Crete evacuation. The retreat to Egypt was a tactical move to regroup for another day.

The lack of air support from the RAF is seen as a huge factor in the loss of Crete, by many historians such as Matthew Wright and Ian Stuart. In their view, not only could the RAF have easily operated from Crete with its three brand-new aerodromes, but had the RAF put even the slightest bit of pressure on the *Luftwaffe* before and during the invasion, the paratrooper drop could have been a dismal failure on the first day. German soldiers floating down to Crete would have been mown down by the thousand by any number of RAF fighters.[20]

During the evacuation, Admiral Cunningham was determined that the 'Navy must not let the Army down.'[21] When Army officers expressed concerns that he would lose too many ships, Cunningham said that 'It takes three years to build a ship, it takes three centuries to build a tradition'.[22] In some senses, the Royal Navy was fortunate. It might have suffered worse losses had not *VIII Fliegerkorps* been transferred for action under Operation *Barbarossa* before the battle finished.

Despite the long delay in issuing evacuation orders, the Royal Navy was able to embark approximately 14,800 men and return them to Egypt. The evacuation was conducted over four nights, suffering losses from German aircraft attacks. Five thousand British and Allied soldiers were left behind.[23]

Despite the paucity of RAF forces in Crete, No. 33 Squadron relocated there after the fall of Greece mainly with Gladiators and

Hurricanes. The Squadron spent most of the war in the Middle East but was in action at the time of the Battle of Crete, after which the remnants of its force were evacuated to Egypt. Severe losses meant that they were compelled to amalgamate with No. 80 Squadron. They attempted to save the airfield at Maleme without success, resorting to hand-to-hand combat with the invading German forces. The squadron later played a significant role in the Desert War, including at El Alamein.[24]

With George's appointment to Crete, he was to rub shoulders with another rugby man in the shape of Jack Griffiths, ADC to General Freyberg, both of whom were New Zealanders and, in Griffiths' case, a former All-Black captain. Griffiths was later to be awarded the Military Cross. In fact, his debut for the New Zealand All Blacks in 1934 was a year following George's own retirement from international rugby and only four years after the 1930 Lions Tour to New Zealand.[25][26] The evacuation personnel certainly did not lack physical prowess. George's strong physical presence and international experience were to the forefront in his Cairo masters' decision to select him as the man to manage an evacuation. No doubt too, George took time to compare notes with Griffiths on rugby matters.

Beevor alludes to the fact that *Ultra* signals were being received by Freyberg before the Crete invasion. Many sources have pointed to his many tactical and judgment errors at the time, chiefly a controversy over his interpretation of *Ultra* intelligence messages. Beevor states that Freyberg misread the *Ultra* signals and as overall commander, it is indisputable that he must take ultimate responsibility. It must be acknowledged, however, that his decision to be the last to leave during the evacuation was symbolic of his well-known devotion to duty and taking personal responsibility.[27]

Crete had a high-profile foreign visitor during the unfolding conflict in the shape of the son of US President Franklin Roosevelt, a US Army Colonel. Freyberg and Beamish managed to persuade James Roosevelt to leave by Sunderland flying boat two days before the invasion. This was six months before Pearl Harbour and the US was still neutral. All efforts were made to ensure this, as no one wanted to be responsible for impeding the safe passage of such an important individual.[28]

On the night of 20 May, the garrison of Maleme abandoned the airfield because of misunderstood orders. The Germans captured it the following day and began to land reinforcements. In May 1941, there were two functioning airfields on the island, at Maleme and Heraklion, with several more under construction.[29]

More than 9,000 ANZACs and thousands of Greeks were left behind to defend the remaining territory as best they could. They fought on until they were surrounded. The cities of Irakleio and Retimo were taken by the Germans in the following days.[30]

A strange event took place on one of the nights of the evacuation. General Heywood, head of military mission, received orders from Cairo to destroy 30,000 gallons of RAF fuel, potentially valuable to the Luftwaffe. Heywood sent a party of sappers to carry it out by night but found the depot guarded by Greek soldiers. Not wanting to precipitate a certain battle, he left without carrying out the task. Discretion perhaps was considered to be the better part of valour.[31]

Communications were hampered by the layout of the island and by the sparseness and quality of its roads and railways. During the next day, however, through miscommunication and failure of the Allied commanders to grasp the situation, Maleme airfield in western Crete fell to the Germans.[32]

As the remnants of Creforce – the designation for the Allied troops on the island – retreated across Crete's Askifou Plain, the first ships left Sfakia for Egypt. The Germans finally entered Retimo, forcing most of its Australian defenders to surrender. The garrison at Heraklion was evacuated by sea but their convoy suffered heavy losses from German air attacks.[33]

Further east of Sfakia, an evacuation was successfully carried out at Heraklion during the night. A force of 2 cruisers and 6 destroyers sailed from Egypt and managed to embark around 4,000 British troops. Delayed by a damaged ship, the convoy came under air attack on the return voyage to Alexandria. The German aircraft inflicted serious damage, and many of the rescued troops were killed on the tightly packed ships.[34]

On 30 May, plans for the evacuation from Crete had to be scaled down as some of the ships were forced back to Egypt. Tensions rose as decisions were made as to which soldiers should go first. At Creforce HQ, Freyberg and his commanders deliberated over that night's evacuation. Each of the 4 destroyers due to arrive after dark would take 500 men. Both the 4th and 5th Brigades were selected to go, but there was not enough room on the ships for all of 5th Brigade. Brigadier James Hargest reluctantly chose 21st Battalion to stay behind. Another New Zealand unit, 18th Battalion, was ordered to form a perimeter around the beach to make sure that the evacuation was orderly.[35] Later that day, news arrived from Alexandria that the evacuation was to be scaled back. Only 250 men were to be taken on each destroyer because the ships would be exposed to air attacks next day and the risk of casualties on crowded vessels was too great. The reduction in numbers meant that 5th Brigade would be staying another night. More bad news was to come. Only 2 destroyers arrived to continue the evacuation. Despite the lack of space, 1,400 men were taken off that night. The entire 4th Brigade embarked behind an armed cordon put in place to prevent desperate stragglers from rushing the ships.[36] During the night, Sunderland flying boats arrived to take Freyberg and other senior staff officers, including George Beamish, back to Egypt. This was not to be the last encounter with Freyberg for George, as the New Zealander was to play a significant role at the Second Battle of El Alamein where George was also stationed, over a year later.

At dawn on 31 May, there were still some 9,000 men in and around Sfakia waiting to be evacuated. Time was fast running out. General Wavell, conscious of mounting naval and troop losses, decided that the evacuation that night would be the last. More than half the remaining members of Creforce were evacuated from Sfakia. Lack of space on ships combined with a scarcity of supplies meant that 6,500 troops were left behind on Crete to face inevitable capture by the Germans. Four destroyers were initially allocated to this operation. When the New Zealand Prime Minister Peter Fraser, who was in Egypt, learned that 31 May was to be the final night of the evacuation, he urged Admiral Cunningham to send an additional ship. The loss of men on Crete would be a crushing blow to New Zealand's war effort, Fraser argued. Cunningham's response was to order that the cruiser HMS *Phoebe* return to Crete.[37] With room only for an estimated 3,500 men, priority was given to infantry units. By the time the ships left, around 4,000 troops had been squeezed on board.

By 31 May, the evacuation was drawing to a close and the commandos, running low on ammunition, rations and water, fell back towards Sphakia too. Lieutenant-colonel Robert Laycock and some of his headquarters, including his intelligence officer, the writer Evelyn Waugh, managed to get out on the last ship to depart. The vast majority of the commandos were left behind on the island.[38] Although some of them were later able to make their own way back to Egypt, by the end of the operation about 600 of the 800 commandos sent to Crete were listed as killed, missing or wounded. Only 23 officers and 156 others managed to get off the island.[38]

With Maleme airfield secured, the Germans flew in thousands of reinforcements and overwhelmed the western side of the island. This was followed by severe British naval losses due to intense German air attacks around the island. After seven days of fighting, the Allied commanders realised that so many Germans had been flown in that any hope of an Allied victory was gone. By 1 June, the evacuation of Crete by the Allies was complete and the island was under German occupation. In light of the heavy casualties suffered by the elite 7th *Flieger* Division, Hitler forbade further airborne operations. General Student would dub Crete 'the graveyard of the German paratroopers' and a 'disastrous victory'.[39]

On the morning of 1 June 1941, the 5,000 Allied troops left at Sfakia realised that they had been abandoned. Their trek over the mountains of Crete had been for nothing. Bewildered and angry, they now faced the prospect of captivity. On that morning, the exhausted remnants of Creforce formally surrendered to the Germans and began a depressing march back across the mountains – 6,500 Commonwealth troops were captured. By the end of December 1941, only an estimated 500 troops remained on the island. While scattered and disorganised, these men and their Greek allies would continue to harass German troops on Crete long after the withdrawal. These acts of selfless courage were not forgotten by the Greeks after the war.[40]

A somewhat frantic scenario played out after the fall of Crete, with blame and counter-blame among the British forces for its collapse. Many at the time suggested that the German invasion could have been repelled and that tactical and leadership faults were responsible. Two senior Army officers, Brigadiers Hargest and Puttick, were said to be remiss in not preventing the Germans from seizing the key airfield in Maleme. Attention also focused inevitably on the overall commander, General Freyberg. Tedder, however, was strongly of the view that the lack of secure air bases was the main reason for Crete being lost.[41] In the fighting for Crete, the Allies suffered around 4,000 killed, 1,900 wounded, and 17,000 captured. The campaign also cost the Royal Navy 9 ships sunk and 18 damaged. German losses were 4,041 dead or missing, 2,640 wounded, 17 captured, and 370 aircraft destroyed. Despite the pressure he was under, George Beamish made the best of his task, managing to save considerable manpower and equipment to fight another day.[42]

Among those to escape later from the advancing Germans was Evelyn Waugh, an army major in the conflict. A biting satirist of the war, Waugh was to draw on his experiences in Crete in his later writings, including his trilogy *Sword of Honour*. George, as a winner of the Cranwell iteration of the Sword of Honour would, no doubt, have been wryly amused at Waugh's creation.[43]

With the whole of Greece in German hands, the Axis now had complete control over the Balkans. George II of Greece went into exile in London. Greece would remain occupied by the Germans until they abandoned the Balkans in 1944. Hitler would later blame the failure of Operation *Barbarossa* on Mussolini's inability to conquer Greece in 1940. As the long campaign in Greece had delayed *Barbarossa*, that campaign only started in the summer of 1941 and continued into the deadly winter months.

Having continued to hold key commands for the remainder of the war following Crete, Freyberg owes a lot to George Beamish for his efforts in spiriting him away to safety in Egypt after the Cretan debacle. At times, George Beamish seems to have been cast in the role of an RAF 'one-man band' in Crete. The image of 'Hercules', George's nickname at Cranwell, with the globe on his shoulders immediately comes to mind –or perhaps, it could have been Sisyphus eternally rolling a boulder up the mountain. Both were ancient Greek mythical heroes, yet George was faced with a very real and current Greek tragedy. George had a huge responsibility placed on him as a Group Captain dealing with generals and admirals. One might also question the wisdom of Middle East HQ in Cairo in appointing him, a middle ranking officer, to such a mammoth task. He was given a mission and was required to deal directly with key generals – maximum responsibility with minimum authority. In the final analysis, however, the overwhelming strength of the German invading force would surely have prevailed no matter who oversaw the evacuation.

The most notable RAF squadrons to join battle in Crete are listed in Appendix 4.

The *Luftwaffe* Enemy

Because of the low level of involvement of the RAF in the defence of Crete in 1941 and the fact that the *Luftwaffe* were put in command of the invasion in that year, it is worth identifying and describing the role of the key *Luftwaffe* players. Among them were several unrepentant Nazis, three Von Blüchers – Napoleon only had to face one, and a Von Richthofen, names that clearly resonate in German military history. At the time of the invasion of Crete in early 1941, the Germans were at the peak of their dominance.

Greece had fallen and the capture of the island of Crete was seen as a mere formality. The RAF and Army presence on the island were insignificant, almost inviting capture. Hitler instructed that Operation *Mercury,* the occupation of Crete was to be the base for conducting an air war in the eastern Mediterranean. At the same time, he was adamant that it should not lead to a delay in Operation *Barbarossa.* In the fullness of time, the short timeline involved in *Mercury* did ensure the smooth transition to *Barbarossa.*

In overall command of the Crete invasion was General Alexander Lohr,[44] an Austrian *Luftwaffe* General, Commander of South Eastern Europe based at Staff HQ. He was responsible for the aerial bombing of Warsaw in 1939 and in December 1941 for the attack on Belgrade. Such was his zeal for the Reich that he refused to surrender when he was ordered to accept unconditional surrender in May 1945. He escaped but was eventually captured a few days later and tried for war crimes in Yugoslavia. He was executed by firing squad in 1947.

On the ground, the most senior operational *Luftwaffe* officer, was Kurt Student,[45] the famous paratrooper general. It was he who led Operation *Mercury* to seize Crete. He introduced the innovation of using gliders quite effectively into the battle, which provoked a bemused reaction from British forces in Crete. General Student became the head of the *Fallschirmjäger* (paratroopers) throughout the Second World War. Before Crete, he was central to the *Luftwaffe's blitzkrieg* attacks on the Netherlands, Belgium and Luxembourg. After the war, he was indicted for mistreatment and murder of Prisoners of War by his men in Crete (but not with crimes against the civilian population) and was found guilty on three charges. He is thought to have involved himself in ex-Nazi groups.[46]

In December 1940, Alfred Schlemm was appointed Chief of Staff of the XI Air Corps under Student, also closely involved with events in Crete and including full knowledge of the massacres.[47] Alfred Schlemm was to go on to serve in Italy and in *Barbarossa.* He was to replace Student as General Kommandant of the *Fallschirmjäger* in the Netherlands in 1943.

Wolfram von Richthofen[48] was a *Luftwaffe* general acting in support of the invasion of Crete. He was from an aristocratic family; his cousins, the brothers Lothar and Manfred von Richthofen, both flying aces, had encouraged him to join the *Luftstreitkräfte* (German Imperial Air Service). His efforts in the early days of the invasion probably saved the initial invasion force, dangerously hemmed in on land, from destruction.

Eugen Meindl[49] was an air general in command of the *Luftwaffe* Storm Regiment during the invasion and capture of Crete in 1941–42. Having been in the *Wehrmacht* for most of his career, he transferred to the *Luftwaffe* in 1940 after Narvik. As head of the *Fallschirmjäger* regiment, he commanded many daring actions during the war, particularly in Crete. His military honours included, the Iron Cross with Clasp and the Knights Cross to the Iron Cross with Oak Leaves and Swords.

When Eugen Meindl took temporary leave in May 1941, Hermann Ramcke took command of the force invading Crete. A dedicated Nazi, troops under his command in Crete were accused of killing Cretan villagers. Meindl was also a commander in the North African Desert Campaign, fighting at El Alamein. His tactical astuteness led him to escaping from Montgomery's forces there. One of the most decorated German officers of the war, he won the Knight's Cross of the Iron Cross with Oak Leaves and Diamonds. He was also rare in having served in the *Wehrmacht,* the Navy and the *Luftwaffe* during his career. After the war, he served a sentence for war crimes he committed in Brest, spending a number of years in prison. On release, his public appearances confirmed him as an unrepentant Nazi.

A report prepared on Hermann-Bernhard Ramcke[50] after the war stated that 'if there was to be such a thing as a list of especially dangerous men to be kept under surveillance [after the war], General Ramcke ought to qualify as one of the first candidates'. While being interrogated at Trent Park in north London, Ramcke boasted about destroying Brest in a conversation with Dietrich von Choltitz, the last commander of German-occupied Paris.

Following a trial, he was found guilty on 21 March 1951, and sentenced to five years and six months imprisonment. He was released after three months imprisonment either on account of his age or due to having already been held in French captivity for five years before the verdict. In November 1952, Ramcke told a group of former SS-men attending a meeting that they should be proud of being blacklisted, while stating that in the future their blacklist would instead be seen as a 'list of honour'. He died in 1968.

Albeit at a lower level of command, the three aristocratic Von Blücher brothers[51] also took part in the Battle of Crete. Their ancestor was the famous Prussian General Gebhard Leberecht von Blücher who arrived late at the Battle of Waterloo, which turned the battle in Wellington's favour. George could not have failed to see the connection with them and his own brothers in the RAF. Uncannily, they all died near Heraklion in Crete on 21 May 1941 - a fact that would have registered with a loyal air family like the Beamishes. Notably, the surviving Von Blücher sister was to name her three sons after her deceased brothers. Both Wolfgang and Hans-Joachim were re-interred at the German War Graves, near Maleme in 1974. Leberecht, the youngest of the three and whose body was never recovered, was commemorated in an official plaque as part of the unfallen near his bothers' plot at Maleme. Even with the *Wehrmacht's* exceptionally high attrition rate on the Russian front, it is unlikely that any German family experienced as many war deaths in such a short time as did the Von Blüchers.

The *Luftlande-Sturm-Regiment* or *Fallschirmjäger* regiment in the *Luftwaffe* took part in the Battle of Crete, and also on the Eastern Front. Used sparingly prior to then, its role in the Battle of Crete was an important part of the German invading force. The regiment did not take part in the invasion of Greece but was kept in reserve until the invasion of Crete. Its airborne invasion of Crete through the use of paratroopers was very costly in terms of casualties. As General Student stated, Crete was the 'graveyard of the paratroops'.[52]

Nazi War Crimes in Crete

During the German invasion of Crete, Allied forces and Cretan irregulars inflicted heavy losses on the *Wehrmacht*. A reprisal was ordered to send a message to the Cretan population not to resist German occupation of the island. A select group of *Fallschirmjäger* was chosen to carry out the civilian reprisal which was composed of four trucks full of German paratroopers from the 3rd Battalion of *Luftlande-Sturm-Regiment 1* commanded by *Oberleutnant* Horst Trebes. On 2 June 1941, the paratroopers arrived at the village of Kondomari. Rounding up the male villagers, between 23 (according to German sources) and 60 men (other sources) were killed by firing squad.[53] The women and children of the village watched as witnesses to the mass murder. It came to be known as the Massacre of Kondomari. As a further reprisal against the Cretans the following day, the 1st Air Landing Assault Regiment of the *Fallschirmjäger* killed 180 inhabitants in the village of Kandanos and razed the village to the ground. It was ordered by Student in reprisal for the participation of the local population in the Battle of Crete that had held the advancing German soldiers for two days. The destruction constituted one of the worst war crimes committed during the occupation of Crete by Axis forces.[54] Nearby villages such as Floria and Kakopetro met a similar fate. Inscriptions in German and Greek were erected on each entry to the village. One read: 'Here stood Kandanos, destroyed in retribution for the murder of twenty German soldiers, never to be rebuilt again.'[55]

After the capture of Crete, Anogeia emerged as a stronghold of the local resistance. Anogeians sheltered British, New Zealand and Australian soldiers and assisted them to escape to Egypt. In early May 1944, the abductors of *Generalmajor* Heinrich Kreipe, led by Patrick Leigh Fermor, spent some time at Anogeia during their march to the south coast of Crete.[57] On 7 August 1944, a German detachment went up to Anogeia in search of forced labour workers. Several dozen locals were taken hostage and forced to march towards Retimo. Anogeian guerrillas and eliminated the German detachment, freeing all hostages. On the following day, in an attempt to save Anogeia from German reprisals, a group of Anogeians under the commands of Captain Bill Moss carried out the sabotage, killing around 30 German soldiers and destroying an armoured car.[58] In the early morning of 13 August 1944, German battalions of the 65th Regiment with a strength of around 2,000 men, moved towards Anogeia. Around 25 villagers, including women, elders and disabled, who refused to abandon their homes, were summarily shot. The village houses were then systematically pillaged, burned and finally dynamited. The pillage and destruction continued for a total of twenty-three days. Out of the 940 houses of Anogeia, none stood intact.[59]

In 1945, Müller, the instigator of the atrocity, was captured by the Red Army in East Prussia. In 1946, he was tried by a Greek court in Athens for ordering atrocities against civilians. He was sentenced to death on 9 December 1946 and executed by firing squad on 20 May 1947.[60]

After the surrender of Germany in 1945, Student was captured by the British. In May 1947, he came before a military tribunal to answer charges of mistreatment and murder of Prisoners of War by his forces in Crete. He was found guilty of three out of eight charges and sentenced to five years in prison. However, he was given a medical discharge and was released in 1948.[56]

Famous Participants in Crete[61]

A considerable number of well-known people took part in the Battle for Crete, either well-known at the time or to become so in their fields after the war. Probably the best known was Evelyn Waugh whose memories of the conflict were recounted in his searing novel, *Officers and Gentlemen*. The account of the battle for Crete by Evelyn Waugh was quite acerbic and controversial for a serving officer.[62] He saw it as symbolic of the collapse of the British ruling class and the manner of the retreat of the officers highlighted that collapse.[63] The writer, Roald Dahl, became an RAF pilot in the Second World War, serving in the Battle of Greece, but injuries prevented him from fighting in Crete.

Famous travel writer and intelligence operative Patrick Leigh Fermor was another famous participant who took an active role in the defence of the island.

On the German side, there was the famous boxer of the 1930s, Max Schmeling. Schmeling was a member of the elite paratroopers, the *Fallschirmjäger,* who served in the German invasion of Crete in 1941 but was injured by shrapnel on the first day of the battle and invalided out.

Lawrence Durrell, the British novelist, was also in Crete for the battle.

Lesser known publicly but equally noted for their contributions were Roy Farran, Charles Upham, John Pendelbury and Geoffrey Cox. Farran was awarded the Military Cross for gallantry in Crete, an award that was slightly tarnished by his being the driver of the car that killed its passenger, the head of 7th Armoured Division, Major General Jock Campbell. Charles Upham was a New Zealand army captain who also served in Crete, receiving a Victoria Cross and Bar for his bravery. Clive Hulme was another New Zealander, who received his Victoria Cross for his actions during the Battle of Crete. Geoffrey Cox was a New Zealander who assisted General Freyberg in intelligence matters in Crete and was to go on to become a renowned journalist and senior TV executive in Britain after the war. Pendelbury was a former public schoolboy who became an archaeologist with a supreme knowledge of Crete which he brought to the British war effort there. After the German invasion in April 1941, he was arrested out of uniform by German gunners and unable to prove he was a soldier, was put up against a wall and shot.

RAF Pilots over Crete

William 'Cherry' Vale was a flying ace of the Second World War. He was credited with 30 enemy aircraft shot down. His 20 kills achieved while flying the Hawker Hurricane and his 10 with the Gloster Gladiator made him the second-highest scoring Hurricane and biplane pilot in the RAF, in both cases after Marmaduke

Pattle. Based in Egypt at the beginning of the war and by then a temporary flight sergeant, Vale flew operations over the Libyan border. In July 1942, Vale was posted to No. 80 Squadron RAF. He saw action over Greece and the Balkans through late 1940 and early 1941, and flew over Crete in May 1941 in defence of the island. On 18 May, Vale was evacuated from Crete to Egypt. He was awarded the Distinguished Flying Cross on 28 March 1941 and Bar on 11 July 1941. His citation states:

> After the evacuation operations from Greece, this officer remained at Maleme aerodrome with some members of his unit. In the course of enemy air attacks on Crete, Pilot Officer Vale proved himself to be a staunch pilot. Frequently against odds, he continued his attacks against the enemy and destroyed four of their aircraft during an attack on the anchorage at Souda Bay. He displayed great courage and determination.

Group Captain Dudley Honor's No. 274 Squadron was sent to Crete in May 1941 in an endeavour to stem the German landings. On 25 May, he and another aircraft were tasked to attack the German-held airfield at Maleme. As he approached, he saw many Italian and German transport aircraft preparing to land. Ignoring the dense flak, he attacked and within a few minutes he had shot down two of the transports laden with troop reinforcements for the island. As he broke away from the enemy airfield, German fighters chased him. His aircraft was badly damaged, became difficult to control and he was forced to ditch into the sea. Some days later, he was noticed by a Sunderland flying boat and rescued. Honor soon rejoined his squadron, which had returned to the Western Desert after the fall of Crete. Shortly afterwards, he was awarded a Bar to the DFC he had been awarded in 1940. The citation recorded his 'great skill' and noted that he had destroyed nine enemy aircraft.[64]

Although Germany was able to capture Crete and secure its oil fields in the East, the number of casualties and equipment lost in the process was extreme. Crete is described as a 'pyrrhic victory', the cost of victory barely worth the reward. In comparison to the 3,000 Allied troops, 7,000 Germans lost their lives. Germany also lost more than 300 planes. Many of the Allied troops remembered only the 'miraculous evacuation'[65] feeling victorious about robbing the Germans of a successful campaign.

Aftermath of Crete Campaign

From his eyrie in Cairo, Tedder could see at once that Crete had proven how traditional sea power had been replaced by the contingencies of air power. While the evacuation to Cairo was a three-pronged combined co-operation, the actual decision to evacuate was made in a telephone conversation between Wavell and Admiral Cunningham. The campaign was also to demonstrate to Tedder, 'the cycle of interdependence' among the three services which was to repeat itself throughout the Second World War and notably in the Desert War.[66] Allied commanders at first worried that the Germans might use Crete as a springboard for further operations in the Mediterranean's East Basin, possibly for an airborne attack on Cyprus or a seaborne invasion of Egypt in support of the German-Italian forces operating from Libya. This would have been devastating for Britain and its empire. After Crete, Hitler resolved never to conduct a major airborne operation again. By contrast, many Allied leaders were impressed by the *Luftwaffe's* airborne forces' performance and moved to create similar formations within their own armies.

Ron Palenski provides a different perspective on the reason for the Allied loss. Palenski believes that the Allies were doomed from the start, in facing the 'best-trained, best-armed and best-led soldiers in the world' and an invasion by air that had never been seen before. It is hard to argue with Palenski in that the Germans had gained in confidence with every one of its many victories in Europe over the previous two years to become an irresistible force.[67]

Some have suggested that the Battle for Crete delayed German plans for *Barbarossa*. The start date of 22 June 1941, however, had been set several weeks before the Crete operation was considered. One view holds that the reasons for the delay of *Barbarossa* owed nothing to the battle of Crete but was because of the need to allow swollen rivers to fall and for airfields to dry out in Poland. According to this view, it appears, therefore, that whatever the British forces' actions at the time, the greatest tactical disaster by the Germans during the whole war was something beyond British control.[68]

The sinking of the *Bismarck* at around the same time as the fall of Crete, distracted a British public in need of a victory; but the loss of Crete, particularly as a result of the failure of the Allied land forces to recognise the strategic importance of the airfields, served as a sharp warning to the British government. Although the Allies lost Crete, the *Ultra* intelligence that a parachute landing was planned meant that heavy losses were inflicted on the Germans and that fewer British troops were captured.[69] As a direct consequence, the RAF Regiment was formed on 1 February 1942 to protect RAF airfields.[70] Much was learned from past mistakes and the role of the air war was to come more sharply into focus over the course of the Second World War. Many of the Australian forces felt bitter about being left behind in the evacuation and a contingent of Spanish Republican combatants were sure that they would face immediate execution on their repatriation to Spain.[71]

Such was the admiration and gratitude of the Greek people and Greek government for the efforts of the British land, sea and air forces during the Battles for Greece and Crete that the Greek Government later bestowed a wide number of awards. Among these was the Order of King George I awarded to George Beamish and others for his overseeing the evacuation of Crete in 1941. The fostering of positive relations between the Allies and the Greeks during and after the Greek conflict, moreover, was likely to have had some bearing on securing Greece within the western sphere post-war.[72]

One cannot disguise the fact that Crete was a retreat painted as a tactical evacuation, similar to Dunkirk in 1940. Another connection with Dunkirk was in relation to the role of the RAF. At Dunkirk, there was a perception on the part of the evacuees on the beaches that the RAF stood off from the conflict. In Crete, equally, the Allied commitment at the very top to its defence was not as wholehearted as many would have expected. In Crete, the reality was that the RAF was severely under-resourced for the defence of a major strategic island. The reality at Dunkirk was more nuanced as the RAF fought many sorties near Dunkirk at the time of the evacuation but out of sight of the beaches. The same benign interpretation could not be said of the RAF's role at the battle for Crete. As Tedder noted, 'a first-class hate was working up (in the Army) against the RAF for having let them down in Greece and Crete'.[73]

Although the Allies lost Crete, the *Ultra* intelligence that a parachute landing was planned meant that heavy losses were inflicted on the Germans and that fewer British troops were captured. Five intelligence lessons learned from the Battle for Crete were:

- the need to plan to ensure continuous availability of intelligence throughout an operation,
- the criticality of communications to intelligence,
- the need for the commander to understand intelligence to use it effectively,
- the problems associated with source protection, and
- the inevitability of ambiguity in intelligence.[74]

The true importance of the Battle of Crete can only be seen in the effect it had upon later events during the war. Crete would affect the course of the war in North Africa, dissuade Allied command from establishing a Second Front, and go some way towards destroying the Mediterranean strategy. Its most significant contribution, however, is the way in which many thought it delayed *Barbarossa*. Holding Crete meant the Germans maintaining a garrison by removing both men and material from the German war effort in the East.

The Allied losses were also staggeringly high, with 15,743 either becoming a casualty, wounded, or a Prisoner of War. It also gave Hitler a solid base for his upcoming battle in the Soviet Union. The Allies were left frustrated after the fight, as they felt it was a battle that they should have won. To make things worse for morale, it was also the first instance of an island being successfully invaded from the air. Beevor described Cretan defiance: 'Boys, old men, and also women displayed a breathtaking bravery in defence of their island.'[75]

Most of Continental Europe was now either in German hands or in alliance with the Nazis. The Nazis were racing through Eastern Europe and the Soviet Union heading toward Moscow. Nothing seemed to stand in their way. Morale was at a very low ebb and the British public were crying out for a victory to turn the tide of the war. It was during George's next assignment in North Africa that this was to happen.

All told, 332,226 men were rescued from Dunkirk. This was deemed by many as a success, however, Churchill cautiously advised, 'We must be very careful not to assign to this deliverance the attributes of a victory. Wars are not won by evacuations.'[76] It demonstrated too the role of the RAF in support of the Army, a policy developed by Tedder and Coningham that was to prove so effective in the Desert War. Although Crete was on a far smaller scale than Dunkirk, the latter held some lessons for Crete. Churchill was perfectly correct in his characterisation of the Dunkirk exercise. Crete too was a judicious retreat but a retreat for all that. Military activity was now to focus on North Africa with all the attendant challenges and opportunities it presented.

After Crete, George Beamish was to be catapulted into a far more critical conflict in terms of the overall war, the Desert Campaign. Being on the razor's edge in Crete, however, was to stand him in good stead professionally. As a postscript to the Battle of Crete, Rolls-Royce, the aircraft engine manufacturers based in Derby, contacted George in 1941 for his opinion on the relative merits of the Hurricane versus the Tomahawk. Having seen both in action in real-life battle in Crete, his views would have been invaluable to the company. Indirectly, it would have elevated George's status among the air fraternity.[77] This discussion between industry and the RAF could be seen as an example of the workings of the 'military industrial complex' coined two decades later by Dwight D. Eisenhower.[78]

7

DESERT WAR (1941–43)

The importance of the Desert War in North Africa for Allied prospects in the Second World War – particularly British prospects – has been rehearsed on many occasions. The collapse of a British presence in Egypt and the Suez Canal would have left the oilfields of the Middle East open to the Axis powers and, ultimately, also to Britain's colonial possessions in India. Churchill, a strong defender of India's position within the Empire and as the war leader, could not countenance such an outcome. It was this underlying aim that predicated British military action in North Africa. The conflict in the North African theatre was to highlight many heroic and memorable individuals on both sides. The public is generally familiar with Montgomery, Alexander and Rommel. However, the figures of Tedder, Coningham and Broadhurst, who spearheaded the RAF's air war during the Desert War, are generally less well-known. No less a figure than Montgomery gave due praise to the RAF in helping to bring about a successful outcome in North Africa, a view also supported by objective post-war analysis.[1]

Arthur Tedder, as head of the hierarchy as RAF Commander-in-Chief Mediterranean and Middle East, was the architect of the air strategy that led to this success. In such regard was Tedder held during the war that in May 1945, Eisenhower deputed Tedder to take the formal surrender of the Germans on behalf of the Allies.

It was during the critical campaigns in Egypt and Libya during 1942 that Tedder successfully co-ordinated his strategic, coastal, and tactical air forces. The success of the air interdiction during the Desert War was the model upon which the Northwest African Air Forces were created following the Casablanca Conference in January 1943. Tedder's model was to prove critical in pushing the Germans out of North Africa and in the ultimate victory in the campaign.[2] The strategy was also to have a direct and concrete effect on the work of George Beamish and his colleagues in the Desert Campaign. Under the chain of command and in a staff role for most of the time, George was in a position to interpret the strategy and ensure others implemented it. The RAF's role in the Desert War, therefore, should be seen as a unit operating under a clear and cohesive strategy.

Earlier in the war, Tedder had been Churchill's default choice as Air Officer Commander-in-Chief of RAF Middle East when his first choice, Air Vice Marshal Owen Boyd, was captured by the enemy. When Churchill met Tedder on a visit to the desert in 1942, he apologised to Tedder for assuming that he was 'a nuts and bolts man'.[3] Tedder was not quite sure what Churchill meant at the time but took Churchill's admission with good grace. The assumption might have been that Tedder was seen as too pedestrian but, as the Desert War was to show, he was far from that and, in fact, he was a master strategist and tactician. Soon after Tedder assumed command in June 1941, he made the following statement that not only characterised his mission in the Middle East, but the future organisation of the Mediterranean Air Command in early 1943 and nearly all future air forces:

> In my opinion, sea, land and air operations in the Middle East Theatre are now so closely inter-related that effective co-ordination will only be possible if the campaign is considered and controlled as a combined operation in the full sense of that term.[4]

The concept itself was certainly not a new one but putting it into practice under the military dogma of the day was easier said than done. Throughout 1942, the co-ordination and flexibility exercised between then Vice Air Marshal Arthur Coningham's Western Desert Air Force (WDAF) and the Eighth Army has been contrasted with the more rigid relationship between the Luftwaffe and German ground forces.[5]

Tedder was appointed as Air Officer Commander-in-Chief, RAF Middle East Command, on 1 June 1941, with the temporary rank of Air Marshal. His appointment turned out to be an inspired move for the positive impact he had on the outcome of the war. He was also fortunate in 'having the ear' of both Chief of the Air Staff, Portal, and his deputy, Freeman.[6]

In a jaunty and familiar way, RAF pilot ace Mike Judd described his first meeting with Tedder before assignment to his squadron.

> The air officer commanding in chief Middle East air force was an unusually intelligent and charming man named Arthur Tedder, who I eventually got to know quite well. He called in an aide whom he asked what squadrons needed a replacement pilot and the aide said that the 238 Hurricane Squadron had just lost a pilot and that I should be posted there as a replacement. I collected a bed roll containing a collapsible bed, washstand and canvas chair, plus two blankets, bought some khaki shorts and desert boots, left my blue uniforms in a suitcase in Shepheard's Hotel and next day set off for Muss as a passenger in a three ton truck.[7]

As head of the RAF Middle East Command, Tedder commanded air operations in the Mediterranean and North Africa, including the evacuation of Crete where George Beamish had acquitted himself well against huge odds in May 1941. Tedder also commanded Operation *Crusader* in North Africa in late 1941. In July 1942, he was promoted to the temporary rank of Air Chief Marshal.[8] Here, he was the overall superior of the tight-knit WDAF team of Air

Marshal Arthur Coningham, his assistant Tommy Elmhirst, Harry Broadhurst of No. 211 Group and George Beamish in his role as Conningham's SASO.

Before this, Tedder had held an appointment at the Ministry of Production under Lord Beaverbrook, owner of *Express* Newspapers and a close cabinet ally of Churchill's. Tedder and Beaverbrook did not see eye to eye, a difficulty which extended too to Tedder's relations with Churchill. In view of this, Tedder was soon transferred to the Middle East Command, a smart move for all concerned.[9] Tedder oversaw the build-up of the Air Arm in the Western Desert, turning it into a highly effective force and key to the Allied victory at the decisive Battle of El Alamein in October 1942.

> His insistence, and that of his immediate subordinates such as 'Mary' Coningham, that the winning of the air battle must take precedence, and that the whole air, sea and land campaign must be run as a combined operation, was fundamental to the desert victory.[9a]

Importantly too, by 1942 he had managed to regain Churchill's confidence by accompanying the PM on a high-level visit to Moscow.[9b] Tedder's view was that air superiority over the battle area was an essential precondition for an effective and sustained contribution by air forces to a land battle. Once a satisfactory air situation was attained, the whole Air Force with all of its available strength could be switched to direct support; in effect, saturating the battlefield with air power.[10] To assure mutual understanding between the services, Tedder believed that a combined land and air plan was required. Army and air commanders, he believed, must work together throughout all stages of drafting, planning and executing their operations. Unity of purpose would be their guide.[11] The accuracy of Tedder's theory was confirmed a year later by the successful partnership of Montgomery and Coningham in North Africa. Tedder's plan was to become the 'Bible' of RAF/Army Desert War operations. Coningham was to laud this strategy of a joint Army/Air Force approach as being of 'fundamental importance… to the combined fighting of the two Services until the end of the War.'[12]

Following the Desert Campaign, Tedder took command of Mediterranean Air Command in February 1943, serving under US General Dwight D. Eisenhower. In that role, he was closely involved in the planning and execution of the Allied invasion of Sicily and the subsequent invasion of Italy. He also suffered the great tragedy of his wife dying in an air crash in early 1943 during the middle of the Desert Campaign. Tedder was appointed Deputy Supreme Commander at SHAEF (Supreme Headquarters Allied Expeditionary Force) in January 1944 under General Eisenhower. A great critic of Montgomery from his desert days, he even called for the latter's sacking. In May 1945, Tedder was given the honour of signing the terms of unconditional surrender of the Germans on behalf of the Allies.

Tedder gave George the welcome compliment of commending his and Coningham's ability to work closely with the Americans in the Desert War on the strength of their earlier successes in that theatre.[13] These accolades were seen as important. Indeed, this kind of commendation would have played no small part in George later being selected as a recipient of the US Legion of Merit. Furthermore, the war was to show, particularly in post-D-Day Europe, the importance of tact and diplomacy at the highest levels of the Allied Command. Portal, the Chief of the Air Staff, was widely seen as the supreme proponent of tact and co-operation in the Anglo-American alliance, mirrored too in the approach of Coningham. Tact and diplomacy were so critical to the development of relations among the Allies.

An early recruit to the importance of air power was Wavell, the Commander-in-Chief, Middle East, who echoed the RAF view on air power to the Prime Minister by stating that: 'The whole position in the Middle East was governed mainly by air power and air bases.'[14] It was obviously important for Tedder that the senior officers in the other Services also accepted his ideas on air power, so having Wavell's imprimatur was a boon. Generally, the Army in North Africa accepted the broad principles of the air power doctrine, while the Royal Navy was, at times, a little lukewarm, as witnessed by the contrasting attitudes of Montgomery and Admiral Cunningham respectively.

Following Crete, George spent a short period as the Officer Commanding a bomber wing. George was an average pilot with none of the adeptness and track record of his brother, Victor. Yet he was a creditable member of a flight team and a good organiser of men. For most of George's career except for a period attached to squadrons, George became mainly a staff RAF officer. He was a quick, decisive, 'can do' sort of man whose skills won him many admirers among the top echelons of the RAF.

By 1941, George was a Wing Commander and by his time in the Western Desert, a Group Captain. From now on, he was in a position to interact with key senior RAF figures and Army personnel who noted with favour his achievements and from which his future career was ultimately to benefit. Although George was to distinguish himself in several subsequent appointments, the one where he had most real-life impact and which tested his capabilities most was his service in the Desert Air Force in North Africa. His two key commanders in the Desert Air Force were Arthur Coningham and Thomas Elmhirst who are discussed in more detail below. George was closely associated with both men throughout the Desert Campaign.

George's immediate predecessor as Senior Air Staff Officer to Coningham was Basil Embry who, although reasonably apt for the position, returned to England in January 1942 and was said to be 'never cast as a second in command to anyone.'[15] He was to go on to become an Air Chief Marshal and a senior figure in NATO. Group Captain Peter Wykeham, a colleague of Embry's, held that: 'He was both charming and rude, prejudiced and broad-minded, pliable and obstinate, dedicated and human.'[16] By contrast, George Beamish got on well with Coningham and his staff, staying in position until the final period of the Desert War. He was very much seen as a stalwart.[17]

Coningham was first Auchinleck's and then Montgomery's air equivalent in the Desert War. He took an interest in George and the two worked closely together during the Desert War. Elmhirst, an associate of Coningham's, also worked closely with George in the desert. Coningham, Elmhirst and Beamish were to form a particularly cohesive and harmonious group 'on the ground' in the desert, each complementing the others' skills. It was essentially the 'engine' of the Western Desert Air Force.

Air Marshal Sir Arthur 'Mary' Coningham fought in the First World War, serving at Gallipoli with the New Zealand Expeditionary Force in 1915. He later joined the Royal Flying Corps in Britain, where he became a flying ace. His nickname, 'Mary' was a corruption of Maori, harking back to his New Zealand background. He accepted the nickname with good grace throughout his career.[18] Coningham is chiefly remembered as the person responsible for developing forward air control parties directing close air support, which he developed as commander of the Western Desert Air Force between 1941 and 1943, and as commander of the Second Tactical Air Forces in the Normandy Campaign in 1944. He is frequently lauded as the 'architect of modern air power through tactical air operations' based on three principles: the necessity of air superiority as the first priority, centralised command of air operations co-equal with ground leadership, and innovative tactics in support of ground operations.[19]

George Beamish gained valuable experience under Coningham, developing good contacts in the process. Coningham never seemed to be entirely comfortable in an environment without the supportive company of both Elmhirst and Beamish. Most evenings, the three would repair to Coningham's tent and discuss the day's events over a drink – a setting which Coningham enjoyed. They would then have supper, which was a relaxed affair as Coningham did not like war talk, nor, as it happened, any blue jokes. During the period, George regularly read *Ultra* intercepts with Coningham, a sharp irony harking back to the fatal failure of Freyberg to do so during the Battle for Crete.[20]

Coningham began the war as an Air Commodore in charge of Bomber Command's 4 Group for two years. Most of his attacks were on Italy and the Ruhr. As an Air Vice Marshal, in July 1941, he was called to Egypt by Tedder to take over No. 204 Group. Two months later, the Group was transformed into the Western Desert Air Force which went on to distinguish itself in the Desert War.[21] Tedder had been impressed with Coningham ever since hearing the story about how the latter had flown across the Sahara from West Africa to Egypt without wireless, indicating his fitness for further service in Africa.[22] He was said by Sir Phillip Joubert, Head of Coastal Command, to be Tedder's most capable assistant in North Africa.[23] Faced with equipment shortages, a hostile desert environment, and superior enemy planes, Coningham's management system, through judicious deployment of his squadrons, gradually achieved air superiority in the North African campaign. While relations were good with Tedder, Coningham often felt the frustration of not having the required planes and equipment. In particular, his force acutely felt the lack of fighters and trained fighter pilots at the end of 1941. It was not until May 1942 that he received his first Spitfires.[24] Given that it was only five months to El Alamein, Coningham and his forces had to make up a lot of lost ground. This frustration was felt throughout WDAF, particularly for 'can do' men of action like George Beamish.

In January 1942, as the Desert War was progressing, George was appointed Senior Air Staff Officer in the Western Desert Air Force. This was the new force designed to take on the challenges in North Africa presented by German and Italian forces. Having been 'blooded' in serious combat in Crete, George was now to be involved in one of the key theatres of the Second World War. His new role was to see him become the 'eyes and ears' of Air Marshal Coningham, in an 'enforcer' role to ensure that Coningham's orders were implemented. Being 'His Master's Voice' gave George considerable clout but equally, his physical presence surely played a big part in this role.

Coningham formed a close relationship with Montgomery, something not everyone was capable of doing. The relationship worked to their mutual benefit and to the benefit of the Desert War's outcome. History could have been quite different had the original person to succeed Auchinleck, General Gott, not been killed the day before Auchinleck's 'retirement'. Yet, cometh the hour, cometh the man and Montgomery seized the opportunity with both hands.

With the exception of one critical incident involving Coningham and General Patton in Operation *Torch,* Tedder had the highest of respect for Coningham's professional abilities.: 'It was a great asset for me to have at the head of the Desert Air Force a commander so able and enterprising and so determined to work closely with the Army Command.'[25] Both seemed to work like clockwork together. As Coningham's 'eyes and ears', George Beamish would also have benefited from this close relationship.

Both Montgomery and Coningham gave their support to joint operations. The dominance of the Allied air force, for example, was a critical factor in the British victory at the Second Battle of El Alamein in November 1942. Coningham's doctrine was fundamental. He believed that the greatest attribute of air power was its ability to speedily concentrate its force. Tactical air power had to be closely co-ordinated with the ground forces, but the Army could not command it.[26] Coningham met Montgomery first in 1942 almost a year after his own arrival in the Western Desert Air Force. Their first meeting was on 16 August when Coningham praised Montgomery by saying, 'we now have a man, a great soldier if I am any judge and we will go all the way with him'.[27] After his victory over Rommel at the Battle of Alam el Halfa, seen by some as Montgomery's greatest victory, Montgomery wrote to Coningham on 3 September 1942. In the letter, he praised the RAF for its co-operation in the battle. Coningham replied on 5 September commending Montgomery on how the victory was won in a 'flawless manner', followed by another reply from Montgomery reiterating the earlier sentiments. In this spirit, that night Coningham brought out a bottle of champagne which he consumed with Elmhirst and Beamish, toasting to the 'Hun's utter confusion'.[28]

At a meeting on 21 August chaired by Montgomery and Coningham, which George also attended, George was given a stern reprimand by Montgomery for entering the tent sucking on his trademark pipe which had long gone out. 'I don't have any smoking at my conferences,' he blasted at Beamish. Beamish's first exposure to the ire of Monty was to be shared over time by Coningham, whose opinion of the great general was to change sharply.[29]

According to *Time* magazine, Coningham was 'a dark, strong-faced, deep-voiced, wise-cracking non-smoking, six-footer from New Zealand. He has a reputation for talent in co-operation – not a notable talent of previous RAF commanders in the Middle East.'[30]

Coningham was one of the truly heroic commanders of the Second World War, instrumental in the success of one of the key battles of the war, El Alamein. He had the complete faith and support of his superior, Arthur Tedder, and had good relations with most senior commanders in the Army. For George Beamish, his time under Coningham's command was a marvellous experience in the crucible of war.

Tommy Elmhirst, Coningham's ASO, felt his superior was stronger on the operations side than the administration side of things. Elmhirst noted the scale of bureaucratic confusion on his arrival in the Western Desert, where he was left to clear things up, and for which he relied to a large degree on George Beamish.[31]

Coningham continued to provide tactical air support for the Eighth Army until they occupied Tripoli in January 1943. In late 1943, he was promoted to Air Marshal and directed tactical air force operations in the Allied invasion of Sicily and Italy following the fall of Tunis and victory in North Africa. In January 1944, Coningham was transferred back to Britain to command Second Tactical Air Force in the North-West European Campaign under Air Marshal Trafford Leigh-Mallory, commanding the Allied Expeditionary Air Forces. During that stint under Leigh-Mallory,

Coningham apparently confided in his senior that 'the whole of the Desert War really revolved around three people: 'Himself, Elmhirst and Beamish'[32] – a huge compliment to George, the most junior among them. This list was conspicuous by the absence of Broadhurst with whom Coningham had some personal animosities, but who did contribute significantly. Critically, Coningham's remark was that of an insider who knew the full picture of the Desert War.

Coningham's relationship with Montgomery deteriorated towards the end of the North African Campaign and deteriorated markedly after the Normandy Landings. Montgomery lobbied Tedder and Eisenhower to have Coningham removed from his post. Tedder intervened, however, on Coningham's behalf, saying his removal would be a 'disaster'. Coningham remained commander of the Second Tactical Air Force until July 1945, when he was appointed Head of Flying Training Command.[33]

Towards the end of the war, Coningham appeared on the front cover of *Time* magazine. 'Making the front cover' of *Time*, both then and now, is a great honour. It was significant that the choice of Coningham was made during the time the Normandy Invasion was in full flow and after his successful Desert Campaign feats became well known to the Americans.[34] Coningham's career ended in August 1947 after thirty years of service. He died in the most tragic of circumstances in January 1948 when the airliner in which he was travelling to Bermuda was lost in the area later known as the 'Bermuda Triangle'. His body was never recovered. A mysterious end for a man of such substance and achievement. He was sorely missed by George Beamish and many others.[35] No better accolade could have been paid to Coningham by the self-effacing Tedder than when, as recorded by R. H. Liddell-Hart, he said, 'the real hero of the Desert War is the New Zealander, "Mary" Coningham'.[36]

At a particularly dark time for Coningham in the Desert War in February 1942, the announcement that Thomas Elmhirst would be his second-in-command was the best of news. Elmhirst had come direct from Air Command in Egypt and the Suez Canal and knew the terrain. He also acted as an invaluable asset in managing to put an administrative shape on Coningham's, at times, rough and ready organisation. Sir Thomas Walker Elmhirst was a senior RAF commander, eventually rising to the rank of Air Marshal. He was appointed the first Commander-in-Chief of the newly independent Indian Air Force in 1947.

He initially served in the Royal Navy in the First World War, seeing action in the Dardanelles. He was part of the first group to join the Royal Naval Air Service in 1915 and, in 1919, he joined the newly formed Royal Air Force. On selection to the Royal Naval Air Service, it is said that Lord Fisher, First Sea Lord at the time, advised the group of recruits that they were likely to 'win either a VC or be killed' in the new service. He said further, 'If you don't want to fly, report back to this office within forty-eight hours.' No one did.[37] In 1941, Elmhirst commanded the Egypt Command Group under Tedder. He then became Second-in-Command of the Desert Air Force under Coningham, a role he continued in through the battle of El Alamein until after the Allied invasion of Sicily.[38]

On his arrival at Gambut, the joint Army/RAF HQ in the desert, the first person Elmhirst was to meet after Coningham, was George Beamish. In a letter to his wife, Elmhirst recounted the details of his arrival. George Beamish, the Senior Air Staff Officer fixed him up with a bivouac alongside his office caravan. 'The tent is only big enough to hold my camp bed, a chair and a suitcase, but I have already blessed you for the purchase of that Dunlop mattress and Jaeger sleeping bag with the little pillow.'[39] He also recounts on 15 May 1942 how he was nearly killed by 'Luftwaffe bullets on a dawn raid in the narrow area near George Beamish's tent'.[40] 'We usually finish work around 8:00 pm and then George Beamish and I join 'Mary' in his very comfortable office-cabin caravan where we have a drink and discuss the day's operations and the delinquency or otherwise of the soldiers.'[41]

Although ten years older, he was a close RAF associate of George Beamish in the Desert War. Both men saw their respective careers prosper as a result of that association.

Elmhirst became Second-in-Command of British Air Forces in North West Europe until the end of the war, serving in D-Day, Normandy, the Ardennes and the advance across France and Germany. He became Assistant Chief of the Air Staff (Intelligence) from 1945–1947, effectively the Head of RAF Intelligence. While Head of the Indian Air Force from 1947, Elmhirst had the responsibility for organising the funeral of Gandhi following his assassination in 1948. By Hindu custom, Gandhi had to be buried the following day. One million people were expected at the funeral. Gandhi was burned at a pyre according to Hindu tradition with his head facing north, like the great Buddah. When first appointed, Elmhirst could scarcely have imagined that this logistical challenge would be one of his duties!

Elmhirst later became the Lieutenant-Governor and Commander-in-Chief of Guernsey from 1953 to 1958 where he organised a royal visit by the Queen. Looking back over his career, he had a colourful and interesting set of appointments.[42]

Western Desert Campaign

The Western Desert Campaign can broadly be divided into two parts. The first part dating from 1940 saw some early successes by the Italians, the emergence of the power of Rommel's *Afrika Korps* and the Allied forces very much on the back foot. The second part starts from the Allied victory at El Alamein in November 1942, includes Operation *Torch*, and concludes in May 1943. In that latter period, the role of the RAF and allied air forces was decisive in securing victory.

In March 1941, soon after the arrival of the *Afrika Korps* in Tripoli to reinforce the Italians, the Axis forces quickly captured the British front line position at El Agheila and by mid-April, had reached as far as Sallum in Egypt. The British held the fortified port of Tobruk, which was besieged by the Axis. Having been informed by General Wavell that the Western Desert Force was vastly inferior to the Axis forces now in Africa, Churchill ordered that a convoy, containing tanks and Hawker Hurricanes, be sailed through the Mediterranean instead of around the Cape of Good Hope to cut forty days off the journey.

The German High Command sent General Friedrich Paulus, later of Stalingrad fame, to North Africa to investigate the situation. On 12 May, Paulus, after witnessing one of Rommel's failed attempts to assault Tobruk, sent a report to *Wehrmacht* HQ describing Rommel's position as weak, with critical shortages of both fuel and ammunition. With Operation *Barbarossa* imminent, Field Marshal Walther von Brauchitsch, Commander-in-Chief of the German Army, ordered Rommel not to advance further or attack Tobruk again.

Through *Ultra* intercepts, the British also received Paulus's report and Churchill, believing that one strong push would dislodge German forces, began to increase the pressure on General Wavell to attack. Wavell quickly prepared Operation *Brevity*, a limited operation with the intention of seizing Sollum, the Halfaya Pass and Fort Capuzzo, then continuing to advance towards Tobruk as far as the supply chain would allow. Its objective was to destroy as much Axis equipment as possible and secure a foothold for the larger Operation *Battleaxe* to be launched once the new tanks were made available.[43] *Brevity* began on 15 May and Fort Capuzzo and Halfaya Pass were captured. The next day, however, William Gott, concerned that his 22nd Guards Brigade would be wiped out if caught in the open should the Germans attack with tanks, decided to pull almost the entire force back to Halfaya Pass and the operation officially ended on 17 May, with only the Halfaya Pass captured.[44]

By the end of May 1941, the fall of Crete meant that the *Luftwaffe* would have additional airfields available to threaten Allied shipping and also to protect their own supply convoys and troops in Cyrenaica. Delaying *Battleaxe* could therefore mean facing stronger Axis opposition.

Under *Battleaxe*, the Allies had 969 casualties, with 122 killed, 588 wounded, and 259 missing. The Germans had 678 casualties, with 93 killed, 350 wounded and 235 missing and the Italians suffered 592 casualties. The British lost 98 tanks and the Axis had roughly 50 disabled. The British lost 33 fighters and 3 bombers against 10 German aircraft. RAF fighter losses were caused by lack of pilot training and the need for continuous air cover; standing patrols could only be maintained by a few aircraft while the bulk were in transit to the battlefield, being repaired rearmed and refuelled.[45]

When Churchill received the news that *Battleaxe* had failed, he sacked Wavell but to save face, Churchill had Wavell exchange duties with General Claude Auchinleck, Commander-in-Chief, India. Wavell's sacking was not the last to be made by a Prime Minister impatient for results and victory in the desert.

In his diary on 20 November 1941, US Air Force General Lewis Brereton highlighted the dictum of German General Johann von Ravenstein that: 'The desert is a tactician's paradise but a quartermaster's hell'.[46] At various times during the Desert War, both the Allies and the Axis experienced supply shortages or bottlenecks, but the flat, barren terrain generally made it easy to plan military and air movements. While air power was probably the critical factor behind the German defeat in North Africa, supply problems also played an important role in eventually strangling the *Afrika Korps* into submission. It was a particular type of war and effectively, the rulebooks on military engagements in the field could, to some degree, be put aside.

By November 1941, the squadron strength of the Western Desert Air Force was up to 30, made up of 14 squadrons of short-range fighters; 2 squadrons of long-range fighters; 8 squadrons of medium bombers; 3 squadrons of tactical reconnaissance aircraft; 1 flight of survey reconnaissance aircraft; 1 flight of strategical reconnaissance aircraft.[47] Auchinleck launched a new offensive, Operation *Crusader,* in November 1941. After a see-saw battle, the 70th Division garrisoning Tobruk was relieved and the Axis forces were forced to fall back.

After receiving supplies and reinforcements from Tripoli, the Axis attacked again, defeating the Allies at Gazala in June 1942 and capturing Tobruk. During Operation *Crusader* in November and December 1941, the Middle East Air Force fought for and gained air superiority, disrupted the Axis supply network, and assisted in the land battle. *Crusader* was intended to relieve the 1941 siege of Tobruk and to destroy the Axis armoured force before advancing its infantry. The plan failed when, after a number of inconclusive engagements, the British 7th Armoured Division was defeated by the *Afrika Korps* at Sidi Rezegh. Auchinleck's determination and Ritchie's aggression had for the time being removed the Axis threat to Egypt and the Suez Canal. Critically, it was *Ultra* intelligence that helped Auchinleck to prevent Rommel's forces from reaching Cairo in the autumn of 1941. While it may have proved a limited success, Operation *Crusader* showed that Rommel's *Afrika Korps* could be beaten and is a fine illustration of the dynamic back-and-forth fighting which characterised the North African Campaign. Geoffrey Cox wrote that *Crusader* was 'won by a hair's breadth', but 'had we lost it, we would have had to fight the battle of El Alamein six months or a year earlier, without the decisive weapon of the Sherman tank'.[48]

In June 1942, in response to the German threat to the Suez Canal in North Africa, General Brereton was transferred to Cairo as the Commander of United States Army Middle East Air Forces in Libya. His small air force was reinforced by the 57th Fighter Group (P-40s) and 12th Bomb Group (B-25s) in July and August, and Brereton drew heavily on the experiences of Coningham's Western Desert Air Force. He became a good example of successful joint UK/US action in North Africa.[49] On 22 October 1942, the US Desert Air Task Force was formed with Brereton in command to support the British offensive at El Alamein and for arriving USAF staff officers to gain experience. Brereton's heavy bombers used the campaign as a proving ground for tactics, particularly pattern bombing against ships. From July 1942 to the end of the war, Brereton had a close association with and was well regarded by

Coningham, who found in him not just a fellow *bon vivant* but an effective air commander on whom he could rely for efficient and competent co-operation. This type of rapport, although far from universal, was essential to the success of inter-Allied co-operation and the winning of the war. Brereton saw action in more theatres than any other senior officer. He also kept detailed notes of his time in the desert which he published after the war as *The Brereton Diaries*, a frank and expansive account of events in the conflict.[50]

During his time in the desert, the impression George gave was of someone absolutely imperturbable. Only shortages of tea and tobacco were said to have caused him discomfort. A later anecdote about George and his creature comforts is related by his nephew Michael, a son of his youngest brother, Cecil. On clearing George's house and personal effects after his death in Castlerock in 1967, Michael and his brother came across random pouches, tins of tobacco and cigars strewn across the house. This was long before public concern over the dangers of smoking, in an era when smoking a pipe was a normal pastime for a man of his age. George's liking for tea in large quantities is also attested to by senior US air officer, Laurence Kuter, a Western Desert colleague, who mentioned that George and an army counterpart based in Operational Control in North Africa 'never seemed to sleep' and survived on 'strong mugs of tea'. Vincent Orange's biography of Coningham indicates that George's tea-drinking habits may have been contagious, as Coningham also developed a taste for strongly brewed sugary tea. George is identified by Kuter as having a 'badly broken nose' which contrasted with his 'gentle, high-pitched voice'.[51] Compared with the more clipped accent of many Englishmen, George's soft Ulster lilt may well have come across this way. The broken nose was either due to activities in the boxing ring, on the rugby field or both. In the midst of *Luftwaffe* bombing and strafing attacks, George is thought to have said to Coningham that anyone who had been at the Battle of Crete as he had, when faced with a setback in the Desert War 'should have no cause for alarm'.[52]

Rank and status mean everything to those in the forces. With this in mind, Tommy Elmhirst objected to a memo from Air Commodore Spencer in the Air Ministry suggesting changes to SASO (George Beamish's rank). Coningham said: 'My SASO is my mouthpiece, but I expect my AOA to act on his own. The scheme puts the SASO a long way from his AOC. I feel he must act at all times in the closest contact.'[53] As the SASO, Beamish and the WDAF's chief role was to act in support of the Eighth Army in the Desert War. Etched forever into the annals of military glory, the Eighth Army was led by some of the most illustrious generals in the Second World War. The names of Auchinleck, Alexander and Montgomery easily trip off the tongue. Less well known are the senior RAF figures who worked closely with their army colleagues in the ultimate victory over the Axis powers in this theatre. Without the role of RAF figures like Tedder, Coningham and Broadhurst, there may have been quite a different outcome. The huge attention focused historically on the RAF in the Battle of Britain and in protecting the North Atlantic sea lanes has tended to overshadow its critical role in the Desert War. For a long time, Montgomery's Eighth Army unfairly took most of the public adulation, until subsequent more balanced analyses gave the proper amounts of credit to the RAF. In particular, the huge success of the fighter-bomber during that conflict was a key factor in overall victory.

An intriguing character, one Walter Monckton, was to cross the landscape of the desert in those years. A lawyer who served as advisor to Edward VIII during the abdication crisis, he was also to play a role in decision making at Cairo during the conflict. Monckton ran the UK's propaganda department in Cairo and had regular contact with Tedder and other senior military figures based in Egypt. He also wrote an abdication document for Egypt's King Farouk, after the King had shown pro-German sympathies. A politician, Monckton was one of those individuals from outside the services who exercised some influence on events in North Africa. George had spent a short period at HQ in Cairo before his appointment to the Desert Campaign and would have been aware of the kinds of activities engaged in by Monckton and others. The Desert War and indeed Crete threw up many interesting and intriguing characters with roles and responsibilities so different from those in their civilian lives.[54]

No. 211 Group RAF

One of the key Air Force Groups in the Desert War was No. 211, commanded by Richard Atcherley and under the overall command of Harry Broadhurst. Air Commodore Richard Atcherley assumed command of the Group on 11 April 1943. The Group was the principal fighter force of the Desert Air Force (DAF) commanded by Broadhurst, and under command of Coningham's Northwest African Tactical Air Force. It included South African, Australian, American and Canadian forces and proved a good example of Anglo-American military co-operation.[55]

In early 1942, Coningham's HQ received a visit from Group Captain R. H. Humphreys concerning the use of *Ultra* intelligence reports. Humphreys revealed key intelligence on the *Luftwaffe's* plans to discontinue night bombing and to deploy their newest fighters in the Desert War. The result was to point to the need for more Spitfires, to which Tedder assented and which was much applauded in the Western Desert. Tedder also expressed his frustration over having to give so many aircraft to India and the Far East when conditions were still difficult in North Africa.[56]

Elmhirst refers to a visit by retired Marshal of the Air Force Trenchard in September 1942 during which mention is made of discipline, parades and the shaving habits of some of the men, mainly Australians. A stickler for discipline, Trenchard was taken aback by the more 'relaxed' conditions in the Desert.[57] In September 1942, George was closely involved in liaison duties with the RAF regiment, amassing and allocating supplies.[58]

On 26 May 1942, the German Operation *Theseus* on the Gazala front was heading towards Tobruk. The Battle of Gazala was fought west of Tobruk from 26 May to 21 June 1942. Axis troops consisted of German and Italian units. Allied forces were mainly British, Indian, South African and Free French. The RAF was heavily committed during the Battle of Gazala in May and June 1942, and by the middle of July, eleven fighter squadrons were at half strength, seven squadrons were still equipped with obsolescent aircraft, and nine squadrons were without any operational aircraft at all. Rommel secretly had the advantage of detailed advance intelligence on the Allies. The most secret data on British 'strengths, positions, losses, reinforcements, supply, situation, plans, morale etc.,' was read by German signals intelligence in Africa, within eight hours of transmission to Washington. The Axis distracted the British with a decoy attack in the north and made the main attack round the southern flank of the Gazala position. The advance succeeded, but the defence of the French garrison of Bir Hakeim, at the southern end of the line, left the Axis with a long and vulnerable supply route around the Gazala line. The Axis forces drove the Eighth Army back over the Egyptian border. Their advance was stopped in July only 140 km from Alexandria in the First Battle of El Alamein. The Eighth Army counter-attack, Operation *Aberdeen*, was poorly co-ordinated and defeated in detail. The British withdrew from the Gazala Line and the Axis troops overran Tobruk in a day. Rommel exploited the success by pursuing the British into Egypt, denying them time to recover from the defeat. As both sides neared exhaustion, the Eighth Army managed to check the Axis advance at the First Battle of El Alamein. From then on, the Axis was on the back foot.[59]

During a visit to the Desert by the Prime Minister, his aide, Teddy Thompson, asked Elmhirst why Gazala was lost: 'It was lost on the polo fields of Poona, while the RAF battle was won on the RAF rugger fields, as the two Air Commodores and two of the four Group Captains had played rugby for the Air Force. In this colourful quote, GB was one of the two Air Commodores.'[60] GB, of course, refers to George Beamish.

In late 1941, the British Eighth Army relieved Tobruk and drove the Axis forces from Cyrenaica to El Agheila. After a two-month delay, German and Italian forces in Libya began to receive supplies and reinforcements in men and tanks, which continued until the end of May, when *Fliegerkorps II* was transferred to the Russian front. Rommel was impressed by the 'all round the clock bombing' by the RAF.[61] Axis commanders knew that the entry of the United States into the war would give the Eighth Army access to an increase in materiel but sought to forestall an Allied offensive before these supplies could be brought to bear. The Axis retreat to El Agheila after Operation *Crusader* reduced the supply distance from Tripoli to 740 km. On 29 January, the Axis recaptured Benghazi and the next day ammunition supply to the front line failed. Air attacks directed by Kesselring against Malta greatly reduced its offensive capacity, allowing supply convoys from Italy to reach Axis forces in Africa with increased regularity.

In February 1942, the Army, Royal Navy and Air Force Commanders-in-Chief in Cairo had agreed that Tobruk should not stand another siege. On 21 June, 35,000 Allied troops surrendered to the Italian General Navarini. With the capture of Tobruk, the Axis gained a port nearer the Aegean–Crete route and a large amount of British supplies. If the British could not stop the Germans in Egypt, they would take the Suez Canal and potentially drive for the oilfields in the Middle East. Hitler rewarded Rommel with a promotion to the rank of Field Marshal. This made Rommel the youngest German officer ever to achieve this rank, adding to his already powerful allure.[62]

The Eighth Army lost 50,000 men killed, wounded or captured, including around 35,000 prisoners taken at Tobruk. Axis casualties were 3,360 Germans and a smaller number of Italian losses. The *Afrika Korps* advanced upon Egypt, while the Eighth Army fell back to El Alamein. Churchill wrote: 'This was one of the heaviest blows I can recall during the war. Not only were its military effects grievous, but it had affected the reputation of the British armies.'[63]

Owen refers to the comments by Churchill in the House of Commons referring to the signal role played by air power in saving British forces during the retreat from Tobruk. After the dust had settled and more reasoned judgement was allowed to prevail, Churchill was able to see the beneficial role of the RAF.[64]

Brereton notes how German 'water rations are down to half a litre a day – it was hard to see how anyone could survive on that' and on 5 July 1942, Brereton refers to rumours that the British were to abandon Cairo. There was panic buying and rumours that Rommel had already booked a suite in Shepheard's Hotel.[65]

After this victory, Mussolini and Hitler believed that they had an opportunity to seize Egypt from the British and close the Suez Canal to Britain. This would have disrupted trade and supply links between Britain and her Empire and greatly weaken its war efforts. Rommel embarked on the all-out invasion of Egypt. He commanded a joint Italian and German spearhead of tanks. The Eighth Army was forced to retreat into north-western Egypt. Here they waited for what they saw as the inevitable attack from Rommel's *Afrika Korps*. Auchinleck dismissed Ritchie on 25 June and assumed command of the Eighth Army.

The *Afrika Korps* advanced into Egypt and made its way by the coastal route in the direction of Alexandria. If he could seize the city, Rommel would have been in a position to challenge the British and their control of the Suez Canal. Auchinleck adopted a defensive posture and waited for the Germans at El Alamein where the Eighth Army was dug in. The first battle took place only 60 km from Alexandria. Rommel launched a direct attack on the British positions. He had superiority in armour and tried to use his panzers to break through the Allied lines. However, Auchinleck had superiority in artillery and his forces had been well dug in, allowing British lines to hold. The Allies denied Rommel victory and critically, stopped his advance to Alexandria.

In August, Auchinleck was replaced as Eighth Army Commander by Gott and as C-in-C Middle East Command by Alexander. Gott was killed when his aircraft was shot down and Montgomery was appointed as his replacement. One feels that Auchinleck fell victim to Churchill's impatience over the lack of a decisive victory in the desert, as Auchinleck by most accounts, was an honourable and creditable general in the Desert Campaign who, if lacking in charisma, had the strong support of his men.

Elmhirst gives an account of a top-level dinner with the Prime Minister, Montgomery, Alanbrooke, Alexander, Coningham and Beamish. Apparently, the brandy was not passed round as Montgomery was not a drinker – it stayed in front of the PM all evening. Churchill said that he had never been in favour, as some were, of hanging the Kaiser. He advised the electric chair for Nazi war criminals.[66]. Churchill's comment suggests some measure of optimism over the outcome of the war even at such a low point, if he was already musing on punishments for the vanquished.

On 1 October 1942, Brereton notes in his diary the need to tighten up security of information at HQ in the desert. German spies were everywhere in the desert. With the Eighth Army offensive at El Alamein pending, it was especially important that any leaks in security or intelligence were firmly plugged.[67]

El Alamein – October 1942

On the eve of the Second Battle of El Alamein on 23 October 1942, the Axis had 76 Italian and 122 German planes available, the British/Allies had 1,585, a ratio in favour of the Allies of five to one. At El Alamein, the Axis could rely only on a fighter or diving bomber force; the RAF instead had a large bombing force available that launched hundreds of raids beyond the Axis lines. The auguries looked good for the British and Allies on the eve of the battle.

The Second Battle of El Alamein was the most important and the most renowned battle of the North African conflict. It was a huge engagement of men and materiel not seen in the desert before. It was a turning point in the war and the first time that the Allies had decisively defeated the Germans on the battlefield. The Germans and Italian were doomed because they lacked a sufficient number of troops, relied on inadequate supplies, and had unrealistic objectives.[68] Rommel directed the planning for the battle. He personally supervised the defensive line that was intended to repel the British counter-attack. He fell ill during the middle of the battle and was away for critical parts of it. He was able to return, however, for the latter stages – but by then, the die was cast.[69]

Close observers of the Battle of El Alamein tend to agree that the outcome of the battle and of the Desert Campaign *in toto* hinged to a large degree on the use of the B-25 bomber and of the Sherman tank, both of which were provided by the US. They were harbingers of close, successful Allied co-operation under Operation *Torch* and for the remainder of the war.[70]

The German strategy was to have a set piece battle, one that would draw the British and their Allies into a war of attrition that would sap their will to fight. Then Rommel with his panzers would launch a counter-attack after which he would go on and seize Alexandria. Such an outcome would have spelled disaster for the Allies.

Montgomery's objective was simple, to break the German defensive line. Once this was broken, the Germans would be forced to evacuate Egypt. Montgomery placed great faith in his numerical superiority in tanks and men. His army also had the support of the Royal Air Force that was increasingly able to dominate the skies and to nullify the threat posed by the *Luftwaffe*. After six weeks of carefully building up the Eighth Army, it was ready to go on the attack in late October. The Allies had some 200,000 men and 1,000 tanks under Montgomery. They faced some 115,000 Germans and Italians with approximately 550 tanks. Montgomery began the attack with a massive artillery barrage against the entire German line. Then he ordered his divisions to attack to the north of the German line and to the south. At this stage, Rommel had returned to Germany for treatment of a lingering illness. His subordinates had followed his plans for the battle very closely while he was away.[71] While Rommel had gained a reputation as a master tactician in the first part of the Desert War, he was at a huge numerical disadvantage at El Alamein which was to overwhelm his own tactical strengths. Montgomery also showed sharp tactical skills in his decision to employ deception in giving the Germans to understand that an attack was to come from the south. Thus, the first thunderous attack at night at El Alamein came as a surprise.

The fighting lasted for ten days. The British advances were slowed down by minefields, where many casualties were sustained and many tanks lost their tracks as they advanced. The battle depressingly began to resemble a First World War battle. The German commander, General Stumme, went forward to inspect the line but died of a heart attack. He was replaced by his subordinate Major General Wilhelm Ritter von Thoma who managed to steady the line and ordered the panzers into battle. The Germans suffered many losses, but Thoma continued to order further counter-attacks.[72]

Having recovered around the middle of the battle, Rommel returned to North Africa. He stiffened the German and Italian resistance, but the Axis Divisions had sustained huge losses and the defensive line began to crumble. Montgomery ordered his forces to attack on a broader front and during this assault, Von Thoma was killed. Rommel asked Hitler for permission to retreat. Initially Hitler refused, but he later gave his consent. This withdrawal probably saved the Germans and Italians from complete annihilation.

The result of the two Battles of El Alamein was a decisive victory for the Allies. Rommel's Axis forces suffered catastrophic losses and the *Afrika Korps* was never again to pose a threat to the Allies in Egypt. As Churchill said: 'Before El Alamein there were no victories, after it there were no defeats.'

The Axis forces never had enough supplies because of the Allies' ability to restrict Axis shipping. Rommel had insecure supply lines, although he could source his fuel from Libyan oil fields. The Axis Army in Egypt also had overextended supply lines, preventing the arrival of reinforcements to replace losses in men and material at the First Battle of El Alamein. Crucially, the Axis ran short of key supplies of shells and petrol. By contrast, Montgomery was well-supplied, particularly with the Sherman tank and B-25 bomber.[73]

Historians and the public have long acclaimed the Eighth Army as the victors at El Alamein. However, the RAF also played a key role in the battle. After the First Battle of El Alamein, the British moved new squadrons to the battlefield, keeping up the pressure on the Germans from the skies. During the Second Battle, they had been able to achieve total air superiority. The RAF helped to destroy many of Rommel's tanks. Without this, the panzers could have turned the tide of the battle. Montgomery paid tribute to the RAF and especially lauded the close air support that they provided. This was in contrast to the *Luftwaffe* and the Italian Air Force, which did not offer the Axis ground units any support. The RAF helped to tilt the balance in the Allies' favour.[74] Brereton notes in his diary on 6 November 1942 that the 'backbone of the Axis had been broken at El Alamein' and that the USAF played a strong role.[75] The Battle of El Alamein convinced the British that they could beat the Germans and that Hitler was not invincible. *Ultra* also contributed to Montgomery's success, by providing him with a complete picture of Axis forces, and with Rommel's own action reports to Germany.

In the immediate aftermath of El Alamein, Elmhirst had an argument with George, who, according to Elmhirst, 'is never optimistic and didn't think it was yet time to use such a term as "victory"'.[76] This would tend to fit with other accounts of George's temperament, which was not always easy to deal with.

Tedder refers to the fact that in the three months from August to November 1942, over 200,00 tons of Axis shipping had been sunk and under such conditions, Rommel could not survive.[77] He goes on to quote General von Thoma saying that 'constant bombing by the RAF and raids on airfields did great damage'.[78] British air superiority was complete.

A huge victory such as the Second Battle of El Alamein was inevitably going to lead to a generous awarding of medals, although not all were happy with how it was done. Air Marshal Coningham, despite his critical role in the battle and in the Desert War as a whole, felt aggrieved at not being awarded a knighthood to coincide with that awarded to Montgomery following the battle – he received his several months after Montgomery, a fact that rankled. Elmhirst and Beamish were aware of Coningham's early disappointment over the matter, even though Coningham never talked about it.[79]

Famously, on receiving news of victory at the Second Battle of El Alamein, Churchill declared that church bells, which had been silent since the beginning of the war, could at last ring out in victory. As Churchill famously said some time afterwards: 'Before El Alamein there were no victories and after it, no defeats.'[79a] This was just the tonic the British public needed. Britain and her Allies were to build on the victory gradually over the subsequent months and years.

A wider analysis of the battle since the Second World War has fortunately led to an appreciation of its complex nature, in particular, the vital role of the RAF. Every autumn, a multinational team organises a commemorative event outside El Alamein. In a spirit of inclusivity, it now also includes the Germans. The 2018 event was, in fact, organised by the Germans, happy to play a part in these annual events. The commemoration the previous year in 2017 marked the seventieth anniversary of the battle; according to those who attended the commemoration, it was a memorable event.[80]

Key Role of B-25 Bombers (Mitchell Bombers)
The first B-25s arrived in Egypt and were carrying out independent operations by October 1942. This was fortuitously timed for the beginning of the Second Battle of El Alamein when there were operations against Axis airfields and motorised vehicle columns supported the ground actions. Thereafter, the aircraft took part in the rest of the campaign in North Africa, the invasion of Sicily and the advance up through Italy.

The RAF received nearly 900 Mitchells, using them to replace Douglas Bostons, Lockheed Venturas and Vickers Wellington bombers. By the end of 1942, the RAF had taken delivery of a total of ninety Mitchell marks I and II. Some served with squadrons of No. 2 Group RAF, the RAF's tactical medium bomber force. The B-25s proved to be a vital ingredient in the final victory in the Desert War in their success in achieving the vital air supremacy which ultimately strangled the effectiveness of the *Afrika Korps*.[81]

US Army Field Manual: Map Reading and Land Navigation[82]

The US Army Field Manual points out that tactical mobility and speed are key to successful desert operations. Most deserts permit two-dimensional movement by ground forces similar to that of a naval task force at sea. Speed of execution is essential. Everyone moves farther and faster on the desert. The sand, hard-baked ground, rocky surfaces, thorny vegetation, and heat generally found in the desert impose far greater demands for maintenance than in temperate regions. It may also take longer to perform that maintenance.

Both sides and their respective services would have been conscious of these facts. The challenges would have been more evident for ground forces than the air forces, but vast dust storms could affect pilot visibility. Rommel had formerly been the master of 'speed of execution', gaining a legendary status in the process. By El Alamein, the Allies had evened out the account.

Allied Pursuit of Rommel

El Alamein exacted a heavy toll on Rommel's army. The pursuit of his army's remnants continued westwards in North Africa. A stream of lorries carrying petrol, ammunition and supplies was racing after the advancing tanks of the Eighth Army as they continued down the coast road out of Egypt. Finally, the Axis forces had been ejected from Egypt.

Bombers attacked Benghazi and Tobruk and 20,000 enemy troops were captured. The capture of Benghazi was a significant position along the line. And the capture of a port meant the resupply problem was significantly eased. Now the pursuit would be through Libya to meet up with the Americans in Tunisia.[83]

After the fall of Benghazi as the Eighth Army pursued Rommel across the Desert, Elmhirst noted in his diary on 5 December 1942 that 'Mary' Coningham suggested Elmhirst take George Beamish and two other air officers, Pug and Brereton, around Benghazi to 'see the sights'. He lent them his open-top car. Elmhirst noted how he encountered 'total destruction everywhere'. Clearly, what Coningham had in mind was not the 'fleshpots' of Benghazi but the devastation caused by Allied bombing.[84]

The Key Strategic Role of Malta[85]

Discussion of the North African war would be incomplete without mention of the role of Malta. Throughout the war, military forces on Malta remained capable of disrupting Axis supply lines to North Africa. It was crucial, therefore, for the Axis to neutralise Malta.

On 1 June 1941, Air Vice Marshal Lloyd was appointed Air Officer Commanding in Malta, with the difficult task of protecting the island from German and Italian air attacks as well as attacking Axis shipping delivering supplies to Rommel's *Afrika Korps* in North Africa. He was assigned to RAF headquarters in the Middle East as Senior Air Staff Officer in 1942 and commanded the Northwest African Coastal Air Force and then the Mediterranean Allied Coastal Air Force in 1943. His role there was to carry out harrying of enemy transport by land and sea.

Early on in the war, the island had attracted the attention of the Italian Air Force. Malta had only twenty-four Hurricanes when the *Luftwaffe* took over from the Italians in efforts to neutralise Malta. It was critical for the island to receive Spitfires, more manoeuvrable than the Hurricane and superior to the Me 109.

Operation *Pedestal* was the British operation to carry supplies to the island of Malta in August 1942. From 1940 to 1942, the Axis had conducted the Siege of Malta with air and naval forces in attempts to starve out the island. Despite many losses, enough supplies were delivered for Malta to resist, although it had ceased to be an offensive base for much of 1942. As part of Operation

Pedestal, 126 Spitfires were eventually delivered through Gibraltar and on aircraft carriers. Coningham, Elmhirst and George Beamish were at the centre of this exercise and conscious of its overall importance in the conflict. These Spitfires were successful in downing many Axis planes.

In March and April, the *Luftwaffe* engaged in ferocious night and day bombing of the island, causing much death and destruction. As many as 7,000 people were killed in defence of Malta. Rommel, in his reports to Hitler, claimed he was never in any doubt that North Africa could only be held for any length of time if the Axis possessed Malta.[86] For Kesselring, in order to guarantee supplies, the capture of Malta was essential, and now it was no longer possible in June 1942.[87]

The Siege of Malta was eventually broken by the Allied re-conquest of Egypt and Libya after El Alamein and by Operation *Torch*, which enabled land-based aircraft to escort merchant ships to the island. In August 1942, with Malta still besieged, 35 per cent of Axis convoy shipping to North Africa was lost. In September, with Malta supplied, Allied forces sank 100,000 tons of Axis shipping, contributing to Axis paralysis during the Second Battle of El Alamein and Operation *Torch*. Operation *Pedestal* was a strategic victory, raising the morale of the people and garrison of Malta, averting famine and inevitable surrender.[88]

Air Superiority[89]

In a document produced by the Australian Air Force (*The Air Campaign: Planning for Combat* by Col John A. Warden III, National Defence University Press Publication, 1988) the doctrine of air superiority is well set out (while debatable). It echoes, many decades after the event, the kind of outlook and strategy that Tedder and Coningham set out for the Western Desert Air Force in the Second World War.

Air superiority is a necessity. Since the German attack on Poland in 1939, no country has won a war in the face of enemy air superiority, no major offensive has succeeded against an opponent who controlled the air, and no defence has sustained itself against an enemy who had air superiority. Conversely, no state has lost a war while it maintained air superiority, and attainment of air superiority consistently has been a prelude to military victory... To be superior in the air, to have air superiority, means having sufficient control of the air to make air attacks on the enemy without serious opposition and, on the other hand, to be free from the danger of serious enemy air incursions.

Germany destroyed Poland's air force in the first days of the campaign. From then on, the Germans were able to use their air forces to interdict, to attack ground troops, and to soften positions for subsequent movement on the ground. Nine months later, Germany did the same thing in France, when the *Luftwaffe* won air superiority in two days.

The Allies frequently had numerical superiority in the Western Desert but never before had it been as complete as at El Alamein. With the arrival of Sherman tanks, Mitchells, 6-pounder anti-tank guns and Spitfires, the Allies gained a comprehensive superiority. Montgomery perceived the battle as an attrition operation, similar to those fought in the First World War and correctly predicted the length of the battle and the number of Allied casualties. Allied artillery was superbly handled and Allied air support was excellent, in contrast to the *Luftwaffe* and the Italian air force, *Regia Aeronautica*, which offered little or no support to ground forces, preferring to engage in air-to-air combat.

Air supremacy had a huge effect on the battle and not only because of its physical impact. As Montgomery later wrote,

The moral effect of air action [on the enemy] is very great and out of all proportion to the material damage inflicted. In the reverse direction, the sight and sound of our own air forces operating against the enemy have an equally satisfactory effect on our own troops. A combination of the two has a profound influence on the most important single factor in war—morale.

—Montgomery[90]

Blair Mayne

An account of the life and times of George Beamish would be incomplete without some reference to Blair 'Paddy' Mayne. Like George, he was from Northern Ireland and was a noted combatant in the Second World War, also fighting in the Desert Campaign, but, in his case, with the Army and the Special Services. He was one of the original group of men in the Special Air Services (SAS) founded during the war by Colonel David Stirling. By the war's end, Paddy had reached the rank of Lieutenant Colonel with a string of military exploits to his name. He was also a noted rugby international with six caps for Ireland between 1936 and 1938. He represented the Lions on tour in South Africa in 1938 where he was to cement his reputation as a tearaway with a number of wild exploits, but also with some solid performances on the pitch. Also like George, he was a good all-round sportsman, showing talent in cricket, golf, boxing and marksmanship from an early age. Like George, he was essentially a solitary figure. There, the comparison ends. While George was taciturn, reliable and predictable, a 'play by the rules' man, by comparison Mayne was easily bored and a noted 'hell-raiser' who might have had some lessons in the art for many subsequent rock stars. He never saw a rule he did not want to break, his exploits extending from his rugby to his military career.

While with the Lions in South Africa, he was said to have destroyed a Pietermaritzburg hotel room, reducing its furniture to kindling. Although basically a 'loner', Mayne had the company on that tour of fellow Ulstermen: Sammy Walker (who captained the tour), Harry McKibbin and George Cromey. Mayne was also a senior Freemason which, *prima facie,* seems somewhat at odds with his personality and character in an organisation that prided itself on propriety and secrecy.

One can only imagine how George, noted for not suffering fools gladly, would have reacted had he been Mayne's commanding officer or rugby captain. Such a stickler for the rules was certain to take a tough line with poor behaviour, but the realist in Beamish would also recognised and seen the value in Mayne's exceptional talents.

Mayne was born in 1915 in Newtownards, Co. Down. He was a graduate of Queen's University, where he first established his rugby career. His subsequent club rugby was mainly played for the Malone Club in Belfast. During the Second World War, he was one of the most decorated officers with a Distinguished Service Order (DSO) with three Bars – one of only seven from the war to have received the honour. He was also awarded the Legion d'Honneur and the Croix de Guerre by the French. To his men, he had reached 'god-like' status for his talents and actions. His courage, particularly in the Desert War in direct combat with Italian and German forces, is legendary. However, controversy surrounded him not being awarded the Victoria Cross. He was undoubtedly a prime candidate, but the feeling emerged that he had ruffled just a few too many feathers in his colourful career. It has also been suggested that because an award of a VC requires validation by very senior officers, Mayne's more secretive and independent actions with the SAS were thus harder to validate to the required level. In 2005, fifty years after the Second World War ended, a number of MPs posted an Early Day Motion in the House of Commons calling on the Government to reconsider a posthumous award of the Victoria Cross to Mayne, and others – to date without success.

After the war, he entered the world of bourgeois respectability, working as a solicitor in a respected Belfast legal firm. Such were his credentials that he was eventually appointed Secretary of the Northern Ireland Law Society. He died in a car crash in 1955 at the premature age of forty. He is buried in Newtownards where a plaque and statue in his memory now stands.

In the professional rugby era, players like Blair Mayne simply do not exist anymore. Among Irish players, you have to go back to the likes of Willie Duggan and Moss Keane of the 1980s and even they were tame compared with Mayne, who was the true amateur Corinthian, playing the game for the fun of it with no material reward – a 'character' who was a classic for his time but a symbol of a long-gone era.

George Leaves the Desert

In November 1942 after a hectic period in the desert, George Beamish was replaced initially by Edmund Hudleston and then by Victor Groom as SASO to Coningham at Second Tactical Air Force. Huddleston was an Australian who served in the Middle East Command in a variety of staff roles, so was well equipped to take on the 2TAF role. He was later to become Commander of Allied Forces in Central Europe and Vice Chief of the Air Staff. In terms of RAF internal politics, the Groom appointment was an interesting one as he was a protégé of Trafford Leigh-Mallory, who was on poor terms with both Tedder and Coningham. Groom was confirmed as Group Captain at his appointment, and in June 1943 he was made Air Commodore, participating in the Tunisia and Sicily campaigns. He followed this appointment with a promotion to 2TAF HQ at the rank of Air Vice Marshal. At the conclusion of his time in the desert, Groom returned to Cairo, but was to return to the Desert Theatre during the latter part of the Tunisian Campaign in 1943.[91]

George, himself quite tired from the demanding regime, earned a long-needed period of leave at home, which he would take after visiting Middle East HQ in Cairo. This tiredness was noticed by his colleague Tommy Elmhirst in the final weeks of his desert appointment. As noted earlier, Kuter had remarked on how George could survive on very little sleep and mugs of tea.

George was not away for long, as he would be back soon in North Africa helping in the planning for the Allied invasion of Sicily. It was in November/December 1942 that Elmhirst was called away from the Desert Air team under Coningham, an example of a team that worked harmoniously and effectively. Given the tight-knit group's influence on the Desert War, those involved in the overall Allied war effort had much to be grateful about.

On 29 November 1942, Elmhirst provides a touching description of George's impending departure from his Desert War role.

George Beamish left us for Cairo today and is on his way home, having handed over to his successor, Harry Broadhurst. We had hoped to leave together, but my successor is not to be here for a few days yet. George has been a great stalwart here at the HQ for a year. He is meticulous, cautious and sometimes obstinate and as such, has been the brake required on Mary's temperamental genius and brilliance. It has been a very good contribution. Latterly, George has been a very tired man and once or twice, he and I have had a difference of opinion, both of us have been overworked and irritable if crossed. However, we have had a mostly very successful partnership this last eight months and for two people with strong ideas of their own ... that says a lot as our tracks are always crossing ... George Beamish has been like a 'rock' in troublesome times and as tough as you can make them.

A full appreciation of the Desert Air War would be incomplete without reference to the main combatants on both sides. On the RAF or Allied side were the fighter aces William 'Cherry' Vale, Dudley Honor, Group Captain Clive Robertson Caldwell and Kenneth Cross. On the German side, Kesselring, as both a *Wehrmacht* and a *Luftwaffe* man, was at the head of command. Senior *Luftwaffe* figures included Meindl and Neumann. Their best fighter aces included Marseille, Schroer, Stahlschmidt and Steinhausen, all prolific fighter pilots with a huge number of kills behind them. More detailed information on these figures is included at Appendices 5 and 8.

As Churchill said, El Alamein was the 'end of the beginning'. Spirits had clearly been buoyed among the Desert Forces by the success in preventing German access to Alexandria and Cairo, but much more fighting remained ahead farther west.

8

CASABLANCA AND OPERATION *TORCH* (1943)

Having routed Rommel from Egypt, the Eighth Army and Desert Air Force moved westwards through the desert in pursuit of the 'Desert Fox'. With the landing of US forces in the western part of North Africa, it was surely just a matter of time before the Axis forces were encircled and destroyed.

From 1943 onwards, following major reorganisations agreed at the Casablanca Conference, Tedder was to take overall command of the RAF in the Middle East and North Africa. These matters had been decided at the highest level, that of Roosevelt and Churchill, indicating the key strategic importance of events in the Middle East and North Africa for the future of the Second World War. It also proved to be a very visible example of Anglo-American co-operation, inspiring further examples for the rest of the war. The Casablanca Conference in January 1943 is probably best known for securing adherence by the Allies to the concept of imposing 'unconditional surrender' on the Axis. In relation to Europe, Churchill's plan to invade Sicily and then Italy after the North African campaign was accepted. There was still some fighting to do in North Africa; Tunis was not to fall until the middle of 1943. That said, most could begin to see the writing on the wall.[1]

Operation *Torch*, the Allied campaign in North Africa from late 1942, was the price the Americans paid for inter-Allied harmony and a deferred invasion in Northern Europe. It was clear that *Torch* was not the preferred option for Eisenhower and his top generals. Yet it provided the first opportunity in the war for the Americans to engage with the *Wehrmacht* and to work closely on an operational level with the British, who had been familiar with the desert terrain for several years. It was also a theatre in which air power played a critical role.

After El Alamein, the main strategic target in North Africa for British forces was Tunisia, under Free French control but potentially an ally of the British and Americans under Operation *Torch*. It was the first time British and US troops were to fight together. This was the 'second front' promised by the Allies for some time, to divert German attention and forces away from the Russian front and thus relieve pressure on their Soviet allies. The objective was to capture and control Tunisia, Algeria and Morocco, and then to move on to the Reich's 'soft underbelly' through Sicily and Italy.[2]

Under Eisenhower, over 107,000 forces landed on North African shores in November 1942, just as Montgomery had sealed his victory at El Alamein. Together with British forces amounting to 180,000 in North Africa, Eisenhower had a formidable force under his command. *Ultra* again proved its worth by providing evidence to the Allies that the *Torch* landings in North Africa were not anticipated by the Axis. German overall command was under Kesselring and operationally under Rommel and von Armin, both of whom disliked one another intensely. The former was daring and impulsive while the latter was cautious and conservative, with leadership styles to match. It was a campaign in which a rejuvenated Me 109 and the new Tiger Tank, as well as the Sherman and Churchill tanks, were to play critical roles.

Critical in establishing an Allied beachhead in North Africa was to convince the Vichy French – who were still the colonial powers in Morocco, Algeria and Tunisia – to join in the battle against the Axis powers. This did not happen at first, despite the involvement on the Allied side of General Giraud. Indeed, the *Torch* invasion faced stiff resistance in all three countries after landing, until heavy military pressure led the French to sign an armistice.[3]

Tedder refers to US General Bradley's remarks that 'the *Luftwaffe* ranged the Tunisian front almost unmolested'. Eisenhower told the Chiefs of Staff that 'supplies reaching the Axis through Tunisian ports was a matter of grave concern'.[4] Those who had said that victory was at hand following the rout at El Alamein would have been better advised to have taken George Beamish's counsel in his earlier remarks to Elmhirst after the battle.

At the beginning of *Torch*, George Beamish was to transfer to the new organisational structure devised by Eisenhower to meet the needs of a new inter-Allied command structure. Northwest African Air Forces (NAAF) was formed in February 1943 as a component of the Allied Mediterranean Air Command (MAC). It was primarily responsible for air operations during the Tunisian Campaign and the bombing of Italy. Its objective was to open the Mediterranean sea lanes and help drive the Axis from Tunisia and Africa. Its commander was Lieutenant General Carl Spaatz of the United States Army Air Force. NAAF was created following a reorganisation of the command structure of Allied air forces in the Mediterranean Theatre. The other components of MAC were Middle East Command, AHQ Malta, RAF Gibraltar and 216 Group.

With the conclusion of the North African campaign, Spaatz became deputy commander of the Mediterranean Allied Air Forces reporting to Tedder. He faced many difficulties in his new assignment with the co-ordination of RAF and American Air Forces operations. The solution was to integrate the American and British air operations as quickly as possible. NAAF and the Mediterranean Allied Air Forces were created to solve the question of operational control of the air effort during the African and Mediterranean campaigns. They contributed much to the surrender of Axis forces in North Africa and the invasion of Italy.[5]

In January 1943, US Air Force General Kuter was transferred to North Africa to command the Allied tactical air forces. In February, the RAF Western Desert Air Force reached Tunisia and was merged with the Allied Support Command from North Africa. General Kuter became the American deputy commander in the newly consolidated Northwest African Tactical Air Force and Chief of Staff to Spaatz. During his time in North Africa, he had many encounters with Coningham and his staff, including George Beamish. Apparently, he was quite overwhelmed by George's physical presence, something George had experienced since his rugby days.[5a]

During the Tunisian Campaign, General Henry H. Arnold, Commanding General of Army Air Forces, directed that General Kuter be released from the Mediterranean Theatre and returned to Washington from the day Rommel surrendered. In May 1943, General Kuter returned to become assistant chief of air staff for plans and combat operations.

NAAF was organised on a successful tripartite (or 'tri-force') air interdiction model – consisting of specialised strategic, coastal, and tactical air forces – pioneered by Tedder and Coningham. It was operational between February and December 1943. Effective co-ordination of air and ground forces was a key feature of the tripartite model. The tripartite command structure was regarded as successful; it was therefore retained when NAAF was superseded in December 1943 by the Mediterranean Allied Air Forces. The Northwest African Air Forces had three major combined combat commands:

- Northwest African Strategic Air Force (NASAF) under Major General James H. Doolittle
- Northwest African Coastal Air Force (NACAF), initially under (acting commander) Group Captain G. G. Barrett and, soon afterwards, Air Vice Marshal Hugh Lloyd
- Northwest African Tactical Air Force (NATAF) under Acting Air Marshal Sir Arthur Coningham

To foster co-operation between the British RAF and the American USAAF in particular, the commands listed above and their various sub-commands were intended to have a commanding officer from one air force and a deputy from the other air force. Strong consideration was also given to the concept that air, naval, and ground forces should co-ordinate effectively to provide optimum support of ground troops.[6]

In 1942–43, when the role of air power was still being explored on the battlefield, classic close air support was essentially pioneered and developed by Tedder as Commander-in-Chief of Middle East Command and Coningham as Air Officer Commanding (AOC) of Air Headquarters Western Desert. The importance of flexible co-ordination between air, naval and ground forces took much time to realise let alone implement during the Desert War. It was Tedder who finally realised that every campaign must be planned and executed as a 'joint operation' by all three forces. In particular, the flexibility between Coningham's WDAF and the Eighth Army has been contrasted with the more rigid relationship between the *Luftwaffe* and German ground forces.[7] NAAF was the first official command based upon the 'tri-force' model. Successfully practised and developed during the Tunisian, Sicilian and Italian campaigns, the tripartite model was retained by subsequent Allied air forces for D-Day Normandy and D-Day Southern France. Even some of today's air forces consider the historical precedents of the 'tri-force' model.[8]

George was to return to North Africa under the new Allied structures occasioned by Operation *Torch*, attached to the Second Tactical Air Force under his former superior, Coningham. After the Western Desert campaign, however, he was to return initially to Cairo for a debrief and then, as mentioned previously, for a well-needed period of home leave.[8a]

Coningham could consider himself fortunate in that he worked within a smoothly run command structure headed by Tedder. This compared with his *Luftwaffe* counterpart, Froehlich, who never knew whether he should obey a command from Rommel or Kesselring. This situation also highlighted the functional merits of an independent air force like the RAF.[9] On the ground in the desert, overall German strategy was very much dictated by Rommel with the occasional intervention by Hitler.

The use of RAF air power as a substitute for the army and navy in control operations in British colonies brought about some innovations in command and control measures needed to operate aircraft against ground targets. Operations outside Britain were also a training ground for some of the future leaders of the RAF, especially those who were to go on and gain fame in the realm of tactical air power. Among these were Tedder, Slessor, Coningham and Broadhurst – each of these officers had at some point in the inter-war period served in the colonies where conditions closely replicated those experienced during the Desert War.

Second Tactical Air Force (2TAF)

The RAF Second Tactical Air Force was one of three tactical air forces within the RAF during and after the Second World War. It was composed of squadrons and personnel from the RAF, the air forces of the British Commonwealth and exiles from German-occupied Europe. It was formed on 1 June 1943 in connection with preparations for the Allied invasion of Europe a year later. It took units from both Fighter Command and Bomber Command.[10] Second TAF's first commander was Air Marshal Sir John d'Albiac, who was succeeded by the man most associated with 2TAF, Sir Arthur Coningham. Coningham had great experience of operations supporting fast-moving ground warfare from his command of the Desert Air Force in North Africa and Italy. Fresh from the crucible of the Desert War, he brought a sharpness and dynamism that was to be vital as the war began to play itself out towards endgame. The war was moving in a more collaborative direction, however, particularly with the advent of Operation *Torch*. This meant, inter alia, greater accommodation to US concerns and interests and to the infusion of more US personnel, particularly at the higher reaches of the chain of command.[11] For George, having a head of a mission with whom he previously had worked closely and whom he admired greatly, was a godsend. Montgomery was still a potent factor, however, so inter-service diplomacy remained a requisite skill for George and his associates.[12]

Support was growing for a composite group of all types of aircraft under one air commander who could see the air situation as a whole and co-ordinate support and reconnaissance operations with fighter operations to maintain the situation. On 10 December 1943, Mediterranean Air Command was disbanded and the Allied air forces were again reorganised as the Mediterranean Allied Air Forces (MAAF) with Air Chief Marshal Sir Arthur Tedder as Air Commander-in-Chief.[13]

A senior US Air Force general, John Cannon, who participated in Operation *Torch* and later in Operation *Husky* was not only a colleague but also became a good friend of Coningham's. During *Torch*, Cannon was the commanding general of the XII Air Support Command during the invasion of French Morocco. He moved to Algeria as Commanding General of the XII Bomber Command. He later organised and commanded the Training Command of the Northwest African Air Forces. In May 1943, Cannon became deputy commanding general of the Northwest African Tactical Air Force under Coningham for the Sicilian campaign and the invasion of Italy. In March 1945, he was named air Commander-in-Chief of all Allied Air Forces in the Mediterranean and in May, he became Commanding General of US Air Forces in Europe. Both he and Coningham worked well together across national lines, a welcome contrast for Coningham to his relations with an increasingly difficult Montgomery. Cannon earned four Distinguished Service Medals, Legion of Merit, Bronze Star, Air Medal and decorations from Great Britain, France, Italy, Poland, Yugoslavia and Morocco. He was an excellent example of commitment and co-operation among the Allies.[14]

Another influential participant in the North African air war was General Auby Strickland, a US Air Force general transferred to the North African theatre of operations in July 1942, as commander of the IX Fighter Command. On 22 October 1942, he became chief of staff of the newly organised Desert Air Task Force and later assumed command of that force. He became military governor of Pantelleria, near Sicily, in June 1943, and the following October was named deputy air staff officer of the US component of the Allied Expeditionary Air Forces in England. He was awarded the Distinguished Service Medal for service as chief of staff and later commanding general of the Desert Air Task Force, Ninth USAir Force, from the time of the Battle of El Alamein to the expulsion of the Axis forces from Africa. He received the Legion of Merit for services from 17 June to 26 August 1943, as military governor of the Island of Pantelleria.[15]

In a letter to Tedder about *Benforce* (the attack on Benghazi), George Beamish is mentioned as being in command of four squadrons. This was his first command post in some time after a long stint in staff positions.[16] Tedder notes his happiness with the idea of a joint Army/RAF HQ with Alexander and Coningham. It had changed the whole atmosphere and outlook of British and American air and land forces.[17]

Throughout the North African Campaign, the medium bomber and fighter squadrons of Western Desert Air Force were primarily assigned to either No. 211 Group or No. 212 Fighter Group. No. 211 Group was formed on 10 December 1941 out of Nucleus Group Western Desert. On 11 April 1943, the group reformed as No. 211 Group under the command of Air Commodore Richard Atcherley. No. 211 Group was the principal fighter force of the Desert Air Force commanded by Harry Broadhurst. Desert Air Force (DAF) was a sub-command of Coningham's Northwest African Tactical Air Force. The Group included many units from the South African Air Force, the Royal Australian Air Force and the United States Army Air Forces , with one each from the Hellenic Air Force and Royal Canadian Air Force. Many personnel from other British Commonwealth air forces also served. The fact that the Group worked so effectively is down to strong inter-Allied co-operation.[18]

Operation *Flax* in April 1943 during the Tunisian Campaign was designed to cut the air supply lines between Italy and the Axis armies in Tunisia. Allied commanders of the operation were Tedder, Spaatz, Doolittle and Coningham. George Beamish was also involved in *Flax* from a planning and administrative perspective. *Flax* called for Allied fighters to intercept the aerial convoys over the Sicily–Tunisia strait. Allied units were also briefed to carry out major offensive operations against Axis airfields in Tunisia and the overcrowded staging fields in Sicily. The tactical plan included co-ordinated strikes on Axis airfields, and B-25s and Lockheed P-38 would fly sweeps over the Gulf of Tunis. The RAF and Royal Navy operating from Malta under this Operation took a heavy toll on Axis shipping but Axis supplies were still reaching the besieged *Afrika Korps* by air. By early April, much Axis manpower was also being evacuated by air. Although the Allies held air superiority by this time, *Luftwaffe* transports were operating with impunity during darkness. To prevent this, the Allied Air Forces were ordered to conduct operations against Axis air power by day and night to prevent their resupply or withdrawal. Owing to bad weather and the need to gather intelligence, *Flax* did not begin until 5 April. Although the Axis put up determined resistance and large-scale air battles took place, Allied Air Forces succeeded in destroying the aerial link between Axis-held Sicily and Italy. During the interdiction operation, an air battle known as the 'Palm Sunday Massacre' took place, in which German air transport fleets suffered heavy losses while evacuating forces escaping from the Allied ground offensive. The air operation continued until 27 April and did great harm to Axis logistical support. Operation *Flax* inflicted such heavy losses on the German transport fleets that they were unable to recover. [https://en.wikipedia.org/wiki/Operation_Flax]

Flax had a considerable effect in restricting Axis supplies and logistics. Axis armies and air units in Tunisia gradually ran out of fuel, ammunition and other supplies. Allied air superiority was so overwhelming that *Luftwaffe* personnel climbed into fighter fuselages, or squeezed into the cockpits of Bf 109s alongside the pilot rather than risk flying in transport aircraft.[19]

After the success of *Flax*, Tedder received a message from Churchill commending Spaatz, Coningham, Doolittle and Broadhurst over the victories in Tunisia.[20] Tedder refers to how the Desert Air Force was a good 'team'. Coningham was 'full of initiative, originality and courage. And thoughtful for his men'. Tommy Elmhirst 'made his mark as an ASO and right-hand man to Coningham'. George Beamish was 'imperturbable during exciting moments in the Desert as he was in Greece and Crete.'[21]

Allied forces destroyed 432 Axis transport aircraft during *Flax*. The Germans lost hundreds of crewmen and thousands of tons of cargo. The careful planning of USAF General Doolittle and the close co-operation of the Allied Air Forces created a notable victory. In March 1943, Operation *Pugilist* was launched to destroy the enemy facing the Eighth Army at the Mareth Line and to go on and capture Sfax. *Pugilist* did not succeed but it did lay the ground for the later Operation *Supercharge*.[22]

Three days after the conclusion of *Flax*, *Ultra* code breakers deciphered an order from Goering that all German transport flights to Tunisia were to fly at night. This order by the German command proved too little, too late.

The Battle of El Agheila was a brief engagement in December 1942 between the Eighth Army and Rommel, during the Axis withdrawal from El Alamein to Tunis. It ended with the German-Italian *Panzer* Army resuming its retreat towards Tunisia.

On 4 November 1942, during the Battle of El Alamein, Rommel decided to withdraw west towards Libya. In doing so, he defied the 'Stand to the last' orders of Adolf Hitler, to save the remainder of his force.

Despite the importance of Benghazi to the Axis supply chain, Rommel abandoned the port to avoid a repeat of the entrapment, ordering the demolition of port facilities and materiel in Benghazi. Benghazi was occupied by the British on 20 November. The Axis forces faced many difficulties, including British air superiority. The Desert Air Force attacked Axis columns crowded on the coast road and short of fuel. To delay the British advance at any cost, Axis sappers laid mines in the Mersa Brega area; steel helmets were buried to mislead British mine detectors.[23]

Rommel described disagreements with his political and military superiors and he engaged in bitter arguments with Hitler, Goering and Kesselring. Rommel wanted to withdraw to Tunis as soon as possible and the others wanted him to make a stand on the El Agheila–Mersa Brega line. Mussolini ordered Rommel to stand on the Agheila line to defend Tripolitania, supported by Hitler, who ordered that El Agheila should be held 'in all circumstances'. Rommel's assessment was that he would be able to hold the position only if he received artillery and tank replacements, if the *Luftwaffe* was strengthened and his fuel and ammunition supplies were restored. By this time, all available men and equipment were being diverted to Tunis, following the Allied landings of Operation *Torch,* to prevent Tunisia falling to an Allied advance from Algeria.

Rommel's supply position had not improved: Tunisia was still given priority for supplies but of the ships which were sent to Tripoli to supply the *Panzer* Army in November, three-quarters had been destroyed. Rommel was short of men and equipment and very short of fuel and ammunition. His stated intention, therefore, was to hold out as long as possible but to retire in the face of strong pressure.[24] I. S. O. Playfair, the British official historian, believed an estimated 450 Axis prisoners were killed with 40 casualties on the New Zealand side.[25]

All was not plain sailing in Tunisia, as the *Wehrmacht* showed considerable resilience even after the defeat at El Alamein. The Allied defeat at the Kasserine Pass, was one of the worst Allied defeats of the war. The Allies did re-take the pass some time later, having learned the lessons of better ground to air co-operation. With Montgomery's Eighth Army arriving from the east and the US First Army from the west, the *Afrika Korps* was encircled and eventually surrendered

Fall of Tunis and Victory in North Africa

Operation *Torch* precipitated a crisis in Kesselring's command. He ordered Walther Nehring, the former commander of the *Afrika Korps* to proceed to Tunisia to take command of a new corps. Kesselring ordered Nehring to establish a bridgehead in Tunisia and then to press west as far as possible. By December, the Allied commander, Eisenhower, was forced to concede that Kesselring had won the race; the final phase of *Torch* had failed and the Axis could only be ejected from Tunisia after a prolonged struggle.

At the Battle of the Kasserine Pass, Kesselring's forces gave the Allies a beating, but in the end, strong Allied resistance and a string of Axis errors stopped the advance. Kesselring's efforts to shore up his forces by moving supplies from Sicily were frustrated by Allied aircraft and submarines. An Allied offensive in April finally broke through, leading to a collapse of the Axis position in Tunisia. Some 275,000 German and Italian prisoners were taken. In return, Kesselring had, however, held up the Allies in Tunisia for six months, forcing a postponement of the Allied invasion of Northern France from the middle of 1943 to the middle of 1944.[26]

After the fall of Tunis and the defeat of the *Afrika Corps* in the desert, Coningham, Broadhurst and Beamish arrived in Tunis in the spring of 1943 like three victorious Roman generals looking for suitable billeting. The historical connection between Tunis and ancient Carthage would not have been lost on them. While the two senior men 'took rooms' in the splendour of the ancient royal palace, it is said that George took himself off to the nearby beach, found a beach hut, laid down his kit, opened a camp bed and stayed there during the next fortnight.[27] This was a story so in keeping with the humble, unpretentious side of George. Not for him the pomp and circumstance of military victory. Strong tea, pipe tobacco and rudimentary billets would do nicely, thank you.

In similar vein, Elmhirst indicated in a memo of 17 July 1943 that 'the top team' of Coningham, Elmhirst and Beamish showed they could relax and 'let it all hang out' after the Tunisian campaign. According to Elmhirst's diaries, they 'spent three hours on the beach unclothed while "Mary" told the story from his end and we were told what had been happening.' 'Teamwork' under Eisenhower was also praised.[28] After Elmhirst's departure, Broadhurst was now part of the senior command structure of the RAF under *Torch* and worked closely with Coningham and George Beamish – he reported directly to Coningham. He was to reach great heights in the RAF during and after the war.

Allied casualties in the Desert Campaign were estimated at 76,020 and those for the Axis in the range of 260,000 to 320,000. Many things stand out about that great victory in North Africa. The unshakeable confidence of Montgomery, the apparent infallibility followed by the fallibility of Rommel and his *Afrika Korps*, the role of air power and the plucky resistance of the Eighth Army.[29] The kernel of the victory was the Second Battle of El Alamein. It stands out along with Stalingrad, Kursk and Midway as among the critical and decisive encounters of the Second World War. It was just the tonic for which the British had been waiting for a long time.

Then there was the role of the Spitfire. Although it is more often associated with the Battle of Britain, the Spitfire had a critical role to play in the Desert Campaign. It was vital in ensuring the Allies gained air superiority, thus ensuring ultimate victory in North Africa. The Hurricane was seen to be no match for the Me109 but when sufficient numbers of Spitfires arrived in the desert, it played its part in the 'end of the beginning'.[30]

Axis resistance ended, for all intents and purposes, on 13 May. General Hans-Jürgen von Arnim had been captured with 260,000 prisoners. Fifteen *Wehrmacht* divisions had been destroyed. A victory march was held in Tunis on 20 May 1943 in which units of the First and Eighth Armies and representative detachments of the American and French forces marched past, with bands playing and Generals Eisenhower, Alexander and Giraud taking the salute. Alexander was under orders from Churchill to meet a deadline of 15 May to end the North African campaign. Key factors in the Allies' favour were: their big numerical superiority,

1. Beamish family photograph 1920s, Co. Derry.

2. Model School, Dunmanway, Co. Cork, attended by George Beamish and his brothers. (Courtesy of Patrick Comerford)

3. Coleraine Academical Institute, where Beamish was taught.

4. After graduating from Coleraine Inst., Beamish attended RAF College Cranwell as a flight cadet.

5. George Beamish captaining RAF rugby side 1930s. Douglas Bader at bottom extreme right.

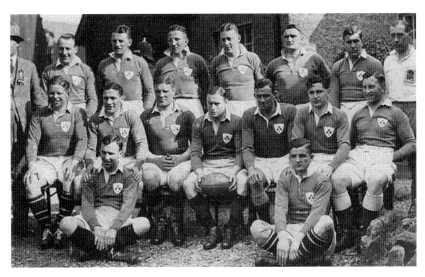

6. George Beamish in Irish rugby team versus Scotland 1933.

7. Beamish was heavily involved in the Battle of Crete. Pictured here are scores of crashed or downed Ju 52s on Maleme airfield early in the conflict.

8. After Crete, Beamish was appointed Senior Air Staff Officer in the Western Desert Air Force. Pictured is the scene at Benina aerodrome after an RAF attack.

9. Damage at Tripoli Harbour caused by the RAF.

10. George Beamish meeting General Dwight D. Eisenhower, 1944.

11. Beamish at Cranwell in 1949.

12. Castlerock.

Above: 13. McGilligan House.

Right: 14. Patrick McDevitt, close friend and golfing partner of George Beamish.

15. Beamish family graves, Castlerock.

16. St. Mary's Churchyard, Articlave, Co. Derry.

their air superiority and their access to *Ultra* intercepts which gave them advance knowledge of Rommel's intentions. The campaign lasted for almost six months and was concluded on 13 May when the famed Desert Rats of Seventh Armoured Division marched into Tunis.

On the fall of Tunis, General Alexander sent a short signal to Churchill as follows:

> Sir, it is my duty to report that the Tunisian Campaign is over. All enemy resistance has ceased. We are masters of the North African shores.[31]

Since the victory at El Alamein, these were the sweetest words to Churchill's ears. The assault on Nazi-occupied Europe could now proceed. The endgame was at last in sight for the Allies.

One of the many reasons for the British victory was undoubtedly air superiority. Since the beginning of the big El Alamein battle, the RAF could replace the losses and strengthen the squadrons already on the line. It was not only a mere numerical superiority: the quality of the RAF planes was superior to all Italian aircraft. The skills and ability of the RAF and Axis pilots were more or less equal, even if it must be said that the Axis' pilots flew and fought in an extremely exhausted mental and physical condition and were always outnumbered. In spite of the Italians fighting in inferior planes, they fought gallantly until their squadrons were decimated.

Citing British intelligence sources, Orange mentions that, 'From 1942 onwards, British forces in North Africa were supplied with more information about more aspects of the enemy operations than any forces enjoyed during any important campaign of the Second World War'.[32] This has been known for some time from information revealed about *Ultra* and codebreaking at Bletchley Park. It also requires the Eighth Army and the RAF to move over in the bed and share its comforts with those shadowy figures who inhabit the netherworld of intelligence.

The Axis campaign in North Africa was characterised by a lack of consistent concentrated logistics support to their forces in the field. The failure was one of the primary reasons that Rommel could not win a decisive breakthrough against the British Eighth Army throughout 1941–1942.[33] The Allies could now focus their attention on Sicily and Italy, happy in the knowledge that the first example of military co-operation in a campaign between the Allies had been a huge success.

Army/Air Force Conflicts

Fighting the Axis enemy was challenge enough without the at times poisonous hostilities among the top brass of the Army and the RAF. These are, to a degree, inevitable among powerful and ambitious figures and have existed since the dawn of time. Yet, they proved costly in terms of misdirected focus and wasted energy. Issuing blame at such a distance is futile, but much of the inter-service hostility tended to focus on the tactics and demeanour of Montgomery.

Montgomery himself wrote in 1943:

Army plus Air ... has to be so knitted that the two together form one entity. I feel very strongly on the whole matter [of Army/Air co-operation], and I know that we can achieve no real success unless each Army and its accompanying Air Force can weld themselves into one entity.[33]

Unfortunately, Montgomery honoured this philosophy more often in word than in deed. He failed even to co-locate his own headquarters with his Air equivalents.

Another issue poisoning relations was the RAF bombing short and causing Allied casualties. This was a well-documented problem, making the RAF unwilling to take on targets too near the front line. Paradoxically, reluctance to accept targets often further aggravated the Army's perception of RAF lack of co-operation. These issues presaged a final breakdown in the relationship between Montgomery and Coningham, which had once been close. John Terraine dates this breakdown from the Second Battle of El Alamein, when Coningham criticised Montgomery for an over-cautious pursuit of the retreating Germans. With the euphoria over El Alamein encouraged by the Government, any public suggestion at the time of disaffection between the Army and the Air Force would have been firmly stamped on.[34]

Carlo D'Este has another and less flattering explanation for the rift between the two senior commanders; Coningham was an ambitious and ruthless man who believed that Montgomery had 'stolen' all of the recognition for the desert victories.[35]

In the desert, the two men had worked in close harmony, living side by side in caravans and closely co-ordinating air–ground actions. When Montgomery gained fame and massive publicity for his victory over Rommel, Coningham felt slighted. From that time forth, relations deteriorated to the point where, in Normandy, Montgomery would deliberately bypass Coningham. This only intensified their bad relations as the frustrated Air Marshal constantly criticised Montgomery's actions.[36] Montgomery reciprocated these feelings and wrote to Brooke just as the Normandy campaign wound up:

> Coningham is violently anti-army and is disliked and despised by all soldiers; my army commanders distrust him and never want to see him ... For my part, I am very distressed about the air set-up.[37]

Who was more at fault in this dispute is unclear. Certainly, Montgomery was a notorious publicity seeker with a sizeable ego, which put off others besides Coningham; Tedder too was no friend of Montgomery's. Carlo D'Este, the US author, concludes that Montgomery also resented being given advice by Tedder. Nor did Montgomery help matters by deliberately by-passing Coningham and dealing directly with Leigh-Mallory on issues concerning the strategic bombers, and directly with Air Vice

Marshal Broadhurst on tactical matters.[37a] For his part, Air Vice Marshal Broadhurst, who apparently managed to establish a very good working relationship with both his opposite number, Lieutenant General Dempsey who was commanding the Second Army, and with Montgomery, felt himself caught between Coningham and Montgomery in a personal grudge match that damaged the war effort.[38] In the second half of July, Tedder actually fomented a plot to try to have Montgomery removed, a prospect Coningham fully supported.[39]

What implications did these disagreements have for Air Commodore George Beamish in his own role in the Desert War? Nothing if not loyal to his RAF superiors, George would have imbibed the same sentiments felt by Coningham. Although the animosities between Monty and the latter came about only late in the North African campaign, George was unlikely to veer from the RAF view that its role in the campaign was somewhat overshadowed by attention on Montgomery and his forces.

As the Tunisian campaign progressed to its conclusion after the fall of Tunis, George worked particularly closely with Coningham and Broadhurst. Seen as a good 'team player', George was hardwired to accept the institutional view. Unlike Broadhurst, he was not senior enough to argue openly with Coningham.

Air Chief Marshal Sir Harry Broadhurst worked closely with Coningham in the Desert War without being particularly 'close' in the sense that Coningham and Elmhirst had been. Tensions arose mainly due to different views on strategic policy. Broadhurst also worked closely with George Beamish who accompanied him and Coningham at key times of the campaign, including the victory arrival in Tunis in early 1943. Broadhurst initially joined the services with the Royal Artillery. It was in 1926 that he joined the RAF, serving first in India and then the North-West Frontier. An accomplished pilot during the Second World War, he was heavily involved in the Battle of France and then the Battle of Britain. Before encountering George, Broadhurst was a close colleague of Victor Beamish as a station commander during the

Battle of Britain and afterwards. He was part of what came to be known the 'Three Bs: Beamish, Bader and Broadhurst' and all three were close to Leigh-Mallory. This would have helped in his relationship with George in the desert. In late 1942, Broadhurst was posted to the Middle East and became a supernumerary Senior Air Staff Officer (SASO) with Beamish and eventually SASO to Coningham, while commander of the Desert Air Force. Broadhurst took command of the DAF in January 1943 then becoming, at the age of thirty-eight, the youngest Air Vice Marshal in the Royal Air Force. He quickly perfected the way he perceived that fighter aircraft ought to be employed as ground support fighter-bombers. His fighter squadrons were trained intensively to strafe and bomb German and Italian vehicles, tanks, transport and communication lines. This aerial cover of the Eighth Army won the approval and appreciation of Montgomery and would form the basis of the ground attack principles used during the D-Day landings.[40] Broadhurst's enthusiastic backing of the Army and his frank opinions did not always go down well with his superiors in the RAF. He returned to the UK in 1944 to command No. 83 Group, part of the Second Tactical Air Force. In September 1945, he became Air Officer Administration at RAF Fighter Command. In August 1946, Broadhurst was made Air Officer Commanding No. 61 Group and in 1949 attended the Imperial Defence College. After promotion to Air Marshal in July 1949, he became Assistant Chief of the Air Staff in April 1952 and then Commander-in-Chief of Second Tactical Air Force in December 1953 at the rank of Air Marshal. Broadhurst was appointed Air Officer Commander-in-Chief Bomber Command in January 1956. He was promoted to Air Chief Marshal in February 1957, and in 1959 became Commander, Allied Air Forces Central Europe, until March 1961 when he retired from the RAF. After retiring, Broadhurst was appointed Managing Director of Avro Aircraft and of Hawker Sidley Aviation Ltd.[41]

With Tedder, Coningham, Broadhurst and Elmhirst as colleagues, George Beamish was blessed. Their talents, character, sense of duty and colour made them a valued example to the less experienced Beamish. At the end of the North African Campaign, George was only thirty-eight – young by any standards and with a rosy career in prospect. The end of the war was nowhere in sight, thus requiring holding onto people of the calibre of George Beamish.

The issue of timeliness – getting close support air attacks on target as quickly as possible after Army requests – has dominated consideration of the tactical air support issue down to the present day. In 1943, the US Army had argued that:

> The ability to strike one great blow with all available means requires quick decision, accurate timing, and prompt execution; it is the ultimate function of command, not of co-operation.

US air strategy in the Second World War favoured a more independent role for the air force, lacking in some of the finer points of collaboration evident in the RAF.[42] This led to some conflict but also some mutual tactical learning. Most recently Ian Gooderson, in his analysis of Allied tactical air power, had this to say:

> The British system proved very successful in processing pre-planned air-support strikes, but the more difficult test was how quickly air support could be provided in response to impromptu requests from forward troops, where speed was vitally important. In this respect, both in Italy and in the early stages of the campaign in North-West Europe, the process was simply not fast enough.[43]

On top of these major disagreements, there were real and perceived differences in approach within each organisation. In the RAF, Coningham sought the opinions of more junior officers all the time but when decisions were made, there was strict obedience. In Elmhirst's view, the Army lacked the same organisational discipline. Even Ritchie in the Eighth Army was never sure from day to day if his orders were going to be implemented.[44]

The fall of Tobruk in 1942 – a very low point in British wartime morale – also led to disagreement at the very top of both the Army and the RAF. After Tobruk's fall, Auchinleck stated that the town was of no real strategic value at all and that El Alamein was the key to protecting Egypt and the Canal. These were certainly not the words to endear him to Churchill. For Coningham too, to hear this after pushing the RAF to extremes to defend Tobruk was too much. It was no surprise that he welcomed the eventual replacement of Auchinleck by the arrival of Montgomery in August 1942. Clearly, the top echelons of the Army and the RAF at this time more closely resembled a nest of vipers than a smoothly running military machine.

Lessons from 'Torch'

A major lesson learned in Operation *Torch* was how the use of air power was a most effective offensive weapon. The RAF in North Africa under Tedder concentrated its air power and defeated the *Luftwaffe*. The RAF had an excellent training programme, using bases in Canada, and maintained very high aircrew morale and inculcated a good fighting spirit. The RAF's success convinced Eisenhower that its system maximised the effectiveness of tactical air power. The point was that air power had to be consolidated at the highest level to operate almost autonomously. With one airman in overall charge, air assets could be concentrated for maximum offensive capability.[45] The fundamental assumption of air power doctrine was that the air war was just as important as the ground war. Indeed, the main function of the sea and ground forces, insisted the air enthusiasts, was to seize forward air bases. The idea of combined arms operations on air, land and sea strongly appealed to Eisenhower and MacArthur. Eisenhower invaded only after he was certain of air supremacy, and he made the establishment of forward air bases his first priority. Tedder pointed to the British and American air forces having become one force and not two forces co-operating.[46]

Looking at the two main parts of the campaign in North Africa – that part pre-*Torch* and that during *Torch* – we see a distinct difference. This mainly centres around the number of victories and defeats and bears out Churchill's famous comments about the vital role in Allied victory of El Alamein. In the early part of the North African campaign, there was one defeat after another for the Allies until Second El Alamein. Under *Torch,* however, with the exception of the Kasserine Pass, we see the inevitable path to Allied victory.

Analysis of the information on George Beamish's time in the latter parts of the Desert War and the Tunisian Campaign are helped immeasurably by the collection of notes, memoirs, operations reports and letters in the collection of Air Marshal Sir Thomas Elmhirst, held at Churchill College Cambridge. He, Beamish and 'Mary' Coningham acted as a sort of strategic air trio during the most critical periods in North Africa, setting policy and strategy in conjunction with the Army's ground war. Not only did they work closely together but ate and drank and chatted together with great gusto, usually in Coningham's quarters, as previously mentioned. However, while there was a close bond, Coningham was decidedly the boss, followed by Elmhirst, his ASO, and then Beamish, the SASO.

One of the duties which befell them was to meet visiting dignitaries. The Desert War was a novelty to many and of course, it was where the main action was taking place – enough reason for the great and the good to visit. These included Claire Booth Luce, Randolph Churchill and many others. Even if RAF servicemen may have seen such visitors as tedious intrusions, they would also have been aware of the PR benefits for the RAF. Later in the war (1944,) Elmhirst also cites a letter referring to the possibility of engaging Viscount Stansgate to deliver lectures to Second TAF. Stansgate, an RAF officer himself, was the father of the famed politician, Tony Benn. Benn and his brother both served in the RAF in the war, the latter killed in action.[47]

In a memo of 5 April 1943, Elmhirst talks about how, in his view, the Tunisian Campaign was tougher than the campaign in the Western

Desert. This was because of the excellent team in the Western Desert – including Coningham, Beamish, himself and others – along the chain of command. He also noted how grafting on a military relationship with the Americans with joint commands had its challenges.[48]

On 21 May 1943, Elmhirst notes that Coningham telegrammed to have both men join him at the victory parade in Tunis. They only received the message at the hour of the parade, so couldn't go.[49] After the campaign, Elmhirst refers to the arrival of the official portraitist who gives two-and-a-half-hours each to Coningham, Elmhirst and Beamish – a tradition for victorious warriors.[49a]

Operation Torch resulted in the capture of a staggering 275,000 Axis troops now removed the battlefield – the biggest concentration of captured troops in the Second World War. This compares with 91,000 Germans captured at Stalingrad and helps put the North African Campaign in its proper perspective.

As a strong indicator of the theatre of battle to come, Elmhirst noted in his diary in May 1943 that Coningham and Beamish flew to Algiers for a conference on the invasion of Sicily. The day of 7 July 1943 is earmarked as the beginning of the Sicily invasion.[50]

The success of *Torch* raised several possibilities for the War Office planners. At last, the British Army was on the offensive. Churchill, however, was never satisfied with the amount of ground covered, telling Major General Sir Noel Holmes, the Director of Movements, 'I intended North Africa to be a springboard, not a sofa.'[51] Among the scenarios that were now subjected to 'urgent examination' were projects for taking Rhodes and the Dodecanese Islands, bombing Italy, invading Sicily, sending air squadrons to help the Russians in the Caucasus, 'getting command of the Aegean again' and using Smyrna and the other Turkish ports further north. 'Sicily was the clear, preferred option.'[52]

Owen rightly points to how *Torch* prevented Rommel's defeated army to stage a 'German Dunkirk' by 'air power and sea power from below.'[53] To Tedder, it was a visible manifestation of the success of integrated Allied air power. Brooke wanted to develop operations for the Mediterranean by which he meant attacking either Sicily, Corsica or Sardinia. Meanwhile, the War Office planners 'had immense labour working out the shipping and other connected problems' connected with the next stage of operations. This staff work, which involved Elmhirst and Beamish and many others, was to pay off handsomely later that month. As noted by Owen, *Torch* was 'the first experiment of all in integration from the top down to the bottom level'. To its credit, it worked successfully. It was replicated in further campaigns with some tweaking during the war and it played a part in securing a successful outcome. Depriving the Axis of supplies was another critical factor in the Allied victory. *Ultra* intelligence from Hagelin decrypts, and from *Luftwaffe* and German naval Enigma decrypts, helped sink about half of the ships supplying the Axis forces in North Africa.[54]

Tedder believed that the cumulative effect of air attack from Northwest Africa, Malta and the Middle East was the decisive factor in ending the war in North Africa.[55] The success of Operation *Torch* was to lead to the first step in the Allied offensive on mainland Europe. The Americans, who had originally questioned the wisdom of the North African campaign, could now focus on the European war and the British could say that North Africa was a necessary and successful part of 'softening up' the Axis. The Axis was now severely exposed and this was amply demonstrated in Sicily and in mainland Italy.

9

SICILIAN CAMPAIGN (1943)

Operation *Husky* was the campaign in which the Allies seized Sicily from the Axis powers. Before the invasion, the RAF carried out an intensive air campaign; the operation began with a large amphibious and airborne operation, followed by a six-week land campaign. George Beamish was involved in an intensive period of planning and analysis with other senior officers in preparation for the invasion. Sicily was seen by Churchill as the 'soft underbelly' of the Axis which, after being conquered, would lead to the eventual unravelling of the Reich. While Sicily fell in less than forty days, not for the first time, Churchill's broader expectations were on the optimistic side.[1] It was to take a little longer to unravel the Reich.

Coningham, Elmhirst and Beamish with teams from the Army, Royal Navy and their American counterparts were all involved in planning the attack on Sicily.[2] A brief aside on the principles of military planning and how they relate to the task that George and his colleagues faced is enlightening.

Planning for Husky

After taking home leave, George Beamish returned to North Africa to work with his former colleagues who, under the command of Coningham, were now in the newly structured NAAF and Second Tactical Air Force. During his period in Tunisia, George was appointed to join a planning team for the proposed invasion of Sicily. His time was divided between that task and maintaining a role in 2TAF – an unenviable situation. After the fall of Tunis on 13 May 1943, Beamish and Elmhirst completed two weeks 'hard labour' (on campaign planning for Sicily) at Algiers. Elmhirst alluded to 'Mary' with some frustration, wanting his 'first team in the field'. Elmhirst also refers to the dilemma that 'they are wanted there and with 2TAF on the Tunisian shore simultaneously'.[3]

Tedder noted that advance planning for *Husky* showed how differently the two Allies saw control and command of air forces. Positive relations developed, however.[4] Advance planning for *Husky* had George deeply involved towards the end of *Torch*, interfering with and overlapping his duties in the latter operation to some degree. Planning is an art, but it is also a skill that can be learned. For someone like George, who had spent two years as SASO with Coningham taking a 'big picture' perspective on behalf of his commander, the role was the right one for him and one in which he could further develop his skills. His role in the Desert War, liaising with the other services and the Americans and the 'planning mindset' he had acquired, was excellent training.

It is worthwhile examining the views on planning of Helmuth von Moltke, head of the German General Staff in the latter part of the nineteenth century. He is one of the fathers of modern military planning. Simple, clear and pervasive, his ideas are instructive in the modern era. In modern warfare, Von Moltke believed that no plan survives first contact with the enemy. Moltke favoured independent thinking and decentralised leadership over unquestioning execution of a top-down plan. Von Moltke's main thesis was that military strategy had to be understood as a system of options since only the beginning of a military operation was plannable. As a result, he considered the main task of military leaders to lie in the extensive preparation of all possible outcomes. It is the commander's job to keep his eye on the strategic picture. Hence, flexibility of response was key.[5]

Planning for Sicily was at root a compromise between FDR and Eisenhower on one side and Churchill and the British on the other. It went back to lively discussions between the two sides over whether the 'second front' should commence from Northern Europe or, as desired by Churchill, the Allies should first attack through the Axis' 'soft underbelly'. Churchill won out on this occasion with full American backing. The plan was to invade and subdue Sicily, step onto the Italian mainland and thrust northwards into the heart of the Reich. Then, the invasion through France would take place. In Moltke's terms, the plan was carried out in broad terms, but as in everything, there were hitches along the way particularly the stronger than expected resistance from the Axis in Italy. Acknowledging Moltke again, improvisation was necessary from the Allies.

In the more modern era, a RAND corporation report examines the history of strategic planning efforts in the US Air Force with useful general application. The report issued several recommendations that could be apposite in many planning environments and particularly so in the environments in which George Beamish found himself in the North Africa and Mediterranean theatres of the Second World War as a member of key planning teams. These are set out below.

Encourage ideas from below: Cultivate free thinkers within the ranks and encourage dialogue between them and senior leaders.

Know your environment: Tailor messages to specific audiences and understand the context — social, political, economic.

Development strategy from the top: Get leadership buy-in early in the process of developing the strategy.

Keep the **strategy succinct**, substantive, and sharp.

Focus on the **process as much as the product**.[6]

The first recommendation did not really apply in North Africa and the Mediterranean in an era that was far more hierarchical and subject to tight secrecy, in contrast to the more flat, democratic decision-making of the present. That said, Coningham, while in command of the Desert War air forces, was keen to throw ideas open to debate and encourage officers to make contributions. This approach was a rarity, however 'Knowing your environment' was quite important in so far as the creators of plans and strategies had to convince and persuade wide constituencies (the politicians, the various Allies, the various services, etc.) – a challenging diplomatic task. Senior level 'buy in' was vitally necessary, which meant among both politicians and the military – FDR, Churchill, Marshall, Eisenhower, Brooke, Portal, Tedder and others. At a political level, sign-off was taken at the Casablanca Conference which set the broad terms of the strategy to be filled out over time by the military and officials. As laid out at Casablanca, the strategy was succinct but with a strong emphasis on proper process. This entailed the need for wide consultation, the setting aside where necessary of sectional objectives and the negotiating of inter-Allied differences. Moltke would have commended the broad outline nature of the Casablanca strategy, with the details to be filled out by leaders on the ground.

Much has been written of the good inter-Allied communication and co-operation during the Second World War. This was not always easy to forge but was made much easier by the equable, diplomatic demeanour of Eisenhower as Supreme Commander.

Operation Husky

During the Casablanca meetings in January 1943, the British lobbied in favour of invading either Sicily or Sardinia as they believed either could lead to the fall of Mussolini's government as well as encouraging Turkey to join the Allies. Though Roosevelt was initially reluctant, he conceded to British wishes to move forward in the Mediterranean. Eisenhower was given overall command with Alexander as ground commander. Supporting Alexander would be naval forces led by Admiral of the Fleet Cunningham and air forces overseen by Tedder. The principal troops for the assault were the US Seventh Army under Patton and the British Eighth Army under Montgomery.[7]

Initial planning for the operation suffered as the commanders involved were still conducting active operations in Tunisia. This is borne out by material contained in a file in the National Archives, Kew, on the Sicilian Campaign which confirms that the Tunisian Campaign's requirements meant that most officers could not devote as much time to planning of the Sicily Campaign as was warranted.[8] The operation was the most meticulously planned to date and benefited from the staff experiences gained at Dieppe and North Africa. However, no joint HQ was established to co-ordinate all land, sea and air elements which would have had all the advantages of speedy and effective communications.

An extensive drop of airborne troops in order to soften resistance behind the beaches was judged the best method of attack. Without early possession of key airbases, it was believed the whole operation would be abortive.[9] The plan of attack went through several iterations before it was signed off among the invading Allies. According to Brereton, 160,000 men were set aside for Sicily. There were potential conflicts of interest between the services in the timing of the operation. One concerned the parachutists who needed bright moonlight conditions to land safely. However, these conditions left ships lying off the coast vulnerable to air attack. The matter was resolved in favour of the parachutists, since the Allies had air superiority which would deter the enemy.

On the night of 9 and 10 July, Allied airborne units began landing, while American and British ground forces came ashore 3 hours later in the Gulf of Gela and south of Syracuse. Both sets of landings were hampered by difficult weather and organisational problems. The Allied advance initially suffered from a lack of co-ordination between US and British forces as Montgomery pushed northeast towards the strategic port of Messina and Patton pushed north and west.

Sicily was defended by the Italian Sixth Army and the German XIV Panzer Corps. The total Axis force was about 190,000 Italian and 40,000 German troops – no easy pushover.[10]

Kesselring's Role in Sicily

Allied adversary in North Africa, Kesselring correctly expected that the Allies would next invade Sicily, as a landing could be made there under fighter cover from Tunisia and Malta.[11] He reinforced the six coastal and four mobile Italian divisions there with two mobile German divisions. Kesselring was aware that while this force was large enough to stop the Allies from simply marching in, it could not withstand a large-scale invasion. He therefore pinned his hopes on repelling the Allied invasion of Sicily by an immediate counterattack.

Kesselring hoped that the Allied invasion fleet would provide good targets for U-boats, but they had few successes. Pressure from the Allied air forces drove *Luftflotte* 2 to withdraw most of its aircraft to the mainland.[12] The Allied invasion of Sicily on 10 July 1943 was stubbornly opposed, however. A *Stuka* attack sank USS *Maddox,* a Bf 109 destroyed a tank landing ship, and a *Liberty* ship filled with ammunition was bombed by *Junker 88s* – these were quick, sharp responses not expected by the Allies.[13]

Kesselring himself flew to Sicily on 12 July and decided that the island would eventually have to be evacuated such was the strength of the combined Allied assault. Unable to provide much more in the way of air support, Kesselring managed to delay the Allies in Sicily for another month. Thus, the Allied conquest of the Sicily was not complete until 17 August. Kesselring's evacuation of Sicily, which began a week earlier on 10 August, was seen by many as the most brilliant action of the campaign. In spite of the Allies' superiority on land, at sea, and in the air, Kesselring was able to evacuate not only 40,000 men, but also 96,605 vehicles,94 guns, 47 tanks, 1,100 tons of ammunition, 970 tons of fuel, and 15,000 tons of stores. Like Dunkirk for the British, Kesselring was able to turn an ignominious defeat in Sicily into a face-saving retreat.[14]

Kesselring made the astute observation in March that German fighter planes were better but British bombing was more effective – broadly true.[15]

Husky's Achievements

Strategically, *Husky* achieved the goals set out for it by Allied planners; the Allies drove Axis air, land and naval forces from the island and the Mediterranean sea lanes were opened for Allied merchant ships for the first time since 1941. Mussolini was toppled from power and the way was opened for the Allied invasion of Italy. Hitler cancelled a major offensive at Kursk after only a week, in part to divert forces to Italy, resulting in a reduction of German strength on the Eastern Front. The collapse of Italy led to Germans replacing Italian troops in Italy, resulting in one-fifth of the entire German army being diverted from the east to southern Europe.[16]

In 1937, Mussolini had boasted: 'Sicily is so well-defended on the land, at sea and in the air that it would be a nameless folly for anyone to try to invade her.'[17] The Allied invasion proved him wrong on all fronts. Once ashore, the Allied armies linked up and secured a large beachhead area. Then the Eighth Army drove north, along the east coast of Sicily, to Messina. The Seventh Army covered the Eighth Army's left flank and cleared the rest of the island.

Mussolini had been dismissed by the King and on 3 September, the Italians agreed to unconditional surrender.

Despite the relentless Allied assault, the vast majority of Axis ground forces were able to evacuate safely to the Italian mainland. The Allies were unable to prevent the orderly withdrawal or effectively interfere with transport across the Strait of Messina.

The Sicily campaign had cost the Allies nearly 25,000 casualties. According to several sources, German units lost about 20,000 killed, wounded or captured, but another source says the German forces lost 4,678 men, while 5,532 were captured and 13,500 wounded, making up a total of 23,710 German casualties. The operation destroyed 40 bombers and 196 fighters.[18] Sicily demonstrated again the role of air superiority. Tedder points out that 'by 10 July, the enemy did not have a single airfield operational'.[19] Further, he points out that: 'Our fighters destroyed German and Italian fighters, and bombers attacked centres of communication in Sicily and Southern Italy'.[20] Tedder quotes battle figures that more than half of enemy forces in Sicily escaped by evacuation, but with over 16,000 taken prisoner and more than 30,000 killed. Italian military losses are reported to amount to 4,325, with 32,500 wounded and 116,681 captured, although another source maintains that 118,700 Italians were captured.[21]

Malta's role in the Sicilian campaign in July 1943

It was during the Sicilian Campaign that news of Mussolini's demise on 25 July 1943 reached Malta. While it was a morale blow to many Italians, the Maltese paraded with an effigy of Mussolini in the capital, Valletta, during celebrations marking the end of his rule.

Tedder was clear and adamant that 'At all cost we had to keep open the route from Gibraltar through Malta to Egypt.' He indicated further that 'advances on November and December 1941 lent extra urgency to the Axis decision to neutralise the island in order that Rommel be sustained.'[22] This was reinforced by Hitler and Mussolini's decision to have the island neutralised.

The assault on Sicily brought to Malta more British and American warships and many landing craft. Many infantry battalions also arrived on the island. Allied commanders came to Malta too, to discuss and make preparations for the invasion of Sicily. Montgomery moved his headquarters to Malta at the end of June 1943 and on 4 July, Admiral Cunningham took up personal command at the Naval Headquarters. On 7 July, Eisenhower arrived in Malta. He was joined by Lord Louis Mountbatten, Chief of Combined Operations. On 8 July, Alexander opened a Tactical Headquarters for 15th Army Group. Coningham moved to Malta as well to supervise tactical air operations. Tedder retained his Mediterranean Air Command Headquarters in Tunisia, but he shuttled between North Africa and Malta. He appointed Air Vice Marshal H.E.P. Wigglesworth, a member of his Cairo team, for better liaison with General Eisenhower. Assembled in Malta for the impending invasion of Sicily, there were 23 Spitfire fighter squadrons plus 1 Spitfire PR Squadron and 1 Spitfire TACR Squadron.

Until the eleventh hour, the German High Command still had doubts about the actual location of the intended landings. The German Naval War staff thought it would be Greece, specifically the Corfu–Arta–Pyrgos region on the east coast, even as late as 20 May 1943. Undoubtedly Operation *Mincemeat* played its part in the Allied plan of deception. This was the British secret operation in which a body dressed in the uniform of the Royal Marines officer was put in the sea off the coast of Spain via a submarine. Attached to the body was a briefcase in which were documents purporting to confirm that the Allied landings were indeed to take place on the Greek west coast. The body was recovered by the Spanish and the documents were handed over to the German authorities, as intended.

The early main effort from Malta was directed to the provision of fighter cover for the landing beaches and shipping in the occupied harbours. During the latter stages of the campaign, Allied troops were continually supported by Kittyhawks and US fighter-bombers with little interference from Axis fighters.

By late July, every German aircraft that could be flown had left Sicily, while the Italians retained just twenty-eight fighters, mainly MacchiMC202s. Malta played a vital part in this denouement.[23]

Lessons from Husky

A file in the National Archives at Kew indicates that the main lessons to be learned from the Sicilian Campaign were the need for: unity of command, clarity of control, early beachhead establishment, early build-up of RAF supplies, inter-communication, and minimum paperwork. *Ultra* intelligence in preparation for the invasion was hugely important in providing information as to where the enemy's forces were strongest and that several Allied strategic deceptions had duped Hitler and the German high command.[24] A document by General Eisenhower in the same file pointed to the physical strain of mountain combat, the necessity of conducting rapid infantry operations without normal transport supplies, and the necessity of seizing high ground (as in Tunisia). He also noted how Army/Air Force co-operation was good – information supplied by the Army allowed for the Air Force to make intercepts. This healthy Allied co-operation was also borne out by Tommy Elmhirst's diaries.[25]

Having secured Sicily, the next step was into Italy in a campaign to last longer than many had expected. The war was far from over, but it was already clear that the Allied 'Mediterranean' strategy was the right one. Tedder points to disagreements over the merits of a campaign in Italy. Finally, all were of one mind that an attack on Italy was the best way to exploit the gains of *Husky*. Amphibious landings would have to be preceded by neutralising the enemy's air power, however.[26]

The Allied invasion of Italy was led by two strong egos in the shape of Patton and Montgomery, with the continued support of the RAF and the USAF. The end of the beginning was now starting to look like the beginning of the end.

10

END OF THE WAR AND FINAL POSTINGS

Compared with George's stints in the Desert and in Sicily, his final appointments of the war were relatively quiet and safe ones. His role as ADC to the King was largely ceremonial but Transport Command had the potential of being unexpectedly challenging. Like everyone, George welcomed the end of the war when it came. He was a fairly circumspect person and not one to jump to conclusions too quickly. His comment during the Desert War to Tommie Elmhirst that it was too early to claim victory immediately after El Alamein sums up George's mindset.[1]

Air ADC to King George VI (1944)

George was appointed Air ADC to the King from 1 January 1944 to 1 October 1944.[2] With this nine-month appointment, George was taken out of the 'front line' of active service during some of the most critical events of the war. June 1944 was the month of the Allied invasion of Normandy and the following months saw the Allies advance through France, the Low Countries and into the heart of the Reich. George, however, would have seen his appointment as an honourable duty to his monarch, even if by temperament he would have preferred to have been in the thick of the action. Compared with the years of exertion and physical danger in the desert, George's royal appointment was a complete contrast.

The appointment in the service of the King would not have been given to anyone insignificant. George had a 'good war' and one cannot but feel that recommendations from people of the stature of Coningham and Tedder, who were familiar with and positive towards George, lay behind the decision. Clearly, from the descriptions of the ADCs described below, George came from quite a different background, but it was never to hold him back.

George may not have been aware of it at the time, but it was George VI's father, George V who had intervened to prod the Army and the Royal Navy into accepting the fledgling RAF into the fold of combined services rugby in the 1920s.[3] For this, George could be grateful because along with his spell at Leicester, it was in combined services rugby that George Beamish was able to showcase his talents.

There is no official doctrine on the proper role of an ADC, with custom and tradition, particularly in relation to ADCs to the Monarch, playing a significant role. This would have been the case in George Beamish's Air ADC role to the King in 1944.

Tom March offers some interesting insights, however, in *Aide-de-Camp: A Survival Guide*. Although aimed mainly at the Army, it has a general application across the services. March states that the role of ADC is crucial to the support of a principal, and in return, the ADC gains a sweeping view of command at the highest levels. He states further that,

> There is no single winning formula to surviving as an ADC, but the relationship with the Principal must be personable as well as professional. Like any relationship, that between an ADC and their Principal takes time for trust and familiarity to build. The formula for success will necessarily involve long hours; unfailing diligence; the care and management of relationships on behalf of the Principal; and the near-constant co-ordination of the minutiae of the Principal's life.[4]

George would have been familiar with most of these roles and tasks from his time as SASO to Coningham in the desert. In his ten-month stint as ADC to the King, he acquitted himself well at a time of critical importance in the war. In current day business, the nearest equivalent to an ADC role would be a Personal Assistant or Executive Assistant to a CEO, particularly in the emphasis on relationship development. Naturally, the relationship with the Monarch was deferential, and lacked the familiarity of private sector arrangements, but the need for tact and diplomacy would also have been to the fore.

An interesting anecdote is told of George in his role as ADC being asked to lead the 'Trooping of the Colour'. This was to be carried out on horseback. Unlike most servicemen at the time, George had never ridden a horse and frantic efforts were made to find a horse that suited him. A suitable candidate was eventually found. One can only hope for the horse's sake that it had a broad, sturdy back and didn't answer back to George![5]

Vincent Orange refers to Coningham's loyalty to his former staff members. Coningham was particularly concerned with the plight of George Beamish in the period leading up to the Normandy invasion, enquiring of colleagues whether he could use his influence to secure George a good position.[6] George had very good relations with Coningham, but after the ADC appointment, was quite content with his vital work in Ferry and Transport Command. Although the positions were less glamourous than those in Operation *Overlord*, the supply of aircraft and other military material to Western Europe in the face of attacks from the *Luftwaffe* and the German Navy was a vital task.

Famous Fellow Military ADCs to King George VI

Lord John Gort was Commander-in Chief of the British Expeditionary Force in Western Europe in the months that led up to the evacuation at Dunkirk, where he managed to oversee the evacuation of almost 300,00 British forces across the Channel. He had previously been Chief of the Imperial General Staff (CIGS). He was also decorated in the First World War with the Military Cross, the Distinguished Service Order and the Victoria Cross. After the evacuation (seen as a humiliation by many), Gort was seen as too senior and influential to be dismissed and in 1940 was appointed ADC to the King. He was later appointed Governor of Gibraltar and of Malta and in 1944, as High Commissioner in Palestine. He died in 1946.[7]

Field Marshal Harold Alexander was one of the few truly outstanding senior figures of the Second World War, notably in India, the desert, Italy and post-D-Day Europe. In March 1937, Alexander was appointed as one of the aides-de-camp to King George VI.[8] Following the war, he was appointed Governor General of Canada. In the 1950s, Churchill appointed him Minister for Defence and he became a member of the Privy Council. He died in 1969.

Another interesting link between George and Harold Alexander was the Alexander family's former ownership of the house, Boom Hall in Derry. It was designed for the Alexander family in the eighteenth century and had subsequently been bought by the McDevitt family, a member of which, Patrick, was a good friend and golf companion of George's from Castlerock. The house was named after the 'boom' laid across the River Foyle during the Siege of Derry in 1689, an event central to the subsequent troubled history of Ireland.

George's Final Appointments of the War[9]

George's last two appointments towards the end of the war, were as Air Officer in Command at No. 44 Group and No. 45 Group respectively. These were then known as Ferry Service Group and Atlantic Ferry Group, or later as RAF Transport Command. It was Coningham who was instrumental in George securing these transport command positions. He also contacted the Air Ministry querying why George had not received the recommended CB in the Year Honours list of 1943. George was eventually to receive his CB, showing the power and influence of the ex-Desert Mafia!

RAF Ferry Command was formed on 20 July 1941 to ferry aircraft from the place of manufacture or other non-operational areas, to the front line squadrons. It was subsumed into the new

Transport Command in March 1943.[10] The overall head of that Command during George's tenure was Sir Frederick Bowhill. A highly decorated officer, prior to Transport Command he had been in command of Coastal Command and Ferry Command. Notably, he sighted the position of the German battleship *Bismarck* during the war, and organised arrangements for its sinking.

Ferry Command operated over only one area of the world, rather than the more general routes that Transport Command later developed. The Command's operational area was the north Atlantic, and its responsibility was to bring the larger aircraft that had the range to do the trip over the ocean from American and Canadian factories to the RAF Home Commands.[11]

The North Atlantic sea lanes were still critical for sea trade during the war and were known to be regularly patrolled by U-boats. George, therefore, still had a strategically important role to perform.

In the final period of the war as the Allies progressed through Normandy, one wonders whether George had any thought that this was the land of his Beaumais/Beamish forebears who made the trek to west Cork more than three centuries previously. Dedication to duty and the fact that sentimentalism was not part of his repertoire, meant that it was unlikely to have been more than a passing thought.

George was to become Commander in charge of Technical Command in 1956 at the rank of Air Marshal, his last appointment in the RAF.

George Beamish's Decoration and Awards

In 1955, George was made a Knight Commander of the Bath. He was also awarded the Gold Cross of the Order of King George I of Greece after the Second World War, in recognition of his evacuation activities in Crete.[12] Other major figures who received various categories of this order were: Field Marshal Alexander, Field Marshal Montgomery, Admiral Chester Nimitz of the US Navy, Walter Hallstein, German politician, and Prince Rainier of Monaco.[13]

Since 1942, the US has awarded the Legion of Merit to selected members of the armed forces of foreign nations, based on the relative rank or position of the recipient. George received his Legion of Merit award in 1946 in the impressive form of a signed letter from US President Truman on the advice of General Eisenhower.[14] George had been mentioned in dispatches in the Desert War for his ability to work closely and build strong relations with US forces in the Desert and in the Sicily Campaign. He also came into regular direct contact there with senior figures such as Spaatz, Kuter, Brereton and Doolittle who would have fed back to HQ positive reports about George. His role in strategic planning would also have given him a high profile. The Order of Merit was awarded according to the rank and status of the recipient and at the highest level, there were a number who received the award in the Second World War.

There were also those who fought in the North African campaign who if not famous then, were at least famous subsequently. One who stands out is magician and comedian, Tommy Cooper. Cooper was a trooper in the Royal Horse Guards and a 'Desert Rat' member of the Seventh Armoured Brigade. His trademark 'fez', he picked up in Egypt while entertaining troops with NAAFI.[15] Napoleon once said that an army marches on its stomach, yet comics like Cooper also proved the vital importance of humour.

Field Marshal Lord Carver, later to become Chief of the Defence Staff, was another famous member of the 'Desert Rats'. Enoch Powell also had a distinguished war in North Africa. He was one among two of the most promoted soldiers in the war, entering as a lance corporal and retiring as a brigadier. He was also a high-profile member of MENSA. Powell's talent was recognised early by his superiors when appointed to North Africa, he helped plan the decisive Second Battle of El Alamein. For those who recall Powell as a controversial and divisive politician or a rather donnish classics expert, the extent and nature of his war record must come as surprise.[16]

Assessment of George's Wartime Activities

While there was no steady upward line of progress in George's career, there were a number of significant high points. His time in the Desert War stands out as a period of considerable achievement which helped boost his subsequent career. Undoubtedly, being chosen as the King's ADC was a high honour. His earlier period during the evacuation of Crete, although a double-edged sword, saw him help in mitigating an embarrassing defeat. His later appointments to Transport Command were a little lacklustre for someone who had previously been at the centre of such critical events, but such is the 'lottery' nature of many appointments. Yet, many have argued that the protection of convoys in the North Atlantic from U-boats – a process in which George's ferrying of aircraft to strategic locations assisted – was also a vital element in the eventual winning of the war. The fact that George had survived the war was a bonus in itself when so many airmen including his brother Victor had met their deaths. The official view of George was of a reliable staff officer, tough and imperturbable if not stubborn, while dedicated to the service of others. His close association with people of the calibre of Coningham also worked to his credit. Elmhirst described George as 'a great stalwart and one I admire, but not too easy to work with.'[17]

Importantly too, he was a former combatant who disliked talking about his time in the war – a fact attested to by his younger relatives. This reluctance to talk about war is a character feature of many veterans who have been at the centre of great conflicts. For example, former Chairman of the US Joint Chiefs of Staff, Colin Powell, instructively talked about the horrors of war in the wake of the First Gulf War. No one who had experienced the horrors of war, he said, would lightly enter into it. Powell also referred to the fact that it was most often those who had no experience of war themselves who were the most bullish in seeking armed conflict.[18] In similar vein, the top leaders who George came across during the war, such as Tedder and Coningham, would have been deeply conscious of the need to protect the lives of their forces and to avoid putting them unnecessarily in harm's way. People of their stature knew intimately that war was no joke.

Reserve, modesty and stoicism were all part of the George Beamish makeup. Moreover, his career attests to the fact that those who have experienced the worst horrors of war are usually those least likely to want to talk about it. George's appointments to the ranks of Air Vice Marshal and Air Marshal were yet to come, as well as his appointment as Commandant of Cranwell. At only forty years of age at the end of the Second World War, George had seen and experienced more than most men of his age. He clearly still had a great deal to contribute.

In his role particularly in the Western Desert, George was to some extent 'punching above his weight'. His role there along with his responsibility for the evacuation of Crete in 1941 was hugely important. It put him in close contact with the most senior figures and gave him a high profile. The fact that he had access to all incoming 'Top Secret' *Ultra* intelligence with Freyberg and Coningham, also indicates his key role.[19] George's role in the Western Desert couldn't have been described better than by Tedder himself when after the conflict, he said that success in the Desert War was basically 'down to Coningham, Elmhirst and Beamish'.[20] It also amplifies the general conclusion that Montgomery and the Eighth Army would not have had the successes they had without the role of the RAF.

The umbrella under which George and his colleagues operated was secured by the eminent Chief of the Air Staff Charles Portal who oversaw general air strategy. He was variously described as the 'complete professional', 'the real brains in the Chiefs of Staff', 'the great co-operator' and by Churchill, 'the man who had everything'. Coningham, Elmhirst and Beamish may have been the visible expression of air policy but this was very much the child of Portal.[21] Portal also had a Huguenot lineage, like George. His forebears came to England from France in the seventeenth century, at around the same time the Beamishes arrived in Ireland.[22]

While much of the historical drama associated with the RAF has tended to focus on Fighter Command during the Battle of Britain and on Bomber Command in the closing period of the War, it could be argued that the RAF role in the Western Desert in bringing about, in Churchill's words, 'the end of the beginning' was the truly instrumental campaign in ensuring the path to victory in the war.

Mention at this stage should be made of two famous Englishmen from the world of sport who had roles in the RAF in the war. From the world of football commentary, Kenneth Wolstenholme was a pilot in RAF Bomber Command, flying over 100 missions, some as part of the *Pathfinder* squadron. He was awarded the DFC and Bar. Dan Maskell, the famous BBC tennis commentator, was a rehabilitation officer with the RAF which, although a less glamorous role, was a vital one in helping injured pilots towards recovery.[23]

German Defeat in the Second World War

The Elmhirst papers reveal some interesting notes on suggested reasons for the German defeat in Europe in 1945. Obviously much has been written on the subject, but it is interesting to explore the views of some of the main combatants in the immediate aftermath of the War. A review paper by the Air Staff of SHAEF in 1945 contained among Elmhirst's papers highlights these points. The notes are particularly interesting in that they include the considered views of some of the main principals in the conflict, Field Marshals von Rundstedt, Kesselring and Montgomery.[24]

Von Rundstedt mentioned three key reasons:

Allied air superiority which paralysed movement of German troops
Lack of fuel for tanks and the few planes we had left
Systematic destruction by Allied air forces of rail and road connections.

Kesselring mentioned three reasons:

Allied strategic bombing behind German lines.
Attacks by low-flying Allied fighter aircraft.
Terror raids against German civilians.

Montgomery summed his views in the pithy: 'Before you can attack on land, you must win the battle of the air.'

The views of all three inevitably stem from their own particular military positions, perspectives and experiences, but what links them all is the acceptance of the key role of the air war. Both Montgomery and Kesselring would have been influenced by their own experiences of the Desert War and in Kesselring's case, by his direct command role over the Luftwaffe in that theatre. In Montgomery's case, the close co-operation with the RAF under Coningham leading to the Army's successes in the Desert War despite some bitter disagreements, would have shaped his views on the vital role of air power.

Von Rundstedt's views, while coming from a Field Marshal's perspective, essentially do not differ from the general consensus. It is noteworthy too how the views of Von Rundstedt and Kesselring are so objective and clear-sighted for military leaders of a defeated power.

Although the three sets of comments refer to the war as a whole and the post-D-Day period, observers of the Desert War would also recognise the merit of their logic. The three top leaders identified those factors that, as it happens, were also decisive in North Africa. Air superiority was thus seen to be critical, as Tedder and Coningham had advocated long before.

Commandant of Cranwell 1949–51

Immediately following the War, George was appointed Head of the RAF Selection Board, a key role in relation to RAF appointments. He served there from 1945 to 1947, when he was appointed to the position of Director of Weapons. These two roles he performed at the rank of Air Commodore and Acting Air Vice Marshal.[25] George's return to Cranwell took place on his appointment as Commandant of the College in 1949. This was a fitting result of a successful career and took place at a time when the huge contribution of the RAF to the war would have been firmly embedded in the collective British psyche. It was a post normally held by a senior RAF man for a period of two years.

George's immediate predecessor was Sir Richard Atcherley who, following Cranwell, was made Chief of the Air Staff of the Pakistani Air Force in its fledgling years following independence. Shortly after the death of George's brother Victor, Atcherley was appointed in 1942 as station commander at RAF Kenley, Victor's home station. During the Desert War, he was AOC of No. 211 Group under Coningham's North West African Tactical Air Force, notable for its actions in Libya and in Operation *Husky* in Sicily. He was awarded an Air Force Cross and Bar earlier in the war. Atcherley was one of the early post-war Commandants to shepherd the latest flight cadets into service when the College was fully opened again from 1946. He was to leave the College in fine shape for George to seize the reins.[26]

In some ways, George's appointment as Commandant was the 'crowning glory' of his career. A graduate of the College from the early years, an outstanding rugby player and an RAF man with a distinguished war record who also acted in the personal service of the King, George returned to Cranwell with a certain lustre as Commandant in the latter years of his career. It must have been a pleasure of sorts for George to re-enter Cranwell again twenty-five years after his graduation in 1924. Having distinguished himself there as a cadet on many fronts, there was no doubt that he was one of its most illustrious graduates. By the same token, the staff and cadets would surely have been aware of the achievements of their new Commandant.

George's period of office was in the early post-war years coincided with the recognition that the numerical requirement for servicemen had been reduced considerably. This did not allow, however, for any complacency as Britain and NATO were careful not to let their guard down in the new climate of the Cold War. George's first year in the post saw the first intake of cadets since the war to complete the full course, due to wartime exigencies. Cranwell was used as a flight training school during the war and was only re-opened for cadets in 1946. In the year after George left the Cranwell appointment, a former New Zealand flight cadet published his diaries of his time at Cranwell. Despite their fairly anodyne content, at the time, the diaries caused a flap among officialdom who didn't wish to encourage such independent initiatives.[27]

Of general concern at the time was the low applicant rate to the College. In 1949, 320 places were made available for flight cadets but only 246 candidates enrolled. In some ways, this was understandable as the 'war enthusiasm' had worn off since 1945 and other job opportunities started to open up in the post-war era. These were not problems isolated to Cranwell.[28]

Although George was not involved himself, the Air Ministry was fighting another battle with the Treasury over upgrading the rank of the Commandant of Cranwell from Air Commodore to Air Vice Marshal status. In 1949, the Air Ministry called for the role to be that of an Air Vice Marshal. For three years in the 1930s, the Commandant was, in fact, an Air Vice Marshal, but the post reverted to the original position before the war. This proved another lengthy bureaucratic battle and it was only as late as 1967 that the role was upgraded – a sad irony as this was the year in which George died.[29]

George was the second graduate of Cranwell to hold the post, his immediate predecessor, Atcherley being the first. In his time as Commandant, George maintained the strong training regime at Cranwell, supported by his own example of robust leadership, physical courage, fitness and moral integrity. In those years, the RAF was in the process of consolidating its reputation and standards after the successes of the war. Central to that process was an effective training regime. George's war record and the fact that he was a distinguished graduate and recipient of the Sword of Honour would have enhanced his stature among the staff and cadets at Cranwell. The decision on George's appointment in this sense, reflected his exemplary qualities. Part of the responsibilities of Commandant involved several ceremonial duties. The end-of-year graduation was usually attended by the King or a senior Royal, and making the appropriate arrangements was a duty which George performed seamlessly. In this case, George had a past association of service to the King – his role as RAF aide-de-camp to George VI. More of a 'man of action' by nature than a ceremonial type, George nevertheless acquitted himself well in his role. This past association would also have helped in ensuring the whole Cranwell graduation process ran smoothly. The ADC role and several other appointments certainly did George no harm on his ascent up the RAF ladder.

At that time, Cranwell was a long way from the experience and traditions of Sandhurst and Dartmouth but in a relatively short period, it had managed to put itself on the map and to enhance the reputation of the RAF as a whole. As an institution it had to fight its corner to gain acceptability as did the RAF itself.

In 1950, Prince Henry, Duke of Gloucester, performed the graduation ceremony on behalf of the King. George was in overall charge of ceremonies on the day.

A sad event occurred in January 1950 about a year into George's tenure as Commandant which resonated throughout the RAF community. A young flight cadet died while at Cranwell. He was no ordinary cadet but the son of Lady Tedder, wife of the Chief of the Air Staff, a son from her first marriage.[30] Having worked with Lord Tedder, George would have been quite attuned to the sensitivity of this premature death.

George's deputy at Cranwell was Laurence Sinclair who was a graduate of the College in 1926, two years after George. Sinclair had had a distinguished war record, having been knighted, awarded the DSO and Bar, the George Cross and the US Legion of Merit.[31]

Cranwell was a fine structure that was built over various stages, including, inter alia, the influences of Sir Christopher Wren. A brief look at the main structures gives a flavour of the College. The main building at Cranwell is noted for its distinctive dome, visible from most of the surrounding roads. The Cranwell motto, *Alitum Altrix* (*Nurture the Winged*), can be found in gold print above the main doors of the College Hall Officers Mess.

Prior to the construction of the neo-classical College Hall in 1929, training took place in old naval huts. In the 1920s, the Secretary of State for War, Sir Samuel Hoare battled for a substantial College building. Architects' plans were drawn up in 1929 for the present-day College. After some disagreement, the building plans incorporated design aspects of Christopher Wren's Royal Hospital at Chelsea. In September 1933, the building was completed in rustic and moulded brick. The building has been used for RAF officer training since the then Prince of Wales (later Edward VIII) officially opened it in October 1934. In 1987, the building was given Grade II listed status.[32]

In 1952, two years after George's tenure as Commandant had expired, a College Memorial Chapel was established within College Hall. It was under construction during George's tenure as Commandant. Ten years later, it was relocated to the then new College Church, St Michael and All Angels, which is situated near the south-east of College Hall.

A figure who features in an apparently innocuous way in the annals of Cranwell in 1949, George's first year as Commandant, is John Cairncross, one of the famous Cambridge Five group of spies and traitors. In 1949, the Air Ministry on behalf of Cranwell, were in regular correspondence with the Treasury where Cairncross held a relatively senior and influential position at the time, seeking sanction for the costs of appointment of laboratory assistants to Cranwell. In the correspondence, it is clear that Cairncross is adopting a typically hard Treasury line, resulting in much toing and froing between the two departments with not much quarter being given by Treasury mandarins.[33] In 1951, Cairncross admitted to MI5 to being a Soviet spy, after many years in such sensitive positions as the Cabinet Office, the Foreign Office, MI6, and the Bletchley Park Code Breakers. After the war, he joined the Treasury during which time, he claimed, he had ceased operating as a spy, although KGB reports suggest otherwise. From the time of his confession in 1951, curiously he was never prosecuted but he did lose his civil service position. After the disappearance of

Burgess and McLean to Moscow in 1951, there was clearly huge concern from officialdom over other Soviet moles in the system.[34] It was as late as 1979 that he was publicly exposed as the 'fifth man', during the public exposure of Anthony Blunt as the 'fourth man'. One can only surmise that the bland role of, inter alia, approving increases to staffing in the RAF's training college was the perfect cover for someone involved in the most covert of espionage. As this was at the height of the Cold War, the activities of Cairncross were treated as a major breach of security.[35]

Short was the period of George's appointment at Cranwell, as was the norm. It must have brought back nostalgic feelings to his time in the 1920s when he won the Sword of Honour there. Yet, duty called him elsewhere.

Some famous Cranwell Alumni
Prince Charles, Prince William, Prince Bandar of Saudi Arabia, Rory Underwood, Frank Whittle and Douglas Bader are among Cranwell's most famous alumni. George had played rugby with Bader for the RAF and like George, Rory Underwood also became a rugby international and Lion of considerable renown. In its 100 years of existence, Cranwell has had an impressive list of alumni.[36] Because Cranwell was only founded in 1919, many of the senior RAF leaders in the Second World War had started their careers either in the Army or Navy or in their respective Flying Corps. As time passed, however, Cranwell was to establish itself as the training ground for future senior members of the RAF.

Appointment to Air HQ Habbaniya, Iraq – 1950
In September 1950 immediately following completion of his period as Commandant at Cranwell, George took up his appointment in Air HQ Iraq as Air Officer in Command at the rank of Air Vice Marshal. He was based at RAF Habanniya.[37]

RAF Habbaniya was constructed on the west bank of the Euphrates and opened on 19 October 1936. As well as the airfield, the base included Air Headquarters of RAF Iraq Command, communication facilities, maintenance units, an aircraft depot, an RAF hospital, RAF barracks, the RAF Armoured Car Company depot and fuel and bomb stores.

George's predecessor was Alexander Gray who had served in in the post since 1946. For services during the War, Gray received the French Croix de Guerre and the Distinguished Flying Cross, retiring at the rank of Air Vice Marshal.[38]

Britain had been given protectorate powers over Iraq since the collapse of the Ottoman regime after the First World War. It had retained these powers and responsibilities during the inter-war years and during the Second World War. At times during that period, there were sporadic examples of disruption on behalf of local groups.

Because of fears during the Second World War that the Germans might break out through Egypt and the Suez Canal and thus threaten India and Britain's other possessions in the Far East, maintaining a secure defence in the Middle East was vital. At the time of George's appointment to Iraq at the beginning of the Cold War, while the nature of the threat had changed, the same logic held.

In 1948, the Iraqi government signed a new treaty of alliance with Britain, whereby Iraq was not to take any initiatives in foreign policy contrary to British directions. When the Iraqi prime minister returned from London having concluded this deal, a popular uprising took place in Baghdad, forcing his resignation and the repudiation of the treaty. In the following years, nationalist forces demanded nationalisation of the oil industry. This was the political context in which George arrived in Iraq. As a result, George's time in Iraq was nothing if not eventful. In the years 1950–51, there were several bombings aimed at the remaining Jewish community in Baghdad. In those years, several Iraqi Jews were killed, and their houses stormed. Some pointed to extreme Zionists seeking a *cause celebre*, while others blamed Arab extremists.[39] In 1952, another popular uprising occurred, carried out by students and 'extremists'. The police were unable to control the demonstrators, and the regent called on the army to maintain public order.

The chief of the armed forces general staff governed the country under martial law for more than two months. Although mainly civil power issues, this was the atmosphere in which George was to exercise his role as AOC in Iraq.[40]

Operational RAF squadrons were based at Habbaniya and many aircraft passed through in transit. Roald Dahl was stationed there in 1940, as described in his book, *Going Solo*. The base closed on 31 May 1959 when Britain finally withdrew following the July 1958 Revolution.[41]

Abadan Oil Crisis[42]

During George's tenure in Iraq, the Abadan Oil Crisis began. In 1951 with the nationalisation of the Anglo-Iranian Oil Company (AIOC) by the government of Iran, the British shut down the Anglo-Iranian Oil Company's huge oil refinery in Abadan. It ended with a CIA-orchestrated coup which overthrew the democratically elected government of Mohammed Mosaddeq in 1953, enabling the Shah to rule autocratically for the next twenty-six years.

Churchill's cabinet imposed a series of economic sanctions on Iran, directed the withdrawal of all British personnel from Iranian oil fields and blocked Iran's access to its hard currency accounts in British banks. The AIOC evacuated its technicians and closed down the oil installations, while the British government reinforced its naval force in the Persian Gulf and lodged complaints against Iran before the United Nations Security Council. The Royal Navy eventually blockaded Abadan.

On 25 July 1950, General Brian Robertson became Commander-in-Chief of Middle East Land Forces. George was to work closely with him throughout his tenure. Robertson had fought in the Desert War at the same time as George. In 1943, Robertson was awarded the distinction of Commander of the Order of Bath. He was also involved in the Tunisian campaign and helped plan and implement the Allied invasion of Sicily. In Italy, he was to become a trusted aided and administrator to Field Marshal Alexander.[43] Like George, he was also an ADC to King George VI.

Amidst this febrile atmosphere, nine months into George's appointment in June 1951 as AOC Iraq, he ordered No. 6 Squadron to Shaibah during the Abadan crisis. The UK ambassador to Persia at the time was Sir John Le Rougetel, an experienced diplomat who had served as High Commissioner to South Africa and Ambassador to Belgium.[44] Le Rougetel was replaced by Sir Francis Shepherd in 1951. Shepherd had served in the Great War and joined the diplomatic service in 1920.[45] Due to the oil dispute, Britain did not have an ambassador in place in the years 1952–53. Given the political ramifications of Air HQ's work in Iraq, close liaison by George with the embassy was important.

The crisis ended with the killing of the Iranian Prime Minister and the installation of the Shah, a friend of the West who stayed in power for twenty-five years until he experienced a not too dissimilar fate to his predecessor. Cool heads prevailed in Iraq and Iran, avoiding what could have become a major crisis.

Director-General of Personnel (1952–54)

George went straight from Iraq to be Head of Personnel Services of the RAF. Again, this was a standard staff job and suited to someone in the sunset years of his career. It was a clear contrast to his previous appointment in volatile Iraq. He was an Air Marshal now, so could consider himself one of the 'top brass' too.[46] Nothing notable is cited in the records about this period, except that the RAF was struggling to gain recruits, a challenge it had been facing for some time. Personnel management in the 1950s was a function without all the fancy 'bells and whistles' of Human Resources of the current day. That said, the RAF services were quite proactive in introducing methods to improve systems that assisted the productivity and welfare of their staffs.

RAF Transport Command (1954–55)[47]

The Head of Transport Command was George's second-last appointment before retirement. He took up the position in March 1954.[48] Compared with his stint in Iraq, this was far less political and far more predictable. In essence, it was one of oversight of a massive procurement and logistics operation.

During the Second World War, the Command at first ferried aircraft from factories to operational units and performed air transport. Later, it took over the job of dropping paratroopers from Army Co-operation Command as well. At its head during the War was Sir Frederick Bowhill, under whom George served towards the end of the war. Bowhill served as Air Officer Commanding-in-Chief at RAF Coastal Command, then as Air Officer Commanding RAF Ferry Command, where he identified the likely position of the German battleship *Bismarck*, using a Catalina flying boat, allowing *Bismarck* to be sunk. His last appointment was as Air Officer Commanding Transport Command in 1943 before retiring in 1945.[49]

After the Second World War, Transport Command increased rapidly in size. It took part in several big operations, including the Berlin Airlift in 1948, which reinforced the need for a big RAF transport fleet. The year following Beamish's move to another command, Transport Command were responsible for dropping men and materiel into the Suez Canal war zone in 1956. The principal RAF Transport Command functions of this period were support operations involving the evacuation of military personnel from the Suez Canal Zone prior to and after the Suez Crisis of 1956; casualty evacuation from South Korea during the Korean War and from Malaya during the Malayan Emergency; essential supplies to Woomera, South Australia, and ferrying personnel and supplies out to Christmas Island for the atomic bomb tests carried out by the UK. Even though Britain was not officially at war at the time, many of these operations were of a sensitive and important nature. Such critical operations as the Berlin airlift and the evacuation from the Suez Canal, however, linked the Command with major geopolitical events of the time, enhancing its critical role. It would be wrong for anyone to dismissively refer to Transport Command, as some did, as a mere 'taxi service'. In addition, Transport Command ran scheduled routes to military staging posts and bases in the Indian Ocean region, Southeast Asia and the Far East, to maintain contact between the UK and military bases of strategic importance.[50]

RAF Technical Training Command (1956–58)[51]

Technical Training Command controlled units responsible for delivering aircraft maintenance training and other non-flying training. In 1945, the Command had moved from Berkshire, to Brampton Grange in Cambridgeshire. George was appointed Head in September 1955. Although not as glamourous a position as some of his previous ones, it was to be George's final appointment before retirement. For someone with his devotion to duty, George brought as much effort to this as to any of his previous jobs. It was in this position that George was promoted to Air Marshal.

To someone who had devoted all of his adult life to the RAF, in peacetime and in war, it must have come as quite a blow finally to have to retire at the relatively young age of fifty-three. Many servicemen had gone on to serve as much older men and during the Second World War some had returned to serve having previously retired. Surviving the war was for George (as indeed, for any serviceman) a great blessing; in this regard, the memories of Victor's tragic early death would have been ever present. George's RAF activities had extended from Crete to the Desert War, to the direct service of the King, to command in Iraq and much else in between. He had also greatly enhanced the reputation of the RAF by his exploits on the rugby field at the highest levels. He was also officially recognised with a knighthood from the King and by honours from the US and the Greek Governments. As a member of a fledgling service established shortly before he was recruited, these were all considerable achievements. George and his brothers more than repaid the 'investment' in their future made by their father, Francis, all those years before.

The RAF emerged from the war with a hugely enhanced reputation, due not least to the quality of its pilots and its senior commanders. It is hard to believe that the RAF had only been in existence since 1918. Its role, particularly in the critical Battle of Britain and the dirt and dust of the Desert War helped on by the praise of Winston Churchill, etched that view firmly in the public mind. That Air Chief Marshal Tedder was to take the surrender of the German armed forces in 1945 highlights the esteem in which the RAF and its top commanders were held by Eisenhower and the Allied political leaders.

II

BEAMISH BROTHERS AND SISTERS

Although all four brothers were high-achieving individuals in their own right, it is also true that they were united by their family links. This was how many saw them and how they saw themselves. The two sisters, Eileen and Kathleen, also led fulfilled lives but without the same high-profile career and sporting achievements as the men.

George and his three brothers, Victor, Charles and Cecil, all served in the RAF, becoming known as the 'Flying Beamishes'. Such were their achievements that they became household names in RAF mess rooms up and down the UK.[1] Much has already been written about Victor, the dashing fighter pilot who met a tragic end in aerial combat over France in 1942. His exploits as an ace fighter pilot were plain for all to see.

Less focus, however, has been on the two youngest brothers, Charles and Cecil. Charles was, like George, an accomplished rugby international. Cecil was an excellent golfer. All were imbued with a sense of modesty and reserve; drawing attention to oneself was discouraged. Nothing was ever handed to them on a plate except the encouragement of their parents. Close family members attest to the fact that they all had bad tempers which they were able to control. One can only imagine the effect which the physically imposing George when stirred to anger could have on young callow cadets at

Cranwell. Victor, Charles and Cecil were all handsome men. George was more accurately described as large and imposing and was said to be awkward in the company of women.

It would be fair to say that the relationship between George and his brothers was generally cordial and formal rather than particularly warm. The biggest bonds between them were the careers they chose and the sports they played. This 'distance' was partly due to George's temperament, but it was also the norm among males of the time. No touchy-feely behaviour for George Beamish. It was said by close relatives that the brothers tended to speak with one another only if the need arose. Sometimes there were fallings out and long silences. One thing they had in common was a reluctance to talk about the war – a not uncommon feature of families at the time. For those veterans who lived in Ireland, there was a particular reluctance to discuss it. A more in-depth look at all three brothers will help in filling out the picture of the Beamish family dynamics.

Group Captain Victor Beamish

Like George, Victor was also born in Dunmanway, Co. Cork. He was born in 1903, two years before George. He attended the local Model School where his father Francis was headmaster.[2] By nature, he was a hardy young boy, keen on the outdoors. He was to retain that hardiness throughout his time as an RAF pilot. A notable feature was his humorous approach to life, something the more serious George lacked. Later on, Victor's colleagues at RAF North Weald and RAF Kenley would attest to his relaxed and independent approach to life, a feature that gave his superior and patron, Trafford Leigh-Mallory, constant headaches.[3]

Victor was the first Beamish to go on to secondary school at Coleraine Inst., immediately after which he joined the RAF, entering Cranwell in 1921. As a young man, Victor was encouraged by his father to read *The Times* where, tellingly, he first read about the exploits of the First World War airmen which helped inspire him to join the RAF.[4]

A useful rugby player, Victor did not rise to the same heights of the game as George or Charles; nevertheless, he did secure an Irish trial in the early 1920s. Like George, he showed talent across a range of sports at Cranwell, including rugby, hockey, athletics, boxing and golf. While with the RAF, he also played rugby briefly with Harlequins, Leicester and London Irish.[5] He was a useful boxer too. In an Inter-Squadron Boxing Competition in the early 1920s, he was pitted against and beat the younger George.[6] No quarter was given by either brother and afterwards, the Commandant of Cranwell, Air Commodore Longcroft was heard to say: 'You would never have known they were brothers.'[7]

Showing exceptional talent as a trainee pilot at Cranwell, Victor was appointed to an RAF Squadron in 1923. After several appointments in Britain, he transferred to India from 1925 to 1927. In 1927, he returned to Cranwell as a flight instructor, where he stayed until 1928. He was then transferred to Canada after which he returned to England in 1933, initially to RAF Hawkinge and then to RAF Uxbridge.[8] While at Uxbridge, Victor contracted TB and was obliged to retire. This was a huge blow at the time when TB was so virulent and before the arrival of antibiotics. His subsequent attempts to regain a commission echo the challenges faced by another famous fighter pilot, Douglas Bader, who also came up against the stony response of officialdom. Sheer persistence on both of their parts resulted in them achieving their goals. Both were later to become close colleagues and formidable fighter pilots.

Having recovered his health, Victor was reinstated with full flying status and posted to command No. 2 Armament Training Camp at RAF Aldergrove in Northern Ireland. He was then appointed to command No. 64 Squadron RAF at Martlesham, Suffolk, on 8 December 1937, and then Church Fenton.[9] Victor was promoted to Wing Commander on 1 March 1940 and returned to England to assume the station command of RAF North Weald on 7 June 1940.

Exploding the myth that no RAF aircraft flew over Dunkirk to provide aerial cover for the 1940 evacuation, Victor was himself a pilot there in a Hurricane, specifically on 5 June 1940. Many RAF aircraft were, in fact, deployed to the evacuation.

Victor's patron, Air Chief Marshal Leigh-Mallory, was anxious to ensure that his valuable Wing Commander remained alive. Thus, he discouraged and often forbade Victor from flying – but to little avail. Victor never felt happier than when up in the skies. He once confided to his sister Eileen that: 'I cannot send these boys to do anything I am not prepared to do myself.'[10] This was a measure of the man.

In the Battle of Britain, he flew an incredible 126 fighter sorties, many of them solo in a Hurricane. In 1942, at his own insistence, and at the age of thirty-eight, he was given another fighter station at RAF Kenley.

Victor was awarded the Distinguished Service Order and Bar and the Distinguished Flying Cross. He was formally awarded his DFC by the King in January 1941 and was given the honour of sitting beside the King at lunch afterwards.[11] After the war, George received Victor's ceremonial sword from the time when he was Personal Assistant to the Duke of Abercorn, the Governor-General of Northern Ireland. Victor's Bar to the Distinguished Service Order was awarded on 2 September 1941. Together with George's Sword of Honour, the Beamish family had two official swords in the family.[12]

Victor was also a regular choice by BBC Radio to give broadcasts after notable RAF actions and thus gained a wider public profile. Albeit governed by wartime censorship regulations, the broadcasts were seen as a useful communications tool to maintain public interest and support for the air war. They also attracted a fee, which was always helpful. At the height of his fame, Victor was photographed by the renowned photographer, Cecil Beaton.[13]

Victor was appointed to command RAF Kenley on 25 January 1942. Accompanied by flying ace Wing Commander R. F. Boyd, he took off on the morning of 12 February 1942 on a reconnaissance flight during which they chased two Messerschmitt Bf 109s before sighting part of the German Fleet making its 'Channel Dash'. The ships had been reported 10 minutes earlier by two pilots of No. 91 Squadron RAF, but the report had not been fully believed until such senior confirmation was received.[14] Churchill understandably wanted to know how the first enemy fleet since the Armada in the sixteenth century was allowed to pass through the Channel unchallenged. The 'Channel Dash' thus became the subject of the Operation *Fuller* Inquiry where RAF actions at the time were investigated and Victor himself was questioned and eventually exonerated.[15]

Although discouraged from flying, Victor had three kills in the early months of 1942 while based at RAF Kenley. On 28 March 1942, Beamish was leading the Kenley Wing flying a Spitfire with No. 485 Squadron RAF when he sighted a Luftwaffe formation just south of Calais. With him was friend and colleague Paddy Finucane. Beamish's Spitfire was attacked and damaged by a Messerschmitt. He was last seen entering a cloud near Calais. His body was never recovered. The atmosphere at Kenley in response to the shocking news was grim.[16]

Victor had confided to his sister, Eileen, that his only real dread was the fear of old age. In action, he was totally fearless. Eileen recalls driving Victor to Limavady airfield in Co. Derry in early 1942 after what was to be Victor's last leave home and that he had then had a premonition of his own death in action.[17]

Victor was dashing while George was more pedestrian in his approach. The analogy could be made with the Kennedy family. Joe Kennedy, the eldest son of Joseph and Rose Kennedy was also a fighter pilot who fought in the Second World War and like Victor, was also shot down and killed. Like Victor, he too was the apple of his family's eye. John, a US Navy officer and later to become US President, was the next brother down but not seen as quite as dynamic and heroic as his elder brother. Yet, he survived the war and went on to greater things. One could be talking about the Beamishes.

According to Douglas Stokes, Air Chief Marshal Leigh-Mallory called Victor 'among the greatest fighter pilots of all time'.[18]

This was no mean praise coming from the man who was in overall charge of the Allied D-Day Air Invasion of Normandy.

As the eldest brother and the pathfinder into the RAF, to his family the loss of Victor was heartbreaking. This loss extended to a wide circle of friends and fellow pilots. Of the RAF fighter pilots from Ulster, he was certainly the most illustrious.

Victor died shortly before George took up duty in the Western Desert Air Force where he was to distinguish himself. The responsibility for the remaining Beamish family now fell on George's shoulders. A less charismatic figure than Victor, yet a solid stalwart, he was the one the younger siblings looked up to after Victor's death. Another Beamish death in the highly dangerous environment of the Second World War would have left the Beamish parents inconsolable. Beamish *paterfamilias*, Francis, was a man in his late sixties at the time of Victor's death, suggesting that the family mantle would have passed on to George. With great relief, all the remaining siblings survived the war in rude good health as did both parents.

Group Captain Charles Beamish

Charles was the third of the four Beamish brothers. He also joined the RAF, and during the Second World War was a successful fighter pilot. In this respect, he was more like Victor than George. He rose to the rank of Group Captain by the end of his career, although he and members of his family felt he deserved further promotion.

Like his brothers, Charles was adept at picking up prizes. In his case, in 1927 he won Cranwell's Groves Memorial Prize for the best cadet in the air. Charles was to go on to become an excellent flyer. In 1928, Air Chief Marshal Trenchard, who maintained a keen interest in Cranwell, wrote to Charles' father, Francis Beamish, congratulating Charles on winning the Groves Prize and further commending Victor and George for their achievements. This was a great gesture by Trenchard which succeeded in cementing the Beamish family's further attachment to the RAF.[19]

In 1931, Charles was posted to Hong Kong where he spent a couple of years before returning to the UK in 1932.

An example of filial loyalty involving Charles came up during the time Victor was recovering from TB and seeking to return to the RAF in the mid-1930s. At the time, Charles was stationed at RAF Digby and had a word in the ear of Leigh-Mallory who arranged for Victor to be taken on.[20] This was only the beginning of Victor's renewed ascent to the heights of the RAF. It also forged a sound alliance between Victor and Leigh-Mallory, who was to become one of the most senior and influential men in the RAF. Leigh-Mallory was patron to Victor in the same way that Arthur Coningham later was to become the patron of George.

From 1941 to 1942, Charles was posted to the US as an RAF attaché, a posting he thought saved his life given the high fatality rates for pilots in the RAF. At the end of the war, he was sent to the Far East, responsible for the disbandment of troops.[21] His last RAF years were spent in the UK and in 1948, he retired. He died in 1984 of heart problems, a recurrent malady in the Beamish family.

Like George, Charles was an outstanding rugby player who played for both Ireland and the Lions. His club rugby included playing for NIFC in Belfast, Harlequins and Leicester. With Leicester, he and his three brothers set a club record for players from the same family, a record that was to last for almost sixty years. He was a leading player for Leicester as a prop from 1933.[22]

The following year, a royal Russian prince from St Petersburg, Alexander Obolensky, a prolific winger, also joined Leicester. An exotic figure on the landscape, Charles played with him at the club for a number of years. While Charles played for Ireland, Obolensky went on to have a magnificent career for Oxford and for England. Both he and Charles played for a Midlands side and a Leicestershire/East Midlands side against the All Blacks in 1935.[23]

In 1936, three Leicester men were selected to tour with the Lions. These were Obolensky, Beamish and Gadney who was captain. Obolensky's RAF connection was another bond with Charles and the other Beamishes.[24] Sadly, however, Obolensky was also the first rugby international to be killed in the Second World War. As an RAF pilot, he died when his Hawker Hurricane crashed on a training flight early in the war.

In 1933, Charles gained his first international cap for Ireland against Wales. He turned out in the position of prop and played with his brother George, who was captain of the side.

Charles played twelve times for Ireland and between 1934 and 1938, and nine times for the Barbarians. In 1935, he played on the championship-winning Irish side and later that year, he was selected to play against the touring All Blacks. Despite scoring a try (his only international try and a rare occurrence for a prop) it was not enough, however, to beat the New Zealanders.[25] On the strength of his international performances, he was selected for the Lions Tour to Argentina in 1936. Charles was also a keen shot, a good golfer and keen fisherman.

Like George and Victor, he was born in Cork, attended the Model School and Coleraine Inst. and was a recruit at RAF Cranwell. He died near Templemore in Co. Tipperary in 1984 at the age of seventy-five and is buried in St Mary's Churchyard in Templemore. His wife, Josephine, died in 2017 and she is survived by his son Victor and daughters, Pam, Jo and Valerie. Charles' daughter, Valerie, was a goddaughter of George's. She recalls George making efforts to keep in touch by visits to their home in Tipperary. She also keeps the family flame alight by maintaining a series of family scrapbooks recording events over the years.

Air Vice Marshal Cecil Beamish

Cecil Beamish, the youngest of the four brothers, served in the RAF during the Second World War and was later Director of RAF Dental Services, 1969–1973. Thirteen years separated him from his eldest brother, Victor. He was born in 1915 and died in 1999. He married relatively late in life and had his first child at age forty-two.

Like his elder brothers, he was an accomplished rugby player, playing for London Irish, the RAF and Leicester. His joining

Leicester as the fourth Beamish brother was to set a record that stayed in the club until the twenty-first century. He played for the club up until the outbreak of war in 1939. He also formed the nucleus of a solid Leicester side in the immediate post-war years, bringing his evident earlier experience to the team.[26] It was golf, however, at which Cecil was to excel.

Like all his brothers, Cecil also passed through the excellent academy of Coleraine Inst. He was the first of the Beamishes to pursue a specific profession through the RAF, that of dentistry. He became the Head of the RAF Dental Services from 1968 to 1973.[27]

His golf career was outstanding. He was five-times winner of the RAF Golfing Society's Challenge Cup and, incredibly, seven times winner of the RAF Individual Championship over a period of twenty-four years, 1949–1973, making him the most successful RAF golfer in history.

A very capable administrator, Cecil was Chairman of the Royal Air Force Golfing Society and was captain of the RAF team for many years through the 1960s until his retirement in 1973. Outside the Air Force, Cecil's golf record was also stellar. He was an Irish international, Irish amateur champion and winner of several other amateur events.[27]

With the kinds of expertise and achievements of all the brothers, whether in the RAF or in sport, it is not surprising that they were so well known 'up and down the country'. RAF duties and sporting activity naturally sat comfortably with one another. At the same time, the flexibility and tolerance of the RAF in its treatment of its sporting high-achievers must be recognised. In the era when tours to New Zealand, Australia and South Africa might last many months, the RAF and other services also had to forego the services of their sporting stars for long periods.

In the case of George, his 1930 Tour to New Zealand and Australia lasted for six months. In Charles' case, the 1936 Argentina Tour took three to four months. Cecil who was more prolific at golf than rugby, still was allowed time to play in many key amateur tournaments. The Beamish brothers and many others were rightly seen as RAF assets who could be afforded a few indulgences.

Listowel and the 'Flying Beamishes'

Victor was killed in action in 1942, George died in 1967, Charles in 1984 and Cecil in 1999. When the Listowel Military Tattoo decided in April 2016 to commemorate the 'Flying Beamishes', it had been seventy-four years since all four brothers had been brought together. Given Victor's expertise as a heroic fighter pilot, he received star billing at the Listowel event, even though it was organised with all four brothers in mind. As the only brother to fly a Spitfire, he inevitably attracted the most attention.[28]

George was not a noted aviator but made his mark in many other important ways in the RAF. Charles, who reached the rank of Group Captain and was a noted pilot, did not, however, achieve the same heights as a pilot as elder brother Victor. Equally, Cecil was attached to one of the key ancillary professional services of the RAF with very little scope to engage in the 'derring do' seen by Victor. On paper, there is very little to dispute the sheer drama and excitement of Victor's war record.

A full-size replica *Spitfire,* painted in Victor Beamish's colours, was unveiled by the members of the Beamish family who travelled to Listowel for the event. The Spitfire also passed over the Beamishes' old home town of Dunmanway in a fitting tribute to Victor, and indeed his brothers and sisters who also served.[29]

Beamish Family Connections

George remained a bachelor all his life. He was survived by two brothers and two sisters as well as several nieces, nephews, grand-nephews and grand-nieces. His brother Charles settled in Co. Tipperary with his family. His youngest brother, Cecil, settled in Scotland where, inter alia, he was able to indulge further his passion for golf on some of the finest courses in the world.

George's first sister, Eileen, married and settled in Northern Ireland. For most of her career, she was RAF Dental Officer in Derry at the rank of Flight Lieutenant. She had two daughters, Gail and Roseanne, both of whom live in England.

George's younger sister was Kathleen. Her fiancé died during the war and she remained unmarried, although she had a wide circle of friends and interests, mainly through her golfing interests. She was very devoted to her extended family and took care of her brother George in his dying days. Kathleen continued the Castlerock tradition by remaining there after George died. Also a keen and accomplished golfer, she was a regular sight on the links at Castlerock and a Lady President at that club as well as at Royal Portrush. Eileen was a single handicapper until her seventies and had been Ladies' Captain at Portstewart and Whitehead golf clubs in Northern Ireland. It was Kathleen who was responsible for amassing George's voluminous papers after his death and transferring them to the National Archives at Kew and at the RAF Museum at Hendon.

The Beamish name remains with Cecil's two sons, David and Michael, who live in Scotland, as well as Charles' son, Victor, and daughter, Val, the former in Scotland and the latter living in Ireland.

Although they were not a close family in the sense of being physically near one another, the Beamish family did have a strong sense of all being Beamishes. George himself was emotionally undemonstrative but at the same time, dutiful to his family. By all accounts, he was a dutiful godfather to his niece, Valerie, the daughter of his brother Charles.

The relationship between the brothers were not always harmonious but this did not deter good relations among the next generation down. Charles had some difficulties with George, but he got on well with Victor – a situation not untypical of families. Victor had the 'JFK glamour effect' as the brother who died in his prime, revered by all his family.

Kathleen shared living at 'Rocklea' with George, until she moved out in the 1960s to her own accommodation. It would be fair to say that George was not always the easiest and the arrangement arrived at was seen as acceptable to both.

Interestingly, it appears that the Beamishes had no contact with cousins left behind in west Cork. The break with Dunmanway in 1912 was a clean one when Francis Beamish took his family north. This was not surprising given the distance between the two. In that era, many Irish people who emigrated across the Irish Sea to Britain regularly lost contact with family in Ireland. Moving the full length of Ireland into quite a different culture also provided its own sense of distance.

The wider Beamish clan who settled in Dunmanway in the 1640s, however, have gone to all corners of the globe over the decades and centuries. Some went to Canada, some to Australia and New Zealand, some too to the United Kingdom. In England, there is even a cluster of Beamishes in the Durham area.[31] Long distance emigration like that was not rare for the populace of west Cork, particularly since the Famine. One surviving relative was Frank Beamish, the grandson of Francis's brother who attended the 2016 Listowel Event and had this to say: 'I am very proud of the Beamish story and it is fitting that we remember them and all they achieved both in the air and on the sports field.'[32]

In the immediate post-war years, the village of Castlerock would, allowing for wartime censorship, certainly have been aware of the roles of all the Beamish siblings in the war. George, an Air Marshal and a knight, retired to Castlerock and would have been regarded with some reverence by the local community there. His selection as High Sherriff in 1962 was a great honour to him, his family and to Castlerock.[33] An avowedly Protestant and unionist village with a small number of Catholics living there, there was no mistaking Castlerock as true blue loyal to King and Country.

The last of the immediate Beamish family to pass away was Kathleen in 2014 in a nursing home in Castlerock. She was a well-known figure in the Castlerock community over many years and was closely committed to all her family members.

This impressive family owes much to the far-seeing ambition and determination of their father Francis and mother, Mary. The parents' commitment to education and hard work were the touchstones also of all their children.

One Air Marshal, one Air Vice Marshal, two Group Captains and two Flight Lieutenants – an impressive tally for one family. Their father, Francis, died relatively young but their mother, Mary lived a little longer to see all her children's progress in their careers. It was not surprising that they were well known in RAF stations 'up and down the country'. It is only right, therefore, to treat them as one family entity given their common background, outlooks and careers.

A New Era of Tolerance and Acceptance

Over the years, there had been a reluctance among the Beamishes to talk about matters relating to their military service. This applied to the direct family, sensing the political climate in the South was not yet ready to accept aspects of their tradition. It also applied to more distant cousins reticent about drawing too much attention to themselves. For the first time, these issues were aired in an open, inclusive, informative manner at the Listowel event. Similar events since then, particularly those under Ireland's 'Centenary Decade' (1912–22) suggest that the old inhibitions are gradually dying away. The Beamishes served Britain in war, but there was also no doubt about their pride in their Irish roots.

One of the great features of this era of more openness and transparency about Irish participation in the two World Wars is the greater knowledge and understanding it has generated among families about their own families. This is particularly so with the Beamishes.

The six siblings were tightly united together through their common service in the RAF, yet many of their relatives and fellow countrymen found coming to terms with their histories, challenging. Opening up the book of history has the benefit of laying everything out on the table: no secrets, no evasions. This is not to say that the Beamishes had major 'secrets' to hide: they just came from a more reserved and reticent era.

The barrier to understanding in my estimation was more on the other side: from those who were too fearful of acknowledging more complex narratives and multi-layered histories. Now the genie is out of the bottle, thankfully there is no putting it back.

12

RETIREMENT TO CASTLEROCK

George retired from the RAF in 1958 at the age of fifty-three. Even in that era, it was a relatively young age at which to retire. Few could argue, however, that he did not deserve his retirement or that he had not contributed considerably over the years. There was no doubt that he would settle in Castlerock. No world cruises or safaris for George Beamish. The golf links of the north Derry and north Antrim coasts awaited him.

George retired at a time when the British and European economies were just beginning to move towards a path of growth after the privations and scarcities of the post-war era. Economic progress was quite visible by the early 1960s. World geopolitics, however, were still set rigidly by the tone of the Cold War. In 1958, the Soviets had launched 'Sputnik', a key statement in the superpower battle. Yet, a new era seemed to beckon with the election of John F. Kennedy in 1960. As a military man, George would have been acutely aware of the potential dangers of the Cuban Missile Crisis in 1962 which tested the young President's mettle.

The 1960s was also the era of the hippies and 'the Summer of Love', a phenomenon Air Marshal George was unlikely to have had much truck with. Not too many ex-military men, indeed, would have seen eye-to-eye with that part of the counter-culture. George would have certainly been aware of the US Civil Rights movement, seen as a precursor of civil rights in Northern Ireland.

Yet, things were changing in Northern Ireland. In 1963, Terence O'Neill took over from Lord Brookeborough as premier and was to usher in a more liberal era in Northern Ireland, involving meetings with two Southern premiers, Seán Lemass and Jack Lynch, for the first time since Partition. In the cruel environment of Northern Ireland politics, these bold gestures eventually involved O'Neill paying with his job.

In the year following George's retirement in 1959, the RAF saw the last operational flight of a Sunderland – an end of an era.[1] The Sunderland was the flying boat that had carried General Freyberg and himself during the evacuation of Crete in 1941. In the year before George's retirement, the first British hydrogen bomb was exploded in the Pacific Islands by an RAF Valiant – an indicator that the Cold War remained.[2] As events were to show, the 1960s were to prove an explosive decade on many levels. It involved the escalation of the Viet Nam conflict from the mid-60s and Israel's military victories in the Six-Day War in 1967. Ironically, George was to die of a coronary in the same year as Christian Barnard performed the first successful heart transplant in Cape Town. It was also the era just before the Ulster Troubles were ignited in 1968 in Derry, the year following George's death. While he would have seen the Troubles largely as a 'law and order' issue, George's moderate unionism would have been far more akin to the tolerance of O'Neill than to Paisley.

At only fifty-three years of age, George was far from being an old man when he retired. Much was happening in the world and there was much to keep him occupied. A long and happy retirement seemed to beckon.

The Charms of Castlerock

Castlerock was a very peaceful seaside village which experienced none of the violent outbreaks seen in other parts of the province. In George's time, there were no Troubles and the village was peacefulness itself. On a clear day, you could look across the sea and see the west of Scotland. Further west, the coast of Donegal was easily visible. It was a fairly remote village and its lifeline was being on the main Belfast–Derry train line. It had a post office, a general grocery shop, a hotel, a small petrol station/hardware store, a hairdresser, a newsagent, a fish and chipper, a couple of cafes, a pub, a mobile home park, a few tennis courts and a few Bed & Breakfast establishments. Latterly, it even had a public swimming pool. It had neither a bank nor a library but had weekly visits from Coleraine of a mobile bank and mobile library. The pace of life was slow and peaceful with no desire to change things.

From where George lived on the main street, it was a short walk to the main amenities of the small village. The Church of Ireland building was a few doors down and the post office was just across the road. Further into the village was the Golf Hotel, Taylor's grocery and Cargan's newsagents which doubled as a fish and chipper by night. The train station was situated at the entrance to the village on the main Belfast to Derry line. From there, the golf club was only a stone's throw away.[3]

A refreshing addition to village life from the world of academia was Professor Norman Gibson, a professor of economics at the New University of Ulster at Coleraine. Gibson took an expansive view of the economic and political opportunities open to Northern Ireland, trying to move discussion beyond traditional sectarian mind-sets. He also had good relations with government and academia in the South. Although he was different in his outlook, he was a welcome and popular member of Castlerock life.[4]

Golf on his doorstep

By the time of George's retirement in 1958, Castlerock had a fine golf course, mobile home parks and a resident population of between 200 and 300, which has grown to considerably above that since the 1950s. It has also attracted people from all around Ulster, from Scotland, England and from south of the border.

In George's retirement, when he had the time to play more golf, a triumvirate were to dominate the international game for many years to come: Arnold Palmer, Gary Player and Jack Nicklaus.

All three were to provide George and many others with interest and entertainment as TV golf became more widely available.

An Ulsterman, Fred Daly, who grew up in George's beloved Portrush, became the best Irish player of his era. Daly as the professional at Royal Portrush Golf Club, knew George and all the golf-mad Beamishes very well. Daly was the first Irishman to win the Open Championships in 1947 and the first to play in the Ryder Cup. He remained the only Irish winner of the Open until Pádraig Harrington won it in 2007 and the only Northern Irish major winner until Graeme McDowell won the US Open in 2010. In 1946, Daly won the Irish Open at Portmarnock, becoming the first Irish winner; 1948 was another successful season when he won three events. He was also an eleven-time winner of the Ulster Professional Championship and a winner of the Canada Cup with Harry Bradshaw. He died at his Belfast home of a heart attack at the age of seventy-nine, one of the great golfers of his era.[5]

George's local club, Castlerock Golf Club was founded in 1901. A course expert from St Andrew's was engaged and the original eighteen-hole Mussenden course was designed by the famous Scot, Ben Sayers. Advanced for its time, there were two ladies on the club's inaugural committee. The course was eventually designated a woman's championship course by the Irish Golfing Union where many good female golfers played, including George's two sisters, Eileen and Kathleen. The land for the course was provided by Sir H. Hervey Bruce and Colonel Bruce, scions of Downhill, thus cementing further the family's long-standing association with Castlerock. The course tends not to get the same attention as the more illustrious near-neighbour courses of Portstewart and Portrush, yet to Irish golf legend, Christy O'Connor, it was a 'hidden gem' when he first discovered it in the 1950s.

The Beamish family were leading lights at Castlerock Golf Club, either as players or officially/administratively. George, Cecil, Kathleen and Eileen had all been captains of the club in their day. Kathleen had been Lady President on three occasions. George was fortunate enough to have a stroll of no more than 200 yards from his home at *Rocklea* to the club – the dream of many a retired man. Castlerock's simple layout allowed for such easy access.

The club has had a largely happy and peaceful passage through the years. One exception was an event that took place during its early years. Tragically, a fire consumed the golf clubhouse in 1913, but the prescient and courageous Michael McDevitt, brother of George's close friend Patrick, managed to salvage the Castlerock Cup from the showcase before it was destroyed. Such was the degree of local industriousness that a new clubhouse was completed by July 1914 just as the storm clouds of war gathered over Europe. The controversial introduction by the club of Sunday golf in the 1920s, created some local tensions resulting in damage to some of the greens. Since then, however, the club has had a trouble-free existence.[6]

George Beamish was also a member at Royal Portrush and Royal Portstewart. Like Castlerock, Portstewart was also in County Derry. Portrush was only a short distance further along the coast, but in County Antrim.

Royal Portrush Golf Club was founded in 1888 as 'The County Club'. In league tables of the best Irish courses, it tends to come in second place after Royal Co. Down, yet Portrush has its equally strong devotees. The Open Championship was staged at Royal Portrush only once, in 1951 where Max Faulkner won his only major championship. In that year, Cecil Beamish came a creditable third place among the amateurs. The Open returned eventually to Portrush in July 2019, long overdue.

By the time of the 2019 Open, it was seventy-two years since Northern Ireland had last seen Open Championship golf. The Ulster troubles were the major reason for this. Royal Portrush 2019 has been successful in providing a huge boost commercially for golf, tourism and trade.[7]

Royal Portstewart was founded in 1894 and redesigned by Willie Park Jnr in the 1920s. This championship links course hosted many major amateur and professional championships over the years. It has somewhat stood in the shadows of its neighbour,

Royal Portrush, yet it receives a steady stream of visitors from across the world. To its west, can be viewed Castlerock and to its east, Portrush. All the Beamishes kept connections with both clubs.[8]

Political Overtures

In 1959 as he settled into retirement, George received the proverbial 'tap on the shoulder' from the 'men in grey suits'. These were the grandees of the Ulster Unionist Party looking for a suitable candidate to run in that year's Westminster election. The saga revolved around the deselection of the Ulster Unionist MP for North Belfast, H. Montgomery Hyde, in 1959 and which nearly saw George entering Northern Ireland politics. The year 1959 was a general election year and the North Belfast constituency Unionists were in search of a suitable candidate. George was encouraged to throw his hat in the ring. George's own constituency was Derry/Londonderry, but there was no vacancy there at the time and he was considered a good candidate for the Belfast constituency.

The reasons for Montgomery Hyde's deselection were intriguing. He was attacked for supporting legislation to decriminalise homosexuality in the UK which was being debated in the House of Commons that year. In 1959, this was too much for the deeply religious people of Ulster to accept and thus, the unionists of North Belfast sought a more 'sound' MP to represent them. Montgomery Hyde had been their MP since 1951.[9] It was said at the time that the real reason for Hyde's deselection was for his casting doubt over the sexual orientation of King William of Orange. This imputation had been around for a long time, but never before had a member of the party dedicated to the legacy of King William's political settlement ever voiced such a view. As if Ulster politics wasn't complicated enough, the atmosphere was to be further clouded by doubts over King Billy's sexuality.[10]

One of George's friends, Patrick McDevitt, offered his advice on whether he should enter politics by saying: 'Don't go near that lot'.[11] George did not heed the advice and went ahead to the selection convention anyway. The attractions of George as a candidate were the fact that he represented good traditional Ulster values, he fought in the war and was an illustrious sportsman.

Two candidates came before the selection convention: George Beamish and Stratton Mills. Mills narrowly won, was duly elected in the General Election and represented the constituency until 1974. Mills, in time, became disillusioned with his unionist colleagues, leaving to join the Alliance Party in the 1970s.[12]

Temperamentally, George was unlikely to have warmed to the dissembling and double-dealing necessary in the work of a politician. He was too much of a straight arrow and took the selection convention decision in his stride. The decision not to go into politics – a decision that was essentially made for him – was probably the best for George in retrospect. History has shown that not all military men make that transition to politics despite pressures to do so from the public. Shakespeare's Coriolanus and US General Douglas MacArthur are good cases in point. Perhaps, Patrick McDevitt's advice was right all along.

Rugby Interests

In his retirement, George obviously had more time to devote to leisure pursuits. Among these interests was following his beloved sport of rugby. After his retirement from the game, he was appointed an RAF rugby selector which maintained his direct interest in the game. He was also an avid follower of the then Five Nations Championship in the era before Italy joined to make it the Six Nations.

In George's early retirement years, he would have been pleased to see fellow Irishman, Ronnie Dawson, being selected for the captaincy of the 1959 Lions Tour to New Zealand and Australia. Indeed, since George's own participation on the 1930 Tour, as well as Dawson, there had been two other Irish captains of the Lions, Karl Mullen and Robin Thompson. In more recent years, four more Irishmen have been added to the list – Willie John McBride (1974), Ciaran Fitzgerald (1983), Brian O'Driscoll (2005) and Paul O'Connell (2011).

A figure who cannot have passed George unnoticed was Bill McLaren, doyen of rugby commentators with the BBC from the early 1950s to the early part of the twenty-first century. Proud Scotsman yet a great internationalist, modest and warm, unpretentious and a cornucopia of rugby knowledge, McLaren was cut from the kind of cloth likely to have impressed George. At the time of George's death in 1967, McLaren had many of his best career years to come, but even in the early 1960s, McLaren's would have been a big feature of BBC rugby coverage, his delivery notable for its Borders Scottish burr.[13]

Fellow Lion and Irish international, Ronnie Dawson, stood out in the rugby of the late 1950s and early 1960s. Few could have failed to admire the talents of Tony O'Reilly, particularly in his Lions appearances. Although his career had ended by the time of George's retirement, Jack Kyle was the fly half of his era and accorded star status.

Willie John McBride, fellow Ulsterman, Lion and Irish international, was almost a latter-day George Beamish in physique and presence. Syd Millar was also built from the same cloth. Mike Gibson, the player's player, had a talent recognised across the world. The last four mentioned were all Ulstermen like George.

George met the young Willie John McBride several times as he lived and worked not far from George. Before McBride's departure on a Lions Tour to New Zealand and Australia in 1966, George met Willie John to provide encouragement and give advice for the challenges to be faced 'down under'. Following the 1966 Tour, George and Willie John had further chances to confer until George's death the following year.[14]

A talented player with a short career who George would have admired was another Ulsterman, Ken Goodall. Goodall played for the City of Derry and was capped several times. People in the late 1960s talked about Goodall as if it was the 'Second Coming', until he committed the sin of all sins at the time of migrating to rugby league.

For someone who had experienced the game at the very top, George was in a strong position to gauge the quality of new talent.[15] With his death in 1967, George missed out on the surge in international rugby marked by brilliant Welsh rugby teams of the late 1960s and 1970s and the Lions series wins in both New Zealand (1971) and South Africa (1974).

Rugby in the Professional Era

There is always the danger for the biographer of engaging in the game of 'What if?' with his subject. Wild speculation is to be avoided, yet there is a difference between that and intelligent, informed, evidence-based speculation. Knowing a little about the man, his times and his values can help in this endeavour.

George came imbued with all the trappings of an amateur player in a strongly amateur era. Those who played professional rugby were shunned by their rugby unions. By the time of his death in 1967, rugby union was firmly amateur with no pressures to change. How might George have reacted at the change to professionalism at the top of the game after the 1995 World Cup? Those who recall the change will acknowledge how swift the transition appeared to be. There had been no long period of pressure for change in advance; it just seemed to happen in the wake of the 1995 World Cup. Because of the many examples of hypocritical amateurism that abounded, the change was seen by many as a good thing.

On the principle of the merits of professionalism, one feels that George would have resisted initially, yet would have come around to the idea over time – as did many people. His long career in the services would suggest that he was aware how little was to be gained from going against the flow.

High Sheriff of County Londonderry

George was appointed by the Queen to the position of High Sherriff of the County of Londonderry/Derry in 1962. The appointment was for one year. His appointment was in keeping with previous choices of senior former military figures, politicians or other local worthies for the role. This was the second occasion on which George was called to 'royal service' during his career. Towards the end of the War, he spent nine months as Air ADC to George VI. Thus, he would have been no stranger to the role of protocol and ceremony in his new job.

Since the selection of a Hervey Bruce in the early twentieth century, George was the first person from Castlerock to have been chosen as High Sherriff. His immediate predecessor was Colonel Sir Michael McCorkell and his immediate successor, Vice Admiral Sir Arthur Richard Hezlet, in keeping with the tradition of military selection.[16] Nearer the present day, a successor of George's as High Sherriff was Jean Caulfield MBE who made a career with Age Action NI and who held the office from 2015–16. Coincidentally, she was also from Castlerock and one of George's next-door neighbours. She and her husband lived in the same house formerly owned by the McGilligan family, one of the leading families formerly resident in Castlerock who moved south after Partition. Mrs Caulfield recalls many encounters over the years with the redoubtable Sir George.[17]

One can imagine George applying his total commitment to the role of High Sherriff. While temperamentally he may not have been the 'ceremonial' type, his RAF training would have imbued in him a sense of 'proper form' and in truth, it was not an unduly onerous role.

In his retirement, George bought a small farm in Co. Donegal just across the border. Donegal is a popular holiday spot for people in Northern Ireland given its remoteness and its breathtaking views. His close friends, the McDevitts of Castlerock, had bought a house in the scenic village of Fahan which offered convenient breaks from Co. Derry. It was, thus, for George, a logical move. George's land purchase did not prove a wise investment as the tractor he used to plough the land would not plough over a water meadow on the plot. As a result, George sold it on again six months later.

His investments in the famous local Bushmills whiskey distillery, however, did prove a success as the company went from strength to strength. It was situated not too far from Castlerock. Bushmills holds the distinction of being the oldest extant Irish whiskey distillery in the world. Fond of an occasional tipple himself, George was a good advertisement for the product.

In his retirement, George was often sought out for advice and comment on a range of matters. For example, a writer from Salisbury, Wiltshire, wrote to George in 1959 asking for clarification of details regarding General Freyberg's controversial role in the Battle of Crete. Freyberg was held responsible for not heeding the message in *Ultra* intercepts of when the Germans were to land in Crete.[18]

George also had an impressive address book which included the details of some of the most senior members of the RAF with whom he interacted during his career. To this day, the leather-backed book is still in pristine condition.

A picture of George in his retirement would be incomplete without reference to his trusty dog, Jim. Jim was fiercely loyal to George and was known to chase the young paper boy away from 'Rocklea' if he was late in his delivery. Jim was George's loyal wingman. Pets are said sometimes to take on characteristics of their masters and mistresses. Certainly, Jim was his master's voice! George also had a number of hunting dogs who assisted in the collection of lost golf balls along the Castlerock links course. These beasts might have helped contribute to George's rather fearsome image.

George's Death

George died of a coronary thrombosis on 13 November 1967 at home in Castlerock. As well as his heart problems, he also had debilitating long-term bone injuries from his rugby days which affected his mobility in the final period of his life.

George, by nature, was a hearty eater and a hardy warrior. Family sources attest to the considerable amount of nourishment provided right from the start to the Beamish children by their mother, Mary. Right to the end, George continued with a substantial propensity for food. Even in his retirement, his regular visits to the golf course would have required substantial fuelling. Like most military and sporting men of the era, he would have had little time for health advice that interfered with his lifestyle. A pipe was usually either in his mouth or by his side. A glass of whiskey was also not too far away. A modern-day doctor might have encouraged him to take a few sessions on the treadmill, an idea that would have been preposterous to the rough and ready George. Stent technology, so common now in the treatment of heart disease, was not available then. Overall, the great shame was that he died so soon after his retirement and with so much remaining in him to offer to life.

A year before George's death, he received a touching letter from a former RAF colleague, Jack Wheeler, who served under George at RAF Benson in Oxfordshire. Wheeler extolled George's qualities of leadership and integrity as his CO at Benson and offered to take him to lunch if he happened to be in London. In any era, it is always heartening to receive such 'positive feedback' and for George who was never too demonstrative emotionally, particularly so.[19]

To put his passing in an historical perspective, George died fifty years after the Russian Revolution and 100 years after the Disestablishment of the Church of Ireland, the church he and his family belonged to. It was also the year that the Beatles released *Sgt Pepper's Lonely Hearts Club Band* – a fact that George would have been blissfully unaware of from his perch at 'Rocklea'. Long hair and loud music would not have been George's form.

It was also in that year that one of the most esteemed RAF figures of the Second World War and a man who had the highest regard for George and the rest of Coningham's Desert team, Marshal of the Royal Air Force, Lord Tedder died. Tedder was seventy-six when he died, bringing home how relatively young George was at sixty-two when he died. Tedder suffered the tragedy of losing his wife in an air crash in Egypt in January 1943 – sharing with George the tragedy of having lost a close family member in the air.

George had been ill for some time, however, and in that period that his sister Kathleen came back to 'Rocklea' to look after him. At that time, much less was known than today about the dangers of heart disease. This was particularly so in relation to diet and lifestyle factors. George enjoyed tobacco and was also partial to an 'Ulster Fry' or two. Yet, he had led an exceptionally fit life both as a rugby player and as an active RAF officer. In his final years, he was also an active golfer. On the other hand, there was already a strain of hereditary heart disease among the Beamishes.

Interestingly, George VI for whom George acted as Air ADC, also died of a coronary thrombosis fifteen years before George. He was only fifty-seven. Like George, he was a smoker, a known strong risk factor. The condition was far more prevalent in that era before the availability of wider public information on heart disease. Countries like Ireland and Scotland notably had very high rates of coronary disease by international standards in that era.

Although George lived beside Castlerock's Church of Ireland church, he was buried beside his mother, Mary, at St Paul's, Articlave, about 2 miles from Castlerock. Many years later in 2014, George's remains were joined at St Paul's by those of his youngest sister, Kathleen. A number of days after his death, the *Coleraine Chronicle* gave a long obituary extolling George's life.[20]

Of the other Beamish siblings, Victor was killed in action in 1942 flying over northern France; his body was never found. Charles is buried in Tipperary and Cecil is buried in Scotland. Eileen is buried in Northern Ireland.

The fiftieth anniversary celebrations of the establishment of the RAF took place in 1968, several months after George's passing. How he would have liked to have been at those celebrations held in Abingdon, Oxfordshire. The centenary celebrations in 2018 would also have met with his approval.[21]

In his final will and testament, George left £1,919 – a substantial sum in 1967. He also established a Trust Fund for his nephews and nieces amounting to £16,803 to be activated in 1970. One of these beneficiaries was his niece and goddaughter, Valerie Beamish, the daughter of his younger brother, Charles. Also, in his will were shares for a number of blue-chip companies including: ICI, Distillers, British American Tobacco and Marks and Spencer.[22]

In his passing, Britain and Ireland lost quite an exceptional figure. His life and career depict a sportsman of the highest calibre. He rose to the top of his profession as an RAF officer, serving his country in challenging roles both in peacetime and in war. He may not have been one of nature's diplomats, but his organisational and man-management skills as well as his physical and moral courage, inspired trust at the highest levels and ensured his rapid rise through the ranks of the RAF. His qualities were recognised not only by the British Government, but also by the US and Greek governments for his service during the Second World War.

From Dunmanway, through Castlerock, Cranwell, international rugby tours, through Crete, El Alamein, Royal palaces, Iraq and back again to Castlerock, it was quite an eventful life.

EPILOGUE

Looking back on George Beamish's RAF career raises many questions about the reasons for Irishmen joining the British services during war. In George's own case, factors such as service, allegiance and loyalty would have loomed large. Many others joined for the excitement and travel. Others simply needed the money.

According to the British government, 42,665 Irish citizens volunteered for service with the British armed forces in the Second World War. Research by Richard Doherty suggests that the real figure may have been as high as 66,000.

Throughout the Second World War, the ex-unionist section of the population of southern Ireland proved a reliable source for recruitment. These citizens continued to regard themselves as being part of the British Empire and had a strong sense of allegiance to the King. Typical among this intake were the sons of middle-class Protestant families who had strong family and educational ties to England; for them joining up 'was something that was taken for granted'. Irish officers such as Sydney Watson and Brian Inglis had attended British public schools and knew friends and relatives who were joining up or were enduring the 'Blitz'. In such families, it was common to regard men of military age who stayed in neutral Ireland as 'white feathers' or cowards. There were many reasons why Irish officers decided that the Second World War was their war. Among the officers, a few were idealistic, some were patriotic, some were naïve, and almost all were very young. Their decision to volunteer sometimes derived from a romanticised understanding of what war was like, while for others it came after long consideration of the possible consequences. In short, there was a wide mixture of motives among Irish officers who went to war, as outlined above.[1]

George and his colleagues in the military left a legacy that was ignored and rejected for many decades in Ireland. A fortunate combination of circumstances, however, has helped change the atmosphere into a more positive one. That legacy is now being embraced as part of a more inclusive national narrative in Ireland. The centenary of the 1918 Armistice was marked by many commemorative events in recognition of the contributions of many Irishmen and women. As part of that more inclusive narrative, a large, dramatic metal sculpture of a First World War soldier was erected in the centre of Dublin in the autumn of 2018 to commemorate the war. Despite a minority negative sentiment, the Irish public responded very positively. On their autumn 2018 Tour of Britain and Ireland, the New Zealand All-Blacks placed a wreath in memory of Dave Gallaher, the captain of the first All-Blacks in 1905/6, at a First World War memorial in Dublin. Gallaher was a Donegal native – the county adjacent to George Beamish's home county of Derry – and was killed at Passchendaele (the Second Battle of Ypres) in 1917. The 1905/6 All Blacks are often referred to as the best All Blacks ever. Gallaher's effective captaincy style was said to have been honed during his time fighting in the Boer War.

By temperament, George was quite taciturn and stubborn. Nor was he brimming with social charm. However, he was a good organiser, a 'details' man who required things to be done properly. He was driven by duty – something inculcated in him and his siblings by their mother, Mary. In this light, you can see why his superior officers, such as Coningham, had such high regard for him. Two of his nieces have recollections from their youth of Uncle George always being in his study. He was a serious man and this element of being 'at a distance' was probably in keeping with the man.

George's cousin Ian Beamish from Limerick has remarked how George always seemed to be 'brewing tea'.[2] Knowing George, it probably came in large solid mugs rather than in dainty china. Even in the Western Desert, he became famous as a prodigious tea drinker and was said never to be happier than when he had his tea and his pipe in front of him.

A test of a person's life is often what legacy they leave. George left definite marks on the RAF and on the world of rugby. Within these worlds, there were the mini-worlds of Cranwell, Leicester Football Club, Irish rugby and the Lions fraternity. Not often mentioned, however, is his legacy in Northern Ireland. He and his siblings brought great kudos to Northern Ireland, which in turn responded with pride to their achievements. Religious and political tolerance were also the hallmarks of George Beamish, reflected in his wide base of friends.

He did not leave a family of his own, but he would have been the first to recognise that as a single-minded bachelor and 'man's man', he was probably not made for traditional family life. To some extent, this was compensated for by having a wide family network and throughout most of his career, the RAF was his effective 'family'.

The countryside surrounding George's home and place of rest is not unlike that of Dunmanway, a town surrounded by large tracts of agricultural land some miles from a medium-sized market town. It was as if the wheel of his life had come full circle. He had started out his life in the same town as the famous GAA man and republican Sam Maguire. He migrated from one of the southernmost towns on the island to one of the northernmost. In the process, he met many and achieved much. A meeting between George and Sam as mature men would have been interesting. Their origins were similar, but their individual paths were so divergent.

Would there have been a meeting of minds? It is hard to say. Perhaps the era in which they lived was too close in time to allow for common ground and reconciliation. Could Sam have forgiven George for joining the 'Crown forces'? Equally, could George have accepted someone so directly anti-British? Over time and age, one feels that there would have been some degree of mutual acceptance.

George's sport of rugby had always held a strong position in Cork, the county of his birth, long before George's era. Now, the province of Munster attracts huge support from people of all traditions. Sam's GAA has also gone from strength to strength. Both trends indicate the easing of acrimony and tension and the fact that sport can be a powerful unifying force. The 2004 Six Nations appearance of an English rugby team at Croke Park was welcomed by all, but it might have been a step too far for republicans like Sam Maguire who remembered the atrocities carried out by British forces at the ground in 1920. Reconciliation inevitably takes time.

In this era of professional rugby, we will no longer see a figure like George Beamish again. The ability to pursue a dual life as a professional airman and as a rugby international simultaneously is now a thing of the past. The Corinthian values of people like Beamish so entwined in the amateur game, moreover, have been replaced by the imperatives of professionalism. His 'star' quality may not have been evident from the beginning of his career but evolved gradually over the years. This would have included his award of the Sword of Honour in 1924 and his ascent through the ranks of Leicester, Ireland and Lions rugby.

As he and his brothers were well-known in RAF circles by the 1930s, by the time he was appointed to work with Coningham in the Western Desert Air Force in 1942, he had a reputation that preceded him. He was fortunate to have had excellent chemistry with Coningham. A strong bond of trust and mutual respect developed between the two which was vital in one of the critical theatres of the war.

George would have been happy at the 2016 Listowel Event, particularly at how far Ireland had come in celebrating its broadly patterned past. It would have also been an opportunity to renew contact with his west Cork relatives.

Being innately conservative, he would have had little time for many of the changes of the 1960s, his twilight years. George might have been bemused by certain innovations in the military over the years. The impact on air warfare due to modern technology would surely have impressed him. George, essentially a technocrat by nature, was interested in whether something 'worked' and less in its provenance. How he would have reacted to the arrival of, for example, the drone is a moot point, but he might have taken a poor view on its dispensing with the need for airmen.

Importantly, George embraced the concept that one could be a proud Ulsterman, an Irishman and British all at the one time. For a long time, many would have seen all three together as being incompatible. 'Official' Ireland has now come around to accepting this more complex reality. In turn, a more mature appreciation of Irish achievements has been evident in Britain. Repressing wider and deeper truths is never healthy and it is clear that Ireland itself has benefited hugely from finally 'welcoming into the parlour' people of the background and traditions of George Beamish.

APPENDIX 1

THE BEST FIVE NATIONS PLAYERS OF THE 1920s/ EARLY 1930s ERA

Eugene Davy was an outstanding outside half whose international career for Ireland (1925/1934) coincided almost exactly with that of George Beamish. His combination with scrum-half Mark Sugden is thought by many to have been the most effective in Irish rugby history. He was a stalwart player for Lansdowne FC in the 1920s and 1930s.

In a career spanning thirty-four caps, he scored eight tries and three drop goals. He also managed an Irish team on tour to Australia and became President of the IRFU in 1967/68.

Jack Bassett was a Welsh fullback who played fifteen times for his country. Along with George Beamish, he was selected for the 1930 Lions Tour of New Zealand and Australia. He was first capped in 1929. He had an outstanding tour in 1930, gaining the accolade of the best fullback in the world, having outwitted the great George Nepia on the tour. He faced much criticism after Wales lost to the touring South Africans in 1931 and in his last international match against Ireland the following year, with the Triple Crown in sight, he missed a conversion to win. He never played for Wales again.

Douglas Kendrew was capped ten times for England at prop and was also selected to tour with the Lions on their 1930 Tour. Like George Beamish, he played for Leicester. During the Second World War, he saw action in North Africa and Italy and was awarded the DSO on three occasions for his bravery during that period. In 1963, he was appointed Governor of Western Australia and, later, was made an Honorary Colonel of the SAS.

Sir Carl Douglas Aarvold played on sixteen occasions for England in the centre. He played five times in Tests for the Lions on the 1927 and 1930 tours respectively. He captained England on six occasions. A barrister who became Recorder of London, he presided at the 1965 trial of the infamous Kray twins. In the Second World War, he served in the Royal Artillery and reached the temporary rank of Lt Colonel. He also had the distinction of being President of the Lawn Tennis Association.

Harry Bowcott was first capped for Wales in 1929 while still at Cambridge University. The following year he was selected captain of Wales. He played for Cardiff and London Welsh in succeeding years and was also selected to play on the Lions 1930 tour. On that tour, he played in twenty of the twenty-seven matches and in all four Tests. He partnered Carl Aarvold, also an ex-Cambridge man, in the centre. In his two encounters against Ireland in which he faced George Beamish on both occasions, Wales drew once and lost the second match. Harry Bowcott was the last surviving member of the 1930 Tour, passing away in 2004 at the age of ninety-seven.

Mark Sugden of Dublin club, Wanderers RFC, was capped twenty-eight times for Ireland, making him the country's most capped scrum-half until that figure was exceeded in 1993. He missed only one international between his debut and his final appearance against Wales in 1931. He was considered one of the best scrum-halves ever to play for Ireland and in combination with outside half, Eugene

Davy, formed a lethal pairing. Owing to work commitments, he was, like many others, compelled to turn down a certain selection for the 1930 Lions Tour. Sugden is also credited with inventing the dummy pass and is said to have played in the greatest back line ever for Ireland. George Beamish had the honour of playing in that side. Sugden was also an accomplished cricketer, playing alongside playwright Samuel Beckett for Trinity College, Dublin.

John Siggins was a fellow Ulsterman who played for Belfast Collegians and whose international career started as George's was ending. Like George, he was a No. 8 and was selected to captain Ireland on nine occasions between 1934 and 1936. He played on the same Irish team as Charles Beamish. In 1955, he was appointed to manage the Lions Tour to South Africa. The Lions were captained on that tour by Inst. and Ireland forward Robin Thompson and included the illustrious Tony O'Reilly who made such a mark on the tour.

Bernard Gadney was a scrum-half for Leicester who gained fourteen caps for England between 1932 and 1938. He captained his country on eight occasions from 1936, including that memorable victory against the All Blacks in Twickenham the same year. He also captained the Lions to Argentina in 1936 where the Lions won the series 10–0. Included in that party was Charles Beamish, his fellow Leicester player. During the Second World War, Gadney served in the Royal Navy.

Doug Prentice of Leicester was a close club associate of George Beamish who went on to play for England and to captain the Lions on their 1930 Tour. He played lock, No. 8 and prop and was a good placekicker. While he gained three caps for England and two for the Lions, he also made his name as an administrator when he served as secretary of the RFU between 1947 and 1962. During the Second World War, he served in the Royal Army Service Corps and was taken prisoner.

Willie Welsh was a Scottish player who was capped twenty-one times for his country and played for the Lions on the 1930 tour. He was the only Scot on the tour. A fellow tourist, Welshman Ivor Jones, described him as 'one of the truly great forwards' and a famous rugby commentator, Bill McLaren rated him very highly. A fellow man of the Borders like McLaren, Welsh was said to have been an inspiration to McLaren for his interest in rugby from an early age.

Harry Greenlees was a fellow Leicester player who also played 153 times for Leicester and six times for Scotland. On his debut for Scotland in 1927, the Scots beat the touring Australians at Murrayfield, 10–8. He was appointed Leicester captain in the 1931/32 season while George was still playing for the club. Greenlees was one of a host of Leicester players who reached their potential with international honours.

Roy Kinnear was a Scot contemporary of Beamish who played for Heriots and was capped three times for Scotland and four times for the Lions. He was one of a small crew who defected to rugby league where he prospered. Like George Beamish, he fought with the RAF in the Second World War. In 1942, he collapsed and died while playing rugby for the RAF.

Fernand Taillantou, French international, was born in 1905, the same year as George Beamish. All three of his caps were in 1930. His first cap was against Ireland in Belfast, a match George also played in. Taillantou's career was cut short by a tragic incident. Playing club rugby in 1930, he tackled a young player, Michel Pradie, causing his death from spinal injuries. Taillantou was convicted of manslaughter but was given a suspended sentence of three months in prison plus a 250-franc fine and costs. Many believed the conviction was far too light, even though it was purely an accident. It cannot be said that the individuals George played against were not intriguing.

Despite contrasting social backgrounds, **Yves du Manoir** was a man who had a lot in common with George. A keen rugby player who played for Racing Club and represented France, he was interested in a range of sports. He also showed the dedication to join the French air force. His first cap was against Ireland in 1925 in Belfast, also the date of George Beamish's first cap. On that day, Ireland took the honours, a rare credit in the history of their head-to-head encounters. A flamboyant man, de Manoir was chosen as the man of the match that day. On the day, de Manoir was asked to play for France in Scotland in 1925, he had to decline because of an air force exam involving an actual air flight. Shortly after take-off, the aircraft crashed and killed him. His French colleagues were distraught when they heard the news after the Scottish match. In recognition, Racing Club named its ground after him. De Manoir was without doubt a player with a great future before death tragically took him.

APPENDIX 2

IRISH RUGBY INTERNATIONALS WHO SERVED IN THE SECOND WORLD WAR

Charles Hallaran fought and died in the Second World War serving with the Royal Navy. He played for Ireland fifteen times between 1921 and 1926, overlapping with George at the end of his career and the beginning of George's.

Major Edward William Francis De Vere Hunt served in the Royal Artillery and died in 1941 during the Japanese attack on Hong Kong. He played five times for Ireland between 1930 and 1933, playing on several occasions with George.

Group Captain Reginald Vere Massey Odbert died in 1943 and played once for Ireland in 1928 against France in Belfast. Like George, he too was an RAF man.

Wing Commander Patrick Bernard Coote won one cap against Scotland in 1933, the very last international season for George. Coote died on 13 April 1941, having been shot down in a Bristol Blenheim by a group of Messerschmitts in Greece. Like George, Coote was also an RAF man and represented the service in many illustrious victories. He also played for Leicester on twenty-seven occasions. With his RAF, Leicester and Ireland connections, he had much in common with George, although he was a bit younger in age.

There were several Irish rugby internationals who played for Ireland at around the same time as George who served in and survived the Second World War, as follows:

W.F. Browne played for Ireland twelve times and served in the Duke of Wellington Regiment.

H. McVicker played five times for Ireland and served in the Royal Army Medical Corps.

H. J. Sayers served in the Royal Artillery and won five caps.

V. J. Pike won thirteen caps and served in the Royal Army Chaplain's office.

H. H. Withers with five caps served in the Royal Engineers.

APPENDIX 3

FAMOUS FIGURES INVOLVED IN RAF INTELLIGENCE IN THE SECOND WORLD WAR

Sarah Churchill worked closely on the interpretation of photographs for the 1942 invasion of North Africa, Operation *Torch*. She also attended the Tehran and Yalta conferences with her father.

Christopher Lee was accepted into RAF Intelligence in 1942, spending time in the Suez Canal Zone and Ismailia. Lee's squadron saw action in Egypt, Libya and Tunisia, providing air support to ground forces and bombing strategic targets. After the Axis surrender in North Africa in May 1943, the squadron moved to Zuwarah in Libya in preparation for the Allied invasion of Sicily. They then moved to Malta, and, after its capture by the British Eighth Army, the Sicilian town of Pachino and then Agnone Bagni. Lee was also attached to Special Operations Executive, the Long-Range Desert Group and the SAS during the war.

Denis Wheatley was part of a team that secretly co-ordinated strategic military deception and cover plans. His literary talents led to his working with planning staffs for the War Office. He wrote numerous papers for the War Office, including suggestions for dealing with a possible Nazi invasion of Britain. After the war, Wheatley was awarded the US Bronze Star for his role in the war effort.

Michael Bentine was not physically qualified for flying and was transferred to RAF Intelligence and seconded to MI9, a unit that was dedicated to supporting resistance movements and helping prisoners escape. His immediate superior was the Colditz escapee and future Conservative politician Airey Neave. At the end of the war, Bentine took part in the liberation of Bergen-Belsen concentration camp, an experience which affected him deeply.

APPENDIX 4

MAIN RAF SQUADRONS INVOLVED IN THE BATTLE OF CRETE

No. 805 Squadron – Formed in February 1941 to support a planned invasion of Rhodes, off the coast of Turkey, held by Italians. Squadron leader Lt Cmdr Alan Black Fleet Air Arm. Based at Maleme in north-eastern Crete. That seems to have been the Brewster's only sortie from Crete. When German paratroopers overran Crete at the end of May, the Brewsters were apparently left in the boneyard.

No. 203 Squadron – After the Italian declaration of war in June 1940, No. 203 became heavily involved in the East Africa campaign before moving on to Crete to cover the evacuation of the beleaguered island. The Squadron flew anti-shipping patrols around the Middle and Far East with a variety of aircraft types including Baltimores, Wellingtons and Liberators.

No. 80 Squadron – In February 1941, No. 80 Squadron started to convert to Hurricanes and after evacuation from Greece, the Squadron spent a period in Syria, Palestine and Cyprus before returning to the Western Desert in October flying patrols in the area until the Battle of El Alamein. With the retreat of the *Afrika Korps*, No. 80 was given the task of providing air defence of the long line of communication and coastal convoys supplying the Eighth Army until January 1944 when the Squadron moved to Italy.

No. 30 Squadron – In November 1940, the squadron was sent to Greece to use its Blenheims in both the bomber and fighter roles, but in March 1941 the squadron was re-designated as a fighter unit. After the fall of Greece and the Battle of Crete, it was evacuated to Egypt.

No. 33 Squadron – At the outbreak of the Second World War, No. 33 moved to the Western Desert and took part in active action beginning with the entry of Italy into the war in June 1940. Conversion to ground attack Hurricanes was completed some six months later. With the exception of a time in Greece and Crete in 1941, 33 Squadron remained in the Middle East for most of the Second World War. Equipped initially with the Hurricane, the squadron flew in support of the Army in the Western Desert, including at the Battle of El Alamein before returning to the UK in April 1944 and receiving Spitfires.

No. 112 Squadron – On 16 May 1939, No. 112 reformed aboard the aircraft carrier *Argus* at Southampton for transportation to the Middle East, arriving in Egypt ten days later. Gladiators were received in June and when Italy joined the war a year later the Squadron flew fighter patrols over the Western Desert. In January 1941 No. 112 moved to Greece to provide air defence and fly offensive patrols over Albania. When the Germans invaded Greece, the Squadron provided fighter cover for the Athens area until evacuated, initially to Crete and then back to Egypt.

On 22 April 1941, No. 112 Squadron was ordered to leave for Heraklion, Crete. When the squadron arrived at Heraklion only six of its fourteen *Gladiators* were serviceable. It was decided to send one flight back to Egypt therefore, and on the toss of a coin the eight pilots of 'A' Flight flew out in a Bombay, the flight's ground crew following by sea next day. Ten pilots remained under Flight Lieutenant Fry, hoping to receive early reinforcements of Hurricanes; their strength was rapidly augmented by the arrival of six new pilots from 1430 Flight, recently arrived from East Africa, under Flight Lieutenant J. E. Dennant.

No. 230 Squadron – The basing of Sunderlands from the squadron at Souda Bay for April and May 1941 were intended to assist in evacuating troops from Greece to Crete and from Crete to Egypt. Further reinforcements came with the move out of Greece of the squadrons that had been operating there.

APPENDIX 5

LUFTWAFFE FIGURES IN NORTH AFRICA (1940–3)

Eduard 'Edu' Neumann commanded the famous *Jagdgeschwader 27 'Afrika'* during the North African Campaign from 1941 to 1943.

In the space of three weeks *I. Gruppe, Jagdgeschwader 27* was rocked by the deaths of its three top aces: Marseille, Stahlschmidt and Steinhausen. Morale fell so low that the *Gruppe* was withdrawn to Sicily in October. It returned briefly to North Africa but was withdrawn from the theatre for the final time on 6 December 1942.

Hans-Joachim Marseille known as the '*Star of Africa*', was renowned for his aerial battles during the North African Campaign. With 158 victories, no other pilot claimed as many Western Allied aircraft in North Africa as Marseille.

On 1 September 1942, he claimed seventeen Allied aircraft kills. For this he received the prestigious Knight's Cross of the Iron Cross with Oak Leaves, Swords and Diamonds. A month later, Marseille was killed in a flying accident after his aircraft suffered engine failure.

As Marseille began to claim Allied aircraft regularly, on occasion he organised the welfare of the downed pilot personally, driving out to remote crash sites to rescue downed Allied airmen. JG 27 was moved out of Africa for about a month because of the impact Marseille's death had on morale.

Werner Schröer, the fighter ace credited with shooting down 114 enemy aircraft was the second most successful claimant of air victories after Marseille. However, the end in Africa was nigh, and his Group was evacuated to Crete and the Aegean islands. He was decorated with the Knight's Cross of the Iron Cross with Oak Leaves and Swords.

Hans-Arnold Stahlschmidt was credited with fifty-nine victories against the Allies in North Africa. On 7 September 1942, Stahlschmidt led a *Schwarm* on a fighter sweep south-east of El Alamein. They intercepted a reconnaissance Hurricane but failed to notice another Spitfire and trapped between both flights, two Me 109s were shot down, including Stahlschmidt's. After a search, Stahlschmidt was posted as missing in action. He was the third-highest scoring ace of the war behind Marseille and Schroer. On 3 January 1944, he posthumously became the 365th recipient of the Knight's Cross of the Iron Cross with Oak Leaves.

Günter Steinhausen was a flying ace with forty combat victories to his name and a posthumous recipient of the Knight's Cross of the Iron Cross. He was awarded the *Ehrenpokal der Luftwaffe* (the Honour Goblet) on 5 August 1942, and then the German Cross in Gold on 21 August. On 6 September 1942, on an early morning patrol, Steinhausen shot down a Hurricane near El Alamein for his fortieth victory. However, he was then himself shot down. His body was never recovered.

APPENDIX 6

KEY RAF SQUADRONS UNDER OPERATION *TORCH* (1942–3)

No. 92 Squadron In February 1942, the Squadron was posted to Egypt to join Air Headquarters Western Desert to support the Allies on the ground. No. 92 Squadron provided air cover at the Battle of El Alamein and on 18 April 1943, eleven Spitfires from the squadron flew at the 'Palm Sunday Massacre' during which approximately seventy axis aircraft were disabled or destroyed.[4]

Following the Allied victory in North Africa, the Squadron moved to Malta in June. It went on to provide air cover for the Eighth Army during the campaigns in Sicily and Italy. No. 92 Squadron then followed the armies up the Italian coast as part of No. 244 Wing and No. 211 Group. During the Second World War the Squadron claimed the highest number of victories scored, 317, in the RAF. For most of 1942, it was commanded by the highest-scoring Australian ace of the Second World War, Clive Caldwell who, in turn, was succeeded by Billy Drake, the second-highest behind Caldwell.

Eight aces had served in the squadron, including future Air Marshal Arthur Coningham.

No. 72 Squadron outfitted with Spitfires moved to assist in the evacuation of Dunkirk in 1940. After the Battle of Britain, the squadron was then moved to North Africa to support the Tunisian campaign.

At the start of Operation *Torch* the squadron operated from Gibraltar, before moving to Tunisia. The squadron then advanced with the Allied armies, moving to Malta in June 1943 to prepare for the invasion of Sicily, then in the next month to Sicily and to Italy in September 1943.

No. 93 Squadron reformed in June 1942, as a fighter squadron equipped with the Supermarine Spitfire. After the success of the Allied landings, the squadron moved to North Africa, where it provided fighter cover for the First Army in Algeria and Tunisia. After the end of the campaign in North Africa No. 93 Squadron moved to Malta, and supported the invasions of Sicily and Italy.

No. 112 Squadron. In January 1941, the squadron joined Allied forces in the Battle of Greece. It later took part in dogfights as part of the air defence of the Athens area. With the defeat of the Allied campaign on the Greek mainland, No. 112 Squadron withdrew to Crete and then to Egypt, where it rejoined the North African Campaign, supporting the Eighth Army. For much of the remainder of the war, the squadron was part of No. 239 Wing.

No. 249 Squadron. On 16 May 1940, 249 equipped with Hurricanes, fought in the Battle of Britain. In May 1941, the squadron was transferred to Malta by aircraft carrier. There it formed part of the fighter defences, converting to Spitfires in February 1942. Fighter bomber missions over Sicily began in November 1942 and in October 1943 the squadron moved to Italy.

No. 94 Squadron spent the Second World War serving as a fighter squadron based in and around the eastern Mediterranean. In

May 1941, the squadron finally began to receive its Hurricanes, and in the next month it passed its Gladiators on to the South African Air Force. The Hurricanes were used to fly defensive patrols over Egypt, before in November the squadron moved to the Western Desert, where it became a ground attack unit. In February 1942, the Hurricanes were replaced with Curtiss Kittyhawks. The squadron was not happy with the Kittyhawk, and so in May 1942 it passed its aircraft over to No. 2 Squadron, SAAF, along with several of the pilots including Edwards, and converted back to the Hurricane. Once again, the Hurricanes were used to fly defensive patrols, at least until the period after the battle of El Alamein. At this point, with the Allies advancing west, the squadron was used to provide fighter cover for the essential coastal convoys.

APPENDIX 7

RAF ACES IN
THE DESERT CAMPAIGN

Before the Desert War, **Group Captain Dudley Honor** was a fighter pilot in the Battles of France and of Britain and during the German invasion of Crete in 1941. In January 1941, he ferried his single-engine aircraft across the desert over Nigeria, Chad and the Sudan to Egypt where he joined No. 274 Squadron as a flight commander in the Western Desert. Honor took command of No. 274 in August 1941, and four months later In December 1941, he was promoted to wing commander to lead No. 258 Wing and shot down an Italian fighter near Tobruk. He served on the fighter operations staff in Malta before landing in Sicily and then in Italy.

Group Captain Clive Robertson Caldwell was the leading Australian air ace of the Second World War, credited with shooting down twenty-eight and a half enemy aircraft in the North African Campaign. He was the highest-scoring Allied pilot in North Africa and was awarded the Distinguished Flying Cross and Bar. When Caldwell left the theatre later that year, the commander of air operations in North Africa and the Middle East, Air Vice Marshal Arthur Tedder described him as: 'an excellent leader and a first class shot'. Caldwell claimed twenty-two victories while in North Africa flying P-40s. Caldwell spent the remainder of the War in the South Pacific.

William 'Cherry' Vale was credited with thirty enemy aircraft shot down making him the second highest scoring Hurricane and biplane pilot in the RAF, in after Marmaduke Pattle. Based in Egypt at the beginning of the war, Vale flew operations over the Libyan border and was awarded the Distinguished Flying Cross in March 1941 and Bar in July 1941.

Having previously been awarded the DFC for action in Norway, **Kenneth Cross** was appointed Officer Commanding No. 252 Wing in the Middle East. In January 1943, he was made Air Officer Commanding No. 212 Group and in February 1943 took over No. 242 Group. He made quite a mark as a Group Captain in the North African campaign.

During Operation *Overlord*, he became Director of Overseas Operations (Tactical) in June 1944. After the war, he went to the Air Ministry as Director of Weapons and then as Director of Operations (Air Defence). He went on to be Air Officer Commanding No. 3 Group in 1956, Air Officer Commanding-in-Chief Bomber Command in 1959 and, following his promotion to Air Marshal in 1961, Air Officer Commanding-in-Chief Transport Command in 1963. This latter post was also held by George Beamish in the mid-1950s. He received decorations from the French, the US, the Dutch and the Norwegians. Cross's appointments in the War were mainly operational, compared with George who held mainly staff positions.

No. 92 Squadron: In February 1942, the Squadron was posted to Egypt to join Air Headquarters Western Desert to support the Allies on the ground. Personnel arrived in Egypt in April, but no aircraft were available. Some pilots flew operations with Hurricanes of No. 80 Squadron. Spitfires finally arrived in August and the squadron commenced operations from RAF Heliopolis over the El Alamein sector. No. 92 Squadron provided air cover at the Battle of El Alamein. On 18 April, eleven Spitfires from the squadron flew top cover at the 'Palm Sunday Massacre' during which approximately seventy-five Axis aircraft were disabled or destroyed. Following the Allied victory in North Africa, the Squadron moved to Malta in June. It went on to provide air cover for the Eighth Army during the campaigns in Sicily and Italy, arriving on Italian soil on 14 September 1943. No. 92 Squadron then followed the armies up the Italian coast as part of No. 244 Wing and No. 211 (Offensive Fighter) Group. During the Second World War, the Squadron claimed 317, the highest number of victories scored in the RAF. No. 601 Squadron had battle honours at El Alamein.

German Air Squadrons

Jagdgeschwader 27 was a fighter wing of the *Luftwaffe* during The Second World War. It served in the North African Campaign, supporting the *Afrika Korps*. It had at its service some of the most prolific aces in the Second World War and for much of the Desert War, its kill rate exacted heavy costs on the Desert Air Force.

I. Gruppe, was deployed to Libya to support the *Afrika Korps*, arriving at Gazala during in April 1941. Under the command of Eduard Neumann, it flew its first combat missions over Africa on 19 April, claiming four Hawker Hurricanes, the *Gruppe's* 100th claim of the war for the loss of a single Bf 109 on 19 April. By December, the whole wing was in North Africa.

The unit had an immediate impact on the campaign, which had up until then been dominated by the Desert Air Force. *JG* 27 provided Rommel's army with fighter protection for virtually the whole Western Desert campaign, from late 1941 until November 1942.

Fighting against the Desert Air Force's generally inferior Hawker Hurricanes and Curtiss P-40s, which were often flown by inexperienced and under-trained pilots, the Bf 109s inflicted heavy losses, although serviceability in the harsh conditions and chronic fuel shortages greatly reduced the effectiveness of the unit. It was only with the arrival of sufficient numbers of Spitfires and B-25 bombers to the Desert War that the Allies were able to turn the tide and assert air supremacy.

With the start of *Afrika Korps* offensive, on 26 May, JG 27's fighters were called to play a decisive role during the Battle of Gazala. Aces, Marseille and Schultz played key roles in terms of kills.

In August, a *Schwarm* (group of four) from *5./JG 27* chanced upon a *Bristol Bombay* transport of No. 216 Squadron RAF. The *Bombay* was carrying Lt Gen William Gott, who had been appointed Commander of the Eighth Army only hours previously. Gott and a number of crew members were killed by a strafing gun. His death led to the appointment of Bernard Montgomery and the rest was history.

In late 1942, the Allied superiority in numbers began to tell. In the space of three weeks, *Jagdgeschwader* 27 was rocked by the deaths of three top aces: Steinhausen, Stahlschmidt and Marseille.

Understandably, high combat fatigue and low morale meant the *Stab*, *I.* and *III. Gruppen* of *JG* 27 were withdrawn to Sicily in October, to operate over Malta. They returned briefly to North Africa but then the whole of *JG* 27 was withdrawn from the theatre for the final time in December 1942.

Most of *JG* 27 avoided the final defeat of Axis forces in Africa, in Tunisia. After withdrawing to airfields in western Cyrenica, and having abandoned a large number of its aircraft along the way, the unit passed the remainder of its aircraft to *JG* 77 and were then evacuated from North Africa on 12 November. *II./JG* 27 remained nearly a month longer, based at Merduma airfield. During that month the *Gruppe* lost three pilots killed for six Allied fighters destroyed.

Most historical attention on the Desert War has tended to focus on Rommel and his *Afrika Korps* with the Luftwaffe generally regarded as playing an ancillary role. The *Luftwaffe*, however, always posed a potent threat, particularly with their Me 109s, despite the achievement of air superiority by the RAF in the theatre. Their senior air figures and fighter pilots were of the highest calibre. It was one of the tasks of the small group invited to Coningham's office/caravan each evening including George to guess the thinking and likely strategy of these eminent adversaries.

But what distinguished the Desert Air Force from the *Luftwaffe* was the unity of command under Tedder and Coningham unlike the volatility of Goering and his difficulties with Kesselring. The German efforts in North Africa, moreover, were dominated by the persona of Rommel with the Luftwaffe playing a less prominent role. By contrast, the Allied effort was collegial and co-operative and supported from the very top (Tedder-Coningham and Alexander-Montgomery).

Key *Luftwaffe* Figures in Desert War
Field Marshal Kesselring held the position of Commander-in-Chief South and it was to him that Rommel reported. Kesselring had experience in the army as well as the *Luftwaffe*. His commands during the Second World War included all the main theatres: Poland and France, the Battle of Britain, North Africa, Italy and Operation *Barbarossa*.

Like many ex-Army officers, he tended to see air power in the tactical role, providing support to land operations. Interdiction and close air support were operations that suited the *Luftwaffe's* pre-existing approach to warfare; a culture of joint inter-service operations, rather than independent strategic air campaigns.

He strove to organise and protect supply convoys to provide forces in the Desert with necessary resources. He succeeded in establishing local air superiority and neutralising Malta, which provided a base for British efforts to interdict Axis convoys headed for North Africa. Kesselring managed to deliver an increased flow of supplies to Rommel's *Afrika Korps* in Libya. With his forces thus strengthened, Rommel prepared an attack on the British positions around Gazala, while Kesselring planned Operation *Herkules*, an airborne and seaborne attack on Malta, attempting to secure the Axis line of communication with North Africa.

Kesselring and Rommel had a disagreement over the latter's conduct in the Battle of Bir Hakeim, blamed on poor co-ordination between the air and army and resulting in the evacuation of Bir on 10 June 1942. Later Rommel's successful assault on Tobruk on 21 June helped improve relations.

Following the campaign, Kesselring was awarded the Knight's Cross with Oak Leaves and Swords. In October 1942, he was given direct command of all German armed forces in the theatre except Rommel's German-Italian Panzer Army in North Africa. After the loss at El Alamein, Kesselring was to face the full might of the Allies' Operation *Torch* and the landings in Sicily and Italy, marking the gradual collapse of the Nazi war effort.

After the war, Kesselring was tried for war crimes and sentenced to death for ordering the murder of 335 Italian civilians. The sentence was subsequently commuted to life imprisonment and in 1952 he received an early release on health grounds.

Source: The Memoirs of Field Marshal Kesselring.

Details of those major Luftwaffe figures in the North African campaign under Kesselring are set out at Appendix 5.

BIBLIOGRAPHY

Andrew, C. and Mitrokhin V. *The KGB in Europe and the West – The Mitrokhin Archive*, Penguin Books, London, 2000.

Brooks, Stephen. *Montgomery and the Battle of Normandy*, Army Records Society, Sutton Publishing, Stroud, 2008.

Beevor, A. *Crete – The Battle and the Resistance*, John Murray Publishers, London, 1991.

Bowyer, Chaz. *History of the RAF*, Hamlyn, London, 1977.

Brereton, Lewis H. *The Brereton Diaries – The War in the Air in the Pacific, Middle East and Europe, 3 October 1941–8 May 1945*, William Morrow and Company, New York, 1948.

Chisholm, Hugh, ed. 'Calvados'. *Encyclopædia Britannica (11th ed.)* Cambridge University Press, 1911.

Connolly, Kieran. *Sam Maguire: The Man and the Cup*, Mercier Press, 2017.

Cullen, P. V. *A Stranger in Blood: The Case Files on Dr John Bodkin Adams*, Elliott & Thompson, London, 2006.

Davenport-Hines, Richard. *Enemies Within: Communists, the Cambridge Spies and the Making of Modern Britain*, William Collins, 2018.

Evans, B. *The Decisive Campaigns of the Desert Air Force 1942–1945*, Pen and Sword, 2014.

Hancock, R. *Flight Cadet: Royal Air Force College Cranwell*, Pentland Press, London, 1996.

Farmer, S. and D. Hands. *Tigers 1880–2014: Official History of Leicester Football Club*, The Rugby Development Foundation. Polar Print Group, Nov 1993.

Gladman, B. W. *Intelligence and Anglo-American Air Support in World War Two: The Western Desert and Tunisia, 1940–43*, Palgrave Macmillan UK, 2009.

McKittrick, D. *Lost Lives,* Mainstream Publishing, 1999.

Montgomery Hyde, H., *Walter Monckton*, Sinclair-Stevenson Ltd, 1991.

Murphy B. OSB, and N. Meehan, *Troubled History: A 10th Anniversary Critique of Peter Hart's The IRA & Its Enemies*, The Aubane Historical Society, 2008.

Mussenden Temple and Downhill Demesne, The National Trust, 2008.

O'Connor, Steven, *Irish Officers in the British Forces, 1922–45,* Palgrave, 2014.

Ó Drisceoil, Donal and Diarmuid. *Beamish & Crawford: The History of an Irish Brewery*, Collins, Cork, 2015.

Orange, V. *A Biography of Air Marshal Sir Arthur Coningham.* Methuen, London, 1993.

Owen, R. *Tedder*, Collins, London, 1952.

Probert, H. Air Commodore, *High Commanders of the Royal Air Force*; The Stationery Office, 1991.

Playfair, Major General I. S. O., with Flynn Captain, F. C., Molony, Brigadier C. J. C. and Gleave, Group Captain T. P., Butler, J. R. M., ed. *The Mediterranean and Middle East: British Fortunes reach their Lowest Ebb (September 1941 to September 1942): History of the Second World War United Kingdom Military Series III.* Naval & Military Press, 2004.

Probert, Henry. *Bomber Harris: His Life and Times: The Biography of Marshal of the Royal Air Force Sir Arthur Harris, Wartime Chief of Bomber Command.* Hardcover, paperback or Kindle versions. Frontline Books, 30 Apr 2016.

Ring, A., O'Hara, M., McCarthy, A., Cahalane, M., and Cotter, L. *Dunmanway: A Local History*, Cork, 1995.

Rolf, David. *The Bloody Road to Tunis: Destruction of the Axis Forces in North Africa, November 1942–May 1943,* Greenhill Books, 2001.

Sheridan O. *Propaganda as Anti-History: Peter Hart's The IRA and its Enemies Examined.* The Aubane Historical Society, Cork, 2008.

Stokes, D. *Wings Aflame*, Crecry, London, 1985.

Tedder; Lord A. *With Prejudice*, Cassell & Co. Ltd, London, 1966.

Tyson, Joseph Howard. *The Surreal Reich*, iUniverse, 21 September 2010.

Archives

Elmhirst papers, Churchill College, Cambridge.

National Archives, Kew: RAF papers on the Second World War.

Newspapers

Dáily Telegraph (various issues)

Guardian newspapers (various issues).

Southern Star Newspapers, Skibereen, Co. Cork, Ireland (various issues)

On line resources

1930 Lions Tour to Australia and New Zealand website www.lionsrugby.com/2010/02/22/the-lions-down-under-1930/

1911 and 1926 https://www.historyireland.com/20th-century-contemporary-history/ethnic-cleansing-protestant-decline-in-west-cork-between-1911-and-1926/

Barbarians FC website, http://www.barbarianfc.co.uk/

Will & Testament, William Crawley's Blog, Sunday, 16 December 2012, https://www.bbc.co.uk/blogs/ni

Air of Authority – A History of RAF Organisation – Air Vice Marshal A. E. Borton www.rafweb.org/Biographies/Borton.htm.

Coleraine Grammar School website, http://www.colerainegrammar.com/

Debates in the Irish Senate 2012: Responses by Denis O'Donovan T.D. to the Address of Mr Drew Nelson, Grand Secretary of the Grand Orange Lodge of Ireland, 3 July 2012: https://www.oireachtas.ie/?tab=seanad

Dunmanway School website: http://cork.anglican.org/school/primary-schools/dunmanway-model-school-dunmanway/

Flanlobbus St Mary's Church, Dunmanway website, http://www.fanlobbus.ie/St-Marys-Church-Dunmanway.htm

Hosford, S. (1999): *Dunmanway and District Model School 1849–1999* available at https://durrushistory.files.wordpress.com/2016/01/full_history.pdf

Lansdowne FC website, https://lansdownerugby.com/

National Archives, Kew: RAF papers on the Second World War http://www.nationalarchives.gov.uk

Nauright, John. 'Danie Craven'. *Encyclopædia Britannica*. Britannica.com. *Retrieved 28 December 2013.*

New Zealand History – The Battle for Crete, https://nzhistory.govt.nz/war/the-battle-for-crete

New Zealand Rugby Museum, http://rugbymuseum.co.nz/

Oxford Dictionary of National Biography: www.oxforddnb.com

Patrick Comeford. *Account of the 'Flying Beamish' Event*, Listowel, Co. Kerry, April 2016 – www.patrickcomeford.com

Portrush Golf Club, https://en.wikipedia.org/wiki/Royal_Portrush_Golf_Club

RAFweb, https://www.rafweb.org/

RAF Cranwell, https://www.raf.mod.uk/our-organisation/stations/raf-college-cranwell/

RAF Rugby Website, https://www.rafsportsfederation.uk/sports/raf-rugby-union-association/

Rugby Hall of Fame, rugbyhalloffame.com '*Danie Craven*', archived from the original on 3 November 2006.

RugbyFootballHistory.com

Rugby History Society, http://www.therugbyhistorysociety.co.uk/

Sam Maguire, www.rebelgaa.com/

Seanad Debates, 3 July 2012, https://www.oireachtas.ie/en/debates/debate/seanad/2012-07-03/

NOTES

Chapter 1: Early Years in Dunmanway

1. Hosford, S. *Dunmanway District Model School – 150 Years to Remember*, Cork, 1999: https://durrushistory.files.wordpress.com/2016/01/full_history.pdf

2. Hosford, S.

3. Ring, A., O'Hara, M., McCarthy, A., Cahalane, M., and Cotter, L. *Dunmanway – A Local History*, 1995.

4. Ring. A.

5. Wikipedia Year 1905.

6. *1911 and 1926 Censuses of Population* – 'The decline of the Protestant population in County Cork between 1911 and 1926'; Flanlobbus St Mary's Church, Dunmanway: http://www.fanlobbus.ie/St-Marys-Church-Dunmanway.htm

7. Chisholm, Hugh, ed. 'Calvados', *Encyclopædia Britannica* (11th ed.) Cambridge University Press, 1911.

8. https://www.historyireland.com/early-modern-history-1500-1700/le-projet-dirlande-huguenot-migration-in-the-1690s-by-randolph-vigne/

9. Chisholm, Hugh.

10. https://en.wikiquote.org/wiki/Charles de Gaulle-Fifth Republic

11. Ó Drisceoil, Donal and Diarmuid. *Beamish & Crawford: The History of an Irish Brewery*, Collins, Cork, 2015.

12. *Southern Star* Newspapers, Skibbereen, April 2016.

13. Sheridan, O. *Propaganda as Anti-History: Peter Hart's 'The IRA and its enemies' examined.'* The Aubane Historical Society, Cork, 2008.

14. Murphy B. OSB, and N. Meehan, *Troubled History: A 10th Anniversary Critique of Peter Hart's The IRA & Its Enemies*. The Aubane Historical Society, 2008.
15. www.rebelgaa.com 30 September 2007
16. Connolly, Kieran. *Sam Maguire: The Man and the Cup*. Mercier Press, 2017.
17. Flanlobbus website.
18. www.rebelgaa.com 30 September 2007.
19. Debates in the Irish Senate 2012: Responses by Denis O'Donovan T.D. to the Address of Mr Drew Nelson, Grand Secretary of the Grand Orange Lodge of Ireland, 3 July 2012: https://www.oireachtas.ie/?tab=seanad
20. *Southern Star*, Skibbereen, Co. Cork, 'Dunmanway's incredible Beamish family to be honoured in Kerry Friday', 8 April 2016.
21. Ó Drisceoil, D. and D.
22. Hosford, S. (1999)
23. Ó Drisceoil, D. and D.; www.rockelstad.se/english/hermann-goring.asp.;Tyson, Joseph Howard. *The Surreal Reich*. iUniverse, 21 September 2010.
24. www.patrickcomeford.com *Account of the 'Flying Beamish' Event*, Listowel, Co. Kerry – Patrick Comerford, April 2016.

Chapter 2: Castlerock and Coleraine Inst.

1. National Archives, Kew, *1911 Census of Population*
2. National Archives, Kew, *1911 Census of Population*
3. The National Trust, *Mussenden Temple and Downhill Demesne*, 2008.
4. Willis, B. *Your Place and Mine*. BBC, 14 April 2009.
5. Palmer, G. E. H. *Constitution and Cooperation in the British Commonwealth*. 1934.
6. McKittrick, D. *Lost Lives*. Mainstream Publishing, 1999, p. 315.
7. www.castlerockgc.co.uk
8. royalportrushgolfclub.com
9. Coleraine Grammar School history archived (2008) at the Wayback Machine.
10. Cullen, P. V., *A Stranger in Blood: The Case Files on Dr John Bodkin Adams*. Elliott & Thompson, London, 2006.
11. 'Past Winners of Ulster Schools' Cup', *BBC Sport*, 14 March 2003.
12. Coleraine Grammar School History, Archived 9 May 2008 at the Wayback Machine.

Chapter 3: Joining the RAF – 'The Eagle Takes Flight'
1. Bowyer, Chaz. *History of the RAF*. Hamlyn. London, 1977.
2. RAF College Cranwell website
3. RAF College Cranwell website
3a. Stokes, D.
4. Probert, H. Air Commodore, *High Commanders of the Royal Air Force*. The Stationery Office, 1991.
5. *Southern Star* newspaper, Skibbereen, April 2016.
6. Bowyer, Chaz.
7. RAF Cranwell Cadets' list of kit requirements, 1923: http://www.oldcranwellians.info
8. RAF Cranwell Cadet Sports records, 1923–24.
9. RAF Cranwell Cadet Sports records, 1923–24.
10. RAF Cranwell Cadet Sports records, 1923–24.
11. 'The Rugby History Society of the RAF and Trenchard, Hugh Montague, First Viscount Trenchard *(1873–1956)*', *Oxford Dictionary of National Biography*. Oxford University Press: www.oxforddnb.com.
12. RAF Cranwell Cadet Sports records (1923–24)
13. Elmhirst papers, Churchill College Cambridge, ELMT, 1942, – archived papers of Air Chief Marshal Sir Thomas Elmhirst.
14. www.rafweb.org/Biographies/Borton.htm.
15. Close, A. Slater, G., ed. (1973) *My Warrior Sons*. Military Book Society. pp. 86 to 90 https://en.wikipedia.org/wiki/Amyas_Borton
16. Air Marshal Sir John Baldwin, Air of Authority – A History of RAF Organisation – http://www.rafweb.org/Biographies/Baldwin.htm
17. RAF History – Bomber Command 60th Anniversary, Archived 14 May 2011 at the Wayback Machine.
18. RAF Rugby History Society Newsletter (past issues).
19. RAF web: Air of Authority, Air Marshal Sir George Beamish.
20. Wikipedia: 'The Year of 1923'.

Chapter 4: From Leicester Tiger to British and Irish Lion
1. RugbyFootballHistory.com – Player Numbering/Lettering.
2. www.rugbyrelics.com/Museum/exhibits/Cent-1923.htm – Rugby History Museum.
3. BBC Sports – Rugby Archive.
4. Farmer, S. and Hands, D. *Tigers 1880–2014: Official History of Leicester Football Club*. The Rugby Development Foundation. Polar Print Group, Nov 1993., pp 38–39

5. Farmer, S. and Hands, D., pp 431–38
6. Farmer, S. and Hands, D., p 431
7. Farmer, S. and Hands, D., pp 83–85
8. Farmer, S. and Hands, D. pp 85–86
9. Farmer, S. and Hands, D., pp 82–87
10. Farmer, S. and Hands, D. p 84 and p 435
11. https://en.wikipedia.org/wiki/Charles Medhurst
12. Farmer, S. and Hands, D., p 83–84
13. IRFU Rugby History Archive www.irfu.com
14. Farmer, S. and Hands, D., pp 431–438
15. https://en.wikipedia.org/wiki/Leicester Tigers and Farmer, S. and Hands, D. p 507
16. Irish rugby website: www.irishrugby.ie/history
17. Irish rugby website: www.irishrugby.ie/history
18. Irish rugby website: www.irishrugby.ie/history
19. W. D. and H. O. Wills– www. cigarettecards.co.uk/valuewills.htm
20. Farmer, S. and Hands, D., pp 446 and 450
21. Farmer, S. and Hands, D., p 426
22. Griffiths, J. (1987). *The Phoenix Book of International Rugby Records*. London: Phoenix House.1910–1938: 'The blue jerseys, the Lions named and the crest adopted'.
22a. Letter of Invitation, 1929, from Lions Management re Participation in 1930 Tour to Australia and New Zealand' - copy on www.lionsrugby.com
22b. RTE Radio Documentary on One 'Lions on Tour – the Jersey Returns!' Diary readings by Michael Dunne, grandson of Michael J. Dunne, broadcast on 23 November 2013.
22c. Gallagher, B. *The Rugby Paper, New Zealand Herald*, 2016. https://www.therugbypaper.co.uk/features/columnists/brendan-gallagher/
22d. Gallagher
23. Godwin, T.; Rhys, C. *The Guinness Book of Rugby Facts & Feats*. Enfield: Guinness Superlatives Limited, 1987.
24. Beamish family reminiscences.
25. British and Irish Lions Results on RugbyHistory.com (1930).
26. Gallagher, B., '1930 Lions Tour to New Zealand and Australia', *The Rugby Paper*, 2006. https://www.therugbypaper.co.uk/features/columnists/brendan-gallagher/
27. Warburton, S. (2017): 'The 1930s – White tie and tails...and grappling with sailors and springboks' – https://www.walesonline.co.uk/sport/rugby/incredible-tales-lions-tours-decades-12960922

28. Farmer, S. and Hands, D. pp 96–97
29. Nauright, J. (2013) 'Danie Craven' *Encyclopædia Britannica*. www.britannica.com/biography/Danie-Craven
30. '1931–32 South Africa rugby union tour of Britain and Ireland... https://en.wikipedia.org/wiki/1931–32South Africa rugby union tour and Danie Craven – Wikipedia https://en.wikipedia.org/wiki/Danie_Craven
31. IRFU Rugby History Archives, www.irfu.com
32. Farmer, S. and Hands, D., pp 96–98
33. Farmer, S. and Hands, D., p 108
34. Farmer, S. and Hands, D., p 473
35. Farmer, Stuart (2016)
36. https://en.wikipedia.org/wiki/Rowland Hill
36a. https://en.wikipedia.org/wiki/Rowland Hill
37. https://www.sportspages.com/product/rowland_hill_memorial_match
38. RAF Sports Federation
39. www.raf.mod.uk/rafrugbyunion
40. www.raf.mod.uk/rafrugbyunion
41. RAF Rugby History Society therugbyhistorysociety.co.uk
42. RAF Rugby History Societytherugbyhistorysociety.co.uk
43. RAF Rugby History Societytherugbyhistorysociety.co.uk
44. https://en.wikipedia.org/wiki/Barbarian_F.C.
45. Farmer, S, and Hands, D.
45a. Family reminiscences – August 2017
46. Elmhirst papers
47. IRFU Rugby History Archives www.irfu.com

Chapter 5: Early Years of RAF Service

1. '100 Squadron' Royal Air Force. Retrieved 13 February 2013.
2. Royal Air Force. 13 February 2013.
3. March, P. *Brace by Wire to Fly-By-Wire – 80 Years of the Royal Air Force 1918–1998*. RAF Fairford: Royal Air Force Benevolent Fund Enterprises, 1998.
4. Air of Authority – A History of RAF Organisation https://web.archive.org/web/20120613210157/http:/www.rafweb.org/Estab1.htm
5. Halley, J. J. *The Squadrons of the Royal Air Force & Commonwealth, 1918–1988*. Tonbridge, Kent, UK: Air-Britain (Historians) Ltd, 1988.
6. https://en.wikipedia.org/wiki/No. 45 Squadron RAF

7. Air of Authority – A History of RAF Organisation https://web.archive. org/web/20120613210157/http:/www.rafweb.org/Estab1.htm

8. https://en.wikipedia.org/wiki/RAF Staff College, Andover and Air of Authority – A History of RAF Organisation

9. Downing, Taylor. *Spies in the Sky*. Little Brown Hardbacks, A & C, 2011.

10. Downing, Taylor.

11. Elmhirst papers.

12. https://en.wikipedia.org/wiki/RAF_Intelligence

13. Winterbotham, F. W. *The Ultra Secret*. New York: Harper & Row, 1974.

14. Winterbotham, F. W.

15. Probert. pp 51–55

16. https://en.wikipedia.org/wiki/Eugene_Esmonde

17. Bowyer, Chaz. *Eugene Esmonde, VC, DSO*. William Kimber & Co., London, 1983.

18. Bowyer.

19. Byrne, M. 'The Ace with the Shamrock'. *Dublin Historical Record*. Published by the Old Dublin Society, Volume LIX, No. 1, Spring 2006. OCLC 400997691

20. Bowyer.

20a. *Dáily Telegraph* of 18 July 1942

21. Bowyer

22. https:/, /en.wikipedia.org/wiki/Paddy Finucane

23. Air of Authority – A History of RAF Organisation – Air Chief Marshal The Earl of Bandon and https://en.wikipedia.org/wiki/ Percy Bernard, 5th Earl of Bandon

24. Air of Authority – A History of RAF Organisation – Air Chief Marshal Sir Edgar Ludlow-Hewitt http://www.rafweb.org/ Biographies/Ludlow-Hewitt.htm

25. https://en.wikipedia.org/wiki/Edgar Ludlow-Hewitt

26. Tedder, Lord A. *With Prejudice*. Cassel & Co., London, 1966, p 163

27. Air of Authority, History of the RAF – Air Marshal Sir George Beamish https://www.rafweb.org/Biographies/Beamish.htm

28. https://ww2ni.webs.com/informationpeople.htm

Chapter 6: Battle of Crete (1941)

1. https://www.thoughtco.com/world-war-ii-battle-of-greece

2. Papagos, A. *The Battle of Greece 1940–1941* (in Greek). Athens: J. M. Scazikis Alpha, 1949.

3. McClymont, W. G. *The Official History of New Zealand in the Second World War 1939–1945.* Wellington, NZ: War History Branch, Department of Internal Affairs, 1959. Chapters 6–22, 'To Greece'.

4. https://en.wikipedia.org/wiki/Battle of Greece

5. Playfair, Major-General I.S.O.; Flynn, Captain F.C.; Molony, Brigadier C.J.C., & Toomer, Air Vice Marshal S.E.; Butler, J.R.M, ed. *The Mediterranean and Middle East: The Germans Come to the Help of their Ally (1941).* History of the Second World War, United Kingdom Military Series. II. Naval & Military Press, 2004.

6. Playfair.

7. Barber, L. and Tonkin-Covell, J. *Freyberg: Churchill's Salamander.* Auckland: Century Hutchinson, 1989.

8. Antill, Peter D. *Crete 1941: Germany's lightning airborne assault.* Campaign series. Oxford; New York: Osprey Publishing, 2005.

9. https://www.scribd.com/document/105076590/Crete-Island-Campaign-1941

10. https://en.wikipedia.org/wiki/Battle of Crete

11. Antill.

12. Beevor, Antony. *Crete: The Battle and the Resistance.* John Murray Publishers, London, 1991. p.88

13. Beevor, p.87

14. Tedder, p 98

15. Beevor, p.99

16. Beevor, p.109

17. Cass F. *A Don at War.* London, 1990.

18. https://www.independent.co.uk/arts-entertainment/obituary-sir-david-hunt-1170946.html

19. https://www.scribd.com/document/105076590/Crete-Island-Campaign-1941

20. Wright, M. *A Near-run Affair – New Zealanders in the battle of Crete, 1941.* Reed Publishing. Auckland, 2000.

21. https://en.wikipedia.org/wiki/Battle of Crete

22. Churchill, W. The Second World War Volume III, 'The Grand Alliance', Chapter XVI Crete: The Battle, (hardcover, paperback and Kindle editions).

23. https://en.wikipedia.org/wiki/Battle of Crete

24. Beevor.

25. Shores, C., Cull, B., Malizia, N. *Air War for Yugoslavia, Greece, and Crete 1940–41.* London: Grub Street, 1987.

26. Luxford, R. Jack Griffiths 'New Zealand Rugby Union', 2016, http://stats.allblacks.com/asp/Profile.asp?ABID=343
27. https://en.wikipedia.org/wiki/Jack Griffiths (rugby union)
28. Beevor, p 81
29. Beevor, p 119
30. https://en.wikipedia.org/wiki/Battle_of_Crete
31. https://en.wikipedia.org/wiki/Battle_of_Crete
32. Beevor, p 46
33. Beevor, p 46
34. New Zealand History on-line: The Battle of Crete
35. New Zealand History on-line: The Battle of Crete
36. New Zealand History on-line: The Battle of Crete
37. New Zealand History on-line: The Battle of Crete
38. https://nzhistory.govt.nz/war/the-battle-for-crete/overview
39. MacDonald, Callum. *The Lost Battle, Crete 1941*. Pan Books, 2002.
40. Antill.
41. Antill.
42. New Zealand History on-line: The Battle of Crete
43. Davin, D. Marcus. *Crete: The Official History of New Zealand in the Second World War 1939–1945* (New Zealand Electronic Text Collection online ed.), Wellington, NZ: Historical Publications Branch, Department of Internal Affairs, Government of New Zealand, 1953. OCLC 1252361
44. https://en.wikipedia.org/wiki/Sword of Honour
45. military.wikia.com/wiki/Alexander Löhr
46. https://en.wikipedia.org/wiki/Kurt Student
47. Feinstein, A. (2011) The Shadow World, Hamish Hamilton.
48. https://en.wikipedia.org/wiki/Alfred Schlemm
49. https://en.wikipedia.org/wiki/Wolfram Freiherr von Richthofen
50. https://en.wikipedia.org/wiki/Eugen Meindl
51. https://en.wikipedia.org/wiki/Hermann-Bernhard Ramcke
52. https://en.wikipedia.org/wiki/Von Blücher brothers
53. Antill.
54. Stroud, R. *Kidnap in Crete: The True Story of the Abduction of a Nazi General*. Bloomsbury, 2015.
55. Stroud, R.
56. https://en.wikipedia.org/wiki/Kurt Student
57. https://en.wikipedia.org/wiki/Razing of Anogeia
58. www.explorecrete.com/history/WW2 Anogia Destruction.html

59. https://en.wikipedia.org/wiki/Razing of Anogeia
60. https://en.wikipedia.org/wiki/Razing of Anogeia
61. Wikipedia entries for Evelyn Waugh, Roald Dahl, Patrick Leigh Fermor, Roy Farran, Max Schmeling, Charles Upham, John Pendelbury, Geoffrey Cox, William Vale and Dudley Honor
62. https://en.wikipedia.org/wiki/Sword_of_Honour
63. Beevor, p 222
64. www.telegraph.co.uk/news/obituaries/1576101/Group-Captain-Dudley-Honor.html.
65. Thompson, P. *Anzac Fury: The Battle of Crete 1941*. William Heinemann, Australia, 2010.
66. Owen p 139–40
67. Palenski, R. *Men of Valour: New Zealand and the Battle of Crete*. Hodder Moa, Auckland, 2013.
68. Willmott, H.P. *The Great Crusade: A New Complete History of the Second World War* (Revised ed.). Washington, DC: Potomac Books, Inc., 2008. pp. 128–129
69. Perlberg, M. *Intelligence Lessons Learned from the Battle for Crete, May 1941*. US Naval War College, Newport, Rhode Island, 1992.
70. https://en.wikipedia.org/wiki/Battle of Crete
71. 'The untold story of heroism of the Spanish who fought in the SAS during WWII' https://www.warhistoryonline.com/instant-articles/churchills.
72. Churchill, W. 'Speech to House of Commons after evacuation of Dunkirk', 4 June 1940.
73. Tedder, p 113
74. Perlberg.
75. Beevor, p 116
76. Churchill, W. 4 June 1940
77. Letter from Rolls-Royce, Derby, to George Beamish 1941.
78. Eisenhower, Dwight D. 'President Eisenhower's Farewell Address', January 17, 1961.

Chapter 7: Desert War (1941–43)

1. Orange, V. *A Biography of Air Marshal Sir Arthur Coningham*. Methuen, London, 1993, p 108.
2. Owen, p 140–41
3. Tedder, p 319
4. Tedder, Lord A. *Air Power in War*. Hodder and Stoughton, London, 1954.

5. https://en.wikipedia.org/wiki/North African campaign

6. Orange, p 77.

7. Judd, M: *Memories 1936–45*. Chapter Five – The Desert acesofww2. com/UK/aces/judd

8. https://en.wikipedia.org/wiki/Arthur_Tedder,_1st_Baron_Tedder

9. Owen, p 121

9a. Owen

9b. Owen

10. Orange, p 79

11. Tedder, p 417

12. Tedder, p 100

13. Orange, p 83

14. https://en.wikipedia.org/wiki/Basil_Embry

15. Tedder, p 417

16. https://en.wikipedia.org/wiki/Arthur_Coningham (RAF officer)

17. Owen, Parts 3 and 4

18. Orange, p 93

19. Air of Authority – A History of RAF Organisation – Air Marshal Sir Arthur Coningham http://www.rafweb.org/Biographies/ Coningham.htm

20. Orange, p 77

21. Orange, p 78

22. Orange, Ch. 8

23. Owen, pp 216–7

24. Orange, p 126

25. Orange, p 106

26. Orange, p 108

27. Orange, p 107

28. Elmhirst papers, ELMT 6/6 and 7

29. Elmhirst papers, ELMT

30. Orange

31. https://en.wikipedia.org/wiki/Arthur Coningham (RAF_officer)

32. ELMT 6/6. *Time* Magazine, 14 August 1944, New York.

33. https://en.wikipedia.org/wiki/Arthur Coningham (RAF_officer)

34. Letter from R. H. Liddell Hart to Field Marshal Cassells, April 1966.

35. Air of Authority – A History of RAF Organisation – Air Marshal Sir Thomas Elmhirst, http://www.rafweb.org/Biographies/ Elmhirst.htm

36. https://en.wikipedia.org/wiki/Thomas Elmhirst

37. Elmhirst papers
38. Elmhirst papers
39. Elmhirst papers
40. https://en.wikipedia.org/wiki/Thomas_Elmhirst
41. Winterbotham, https://en.wikipedia.org/wiki/F._W._Winterbotham.
42. Playfair, https://en.wikipedia.org/wiki/I._S._O._Playfair
43. Playfair
44. *The Brereton Diaries* and africaaxisandallied.blogspot.com/2015/03/desert-war-len-deighton.html
45. https://en.wikipedia.org/wiki/Desert Air Force
46. https://en.wikipedia.org/wiki/Operation Crusader
47. https://en.wikipedia.org/wiki/Lewis H. Brereton
48. https://en.wikipedia.org/wiki/LewisH. Brereton
49. Orange, p 137
50. Elmhirst papers, ELMT
51. Elmhirst Papers, ELMT 2/9
52. https://en.wikipedia.org/wiki/Walter_Monckton and Montgomery Hyde, H., *Walter Monckton*. Sinclair-Stevenson Ltd, 1991.
53. https://en.wikipedia.org/wiki/No. 211 Group RAF
54. Orange, p 93
55. Elmhirst papers, ELMT 2/7
56. Elmhirst papers, ELMT 2/7
57. https://en.wikipedia.org/wiki/Battle of Gazala
58. Elmhirst papers, ELMT 6/6
59. Tedder p 306
60. https://en.wikipedia.org/wiki/Siege of Tobruk
61. Churchill W.S., *The Second World War*. Cassell, London, 1959.
62. Owen, p 161
63. *The Brereton Diaries*. Cairo, 3 July 1942
64. Elmhirst papers, ELMT 6/6
65. *The Brereton Diaries*. 1 October 1942
66. https://en.wikipedia.org/wiki/Second_Battle_of_El_Alamein
67. Chen, P: Second Battle of El Alamein 23 Oct 1942 – 11 Nov 1942
68. https://en.wikipedia.org/wiki/Second Battle of El Alamein
69. https://en.wikipedia.org/wiki/Second Battle of El Alamein
70. https://en.wikipedia.org/wiki/Second Battle of El Alamein
71. *The Brereton Diaries*
72. *The Brereton Diaries*
72a. Winston Churchill, November 1942
73. Elmhirst papers, ELMT 6/6

74. Tedder, p 368
75. Tedder, p 368
76. Elmhirst papers, ELMT 6/6
77. Commonwealth War Graves Commission https://www.cwgc.org/find/find-cemeteries-and-memorials/131900/alamein-memorial
78. https://en.wikipedia.org/wiki/North American B-25 Mitchell
79. Army Field Manual FM 3-25.26 *U.S. Army Map Reading and Land Navigation Handbook.* The United States Army
80. https://en.wikipedia.org/wiki/Second Battle of El Alamein
81. Elmhirst papers, ELMT 6/6
82. https://en.m.wikipedia.org/wiki/Siege of Malta (World War II)
83. Tedder, p 293:
84. Tedder, p 309:
85. Brooks, Stephen, ed. *Montgomery and the Battle of Normandy: A Selection from the Diaries, Correspondence and Other Papers of Field Marshal the Viscount Montgomery of Alamein, January to August 1944,* Sutton Publishing, 2008, and ia.org/wiki/Operation Pedestal
86. www.au.af.mil/au/awc/awcgate/warden/wrdchp01.htm
87. Brooks, S. ed.
88. https://en.wikipedia.org/wiki/Victor Groom
89. Elmhirst papers, ELMT
90. Orange, p 158
91. Elmhirst papers, ELMT 6/6

Chapter 8: Casablanca and Operation *Torch* (1943)

1. https://en.wikipedia.org/wiki/Casablanca Conference
2. Playfair
3. https://en.wikipedia.org/wiki/Operation Torch
4. Tedder, p 386:
5. https://en.wikipedia.org/wiki/Mediterranean Air Command
6. https://en.wikipedia.org/wiki/Mediterranean Air Command
7. Tedder, Ch. 13–19
8. https://en.wikipedia.org/wiki/Mediterranean Air Command
8a. Elmhirst papers, ELMT
9. Owen, p 58
10. https://en.wikipedia.org/wiki/RAF Second Tactical Air Force
11. https://en.wikipedia.org/wiki/RAF Second Tactical Air Force
12. https://en.wikipedia.org/wiki/RAF Second Tactical Air Force
13. https://en.wikipedia.org/wiki/Mediterranean Air Command

14. https://en.wikipedia.org/wiki/John K. Cannon

15. https://www.af.mil/.../105519/brigadier-general-auby-c-strickland

16. National Archives, Kew, AIR/23/6764

17. Tedder, p 404:

18. https://en.wikipedia.org/wiki/No. 211 Group RAF

19. https://en.wikipedia.org/wiki/Operation Flax

20. Tedder, p 415

21. Tedder, pp 215–216

22. https://en.wikipedia.org/wiki/Operation Flax

23. https://en.wikipedia.org/wiki/Western Desert Campaign

24. Playfair

25. Playfair

26. https://en.wikipedia.org/wiki/Operation Torch

27. Orange, p 158

28. Elmhirst papers, ELMT /7

29. https://en.wikipedia.org/wiki/Western Desert Campaign

30. https://en.wikipedia.org/wiki/Desert Air Force

31. http://www.historyofwar.org/articles/campaign_north_african.html Alexander

32. Orange, p 98

33. https://en.wikipedia.org/wiki/Western_Desert_Campaign

33a. Brooks, S.

34. Terraine, J. The Right of the Line: The Royal Air Force in the European War, 1939–45. Hodder & Stoughton, London, 1985.

35. D'Este, C. Decision in Normandy: The Unwritten Story of Montgomery and the Allied Campaign. William Collins, London, 1983.

36. Orange, p 243–45

37. Johnson, P. '2nd TAF and the Normandy Campaign: Controversy and Under-developed Doctrine', Thesis submitted to Department of History in partial fulfilment of requirements for M, The Royal Military College of Canada, Kingston, Ontario, 1999.

38. Johnson

39. Johnson

40. https://en.wikipedia.org/wiki/Harry Broadhurst

41. www.rafweb.org/Biographies/Broadhurst.htm

42. *The Brereton Diaries*, passim

43. Gooderson, I. Air Power at the Battlefront: Allied Close Air Support in Europe, 1943–45. Routledge, 1998.

44. www.rafweb.org/Biographies/Broadhurst.htm

45. Johnson
46. Gooderson
47. Orange p 95
48. https://en.wikipedia.org/wiki/Operation Torch
49. Tedder, p 444
50. Elmhirst papers, ELMT
51. Elmhirst papers, ELMT 6/7
52. Owen, p 206
53. Owen, p 204
54. Owen, p 202
55. Tedder, p 443

Chapter 9: Sicilian Campaign (1943)

1. https://en.wikipedia.org/wiki/Allied invasion of Sicily
2. Elmhirst papers, ELMT 6/7
3. Elmhirst papers, ELMT 6/7
4. Tedder, p 405
5. https://en.wikipedia.org/wiki/Helmuth von Moltke the Elder
6. Cohen, R. 'Air Force Strategic Planning – Past Present and Future', RAND Corporation, Santa Monica CA https://www.rand.org/pubs/research_reports/RR1765.html
7. https://en.wikipedia.org/wiki/Operation Husky
8. File WO/2044363, National Archives, Kew
9. Tedder, p 427–8
10. https://en.wikipedia.org/wiki/Operation Husky
11. https://en.wikipedia.org/wiki/Albert Kesselring
12. https://en.wikipedia.org/wiki/Albert Kesselring
13. https://en.wikipedia.org/wiki/Operation Husky
14. Tedder, p 243–4
15. https://en.wikipedia.org/wiki/Operation Husky
16. *The Brereton Diaries*, 17 August 1943
17. https://en.wikipedia.org/wiki/Operation Husky
18. Tedder, p 445
19. Tedder, p 452
20. Tedder, p453
21. Tedder, pp 244–5
22. https://en.wikipedia.org/wiki/Operation_Pedestal
23. National Archives, Kew, WO/204/4363
24. National Archives, Kew, WO/204/4363
25. Tedder, p 45

Chapter 10: End of the War and Final Postings

1. Elmhirst papers, ELMT
2. www.rafweb.org/Biographies/Beamish.htm
3. RAF Rugby History Society
4. March, T. 'Aide-de-Camp: A Survival Guide,' *The Staff Officers' Handbook*. September 2014, pp.vi–xi
5. Family reminiscences
6. Orange. p 182
7. https://en.wikipedia.org/wiki/John Vereker, 6th Viscount Gort
8. https://en.wikipedia.org/wiki/Harold Alexander, 1st Earl Alexander
9. www.rafweb.org/Biographies/Beamish.htm
10. https://en.wikipedia.org/wiki/RAF Ferry Command and https://en.wikipedia.org/wiki/Air Transport Command
11. https://en.wikipedia.org/wiki/RAF Ferry Command and https://en.wikipedia.org/wiki/Air Transport Command
12. www.rafweb.org/Biographies/Beamish.htm
13. https://en.wikipedia.org/wiki/Order of George I
14. https://en.wikipedia.org/wiki/Legion of Merit
15. https://en.wikipedia.org/wiki/7th Armoured Division (United Kingdom)
16. https://en.wikipedia.org/wiki/7th Armoured Division (United Kingdom)
17. Elmhirst papers, ELMT 6/6 – 19 March 1942
18. Powell, C. *My American Journey*. Ballantine Books, NY, 2003.
19. Orange, p 93
20. Tedder, p 417
21. https://en.wikipedia.org/wiki/Charles Portal, 1st Viscount Portal
22. Probert, H. *High Commanders of the Royal Air Force*. TSO, 1991, pp.26–27
23. Wikipedia entries on Kenneth Wolstenhome and Dan Maskell
24. Elmhirst papers (ELMT 2/14). Review paper by Air Staff of SHAEF of 9 July 1945 entitled 'The Allied Air Offensive'.
25. www.rafweb.org/Biographies/Beamish.htm
26. https://en.wikipedia.org/wiki/Richard Atcherley
27. Hancock, R. *Flight Cadet: Royal Air Force College Cranwell*. Pentland Press, London, 1996.
28. National Archives, Kew, AIR 20/10842
29. National Archives, Kew, AIR 29/2018
30. National Archives, AIR 20/10842
31. https://en.wikipedia.org/wiki/Laurence_Sinclair
32. https://en.wikipedia.org/wiki/Royal Air Force College Cranwell

33. National Archives, Kew, AIR, T 2013/278 and 279
34. Andrew, C. and Mitrokhin V. *The Mitrokhin Archive: The KGB in Europe and the West*. London, Penguin Books, 2000.
35. Davenport-Hines, Richard. *Enemies Within*. Collins, London, 2018.
36. https://en.wikipedia.org/wiki/Category:Graduates of Royal Air Force.
37. www.rafweb.org/Biographies/Beamish.htm
38. https://en.wikipedia.org/wiki/Alexander Gray (RAF officer)
39. https://en.wikipedia.org/wiki/1950–51 Baghdad bombings
40. https://en.wikipedia.org/wiki/1948 Arab–Israeli War
41. https://en.wikipedia.org/wiki/RAF Middle East Command
42. https://en.wikipedia.org/wiki/Abadan Crisis
43. https://en.wikipedia.org/wiki/Brian Robertson, 1st Baron Robertson.
44. https://en.wikipedia.org/wiki/John LeRougetel
45. https://en.wikipedia.org/wiki/BritishAmbassador to Iran
46. www.rafweb.org/Biographies/Beamish.htm
47. https://en.wikipedia.org/wiki/RAF Transport Command
48. www.rafweb.org/Biographies/Beamish.htm
49. https://en.wikipedia.org/wiki/Frederick Bowhill
50. https://en.wikipedia.org/wiki/RAF Transport Command
51. https://en.wikipedia.org/wiki/RAF Technical Training Command

Chapter 11: Beamish Brothers and Sisters

1. Stokes, D. *Wings Aflame*. Crecy, London, 1985, p 8
2. Stokes, p 15
3. Stokes, p 147 and 207
4. Stokes, p 15
5. www.colerainehistoricalsociety.co.uk/Bann Disc
6. Farmer and Hands, p 423
7. Cranwell papers – 1923/24 Cadet Reports
8. https://en.wikipedia.org/wiki/C A H Longcroft
9. Stokes, p 66
10. Stokes, p208
11. Stokes, p208
12. Stokes, p 62–65
13. Stokes, Plate 3
14. Stokes, p 179–87
15. Stokes, p 176–184
16. Stokes, p 206 and Comerford. P. (2016) – www.patrickcomerford.com
17. Stokes, p 210
18. Stokes, p 209

19. Stokes, p 27
20. Stokes, p 56
21. https://en.wikipedia.org/wiki/Charles_Beamish
22. Farmer, S., and Hands, D., p 423
23. https://en.wikipedia.org/wiki/Charles Beamish
24. https://en.wikipedia.org/wiki/Alexander Obolensky
25. Farmer, S., and Hands, D., pp 107–08
26. IRFU Rugby History Archives
27. Farmer, S., and Hands, D., p 431
27a. RAF Golfing Society https://rafgs.org
28. RAF Golfing Society https://rafgs.org
29. *Southern Star*, Skibereen, 8 April 2016
30. Wikipedia – Beamish
31. https://www.beamish.org.uk
32. *Southern Star*, 16 April 2016
33. Discussions with Mrs Jean Caulfield, Coleraine, September 2017.

Chapter 12: Retirement to Castlerock
1. Wikipedia Year 1959
2. Wikipedia Year 1957
3. https://en.wikipedia.org/wiki/Castlerock
4. https://www.timeshighereducation.com/news/people/norman-gibson- Obituary of Prof. Norman Gibson
5. https://en.wikipedia.org/wiki/Fred Daly (golfer)
6. www.castlerockgc.co.uk
7. https://en.wikipedia.org/wiki/Royal Portrush Golf Club
8. https://en.wikipedia.org/wiki/Portstewart Golf Club
9. https://en.wikipedia.org/wiki/H. Montgomery Hyde
10. (i) https://en.m.wikipedia.org/wiki/William III of England (ii) Van der Kiste, 204–205; Baxter, 352; Falkner, James (2004), 'Keppel, Arnold Joost van, first earl of Albemarle (1669/70–1718)', *Oxford Dictionary of National Biography*. Oxford University Press
11. Family reminiscences, 2018.
12. https://en.wikipedia.org/wiki/United Kingdom general election,1959
13. https://en.wikipedia.org/wiki/Bill McLaren
14. Reminiscences of Willie John McBride
15. https://en.wikipedia.org/wiki/Ken Goodall
16. https://en.wikipedia.org/wiki/High Sheriff of County Londonderry
17. Discussions with Mrs Jean Caulfield, September 2016.
18. Letter from J. Spencer to George Beamish re General Freyberg, 1966.

19. Letter to George Beamish from Jack Wheeler, 8 October 1966.
20. *Coleraine Chronicle*, 17 November 1967
21. https://www.fightercontrol.co.uk/forum/viewtopic.php p.277324
22. George Beamish: Last Will and Testament, 1967, Beamish family papers.

Epilogue
1. O'Connor S. *Irish Officers in the British Forces, 1922–45*. Palgrave Macmillan, London, 2014.
2. Beamish family reminiscences: Ian Beamish, 2017.

INDEX

Also available from Amberley Publishing

'The Central Gunnery School was the first of its kind in the world.'
Group Captain Allan Wright

ALASTAIR GOODRUM

SCHOOL OF ACES

THE RAF TRAINING SCHOOL THAT WON
THE BATTLE OF BRITAIN

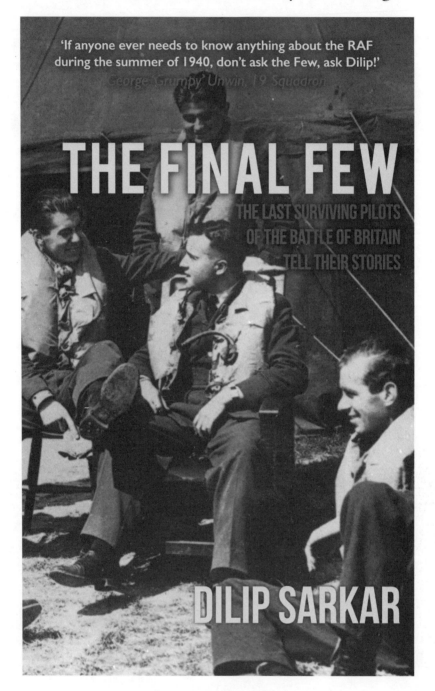

'If anyone ever needs to know anything about the RAF during the summer of 1940, don't ask the Few, ask Dilip!'
George 'Grumpy' Unwin, 19 Squadron

THE FINAL FEW

THE LAST SURVIVING PILOTS
OF THE BATTLE OF BRITAIN
TELL THEIR STORIES

DILIP SARKAR